ENCOUNTERING DIRECTORS

Books by Charles Thomas Samuels

JOHN UPDIKE

A CASEBOOK ON FILM

THE AMBIGUITY OF HENRY JAMES

ENCOUNTERING DIRECTORS

ENCOUNTERING DIRECTORS

by Charles Thomas Samuels

G. P. Putnam's Sons, New York

SBN: 399-11023-2

Library of Congress Catalog

Card Number: 72-79528

Printed in the United States of America

For Erika and Melissa,

*who were kept by it from sufficiently
encountering their father*

Contents

Acknowledgments

The author would like to thank the following for arranging screenings of the various directors' films: *Archives:* Cinémathèque Française; Cinémathèque Royale de Belgique; Cineteca Nazionale; George Eastman House; Library of Congress; National Film Archive of the British Film Institute. *Distributors:* Academy Cinema (London); Avco Embassy Films; Audio Brandon; Contemporary Films/McGraw-Hill; Films Incorporated; Janus Films; Les Films du Carrosse; New Line Cinema; Parc Film; Showcorporation. *Individuals:* Michelangelo Antonioni; William K. Everson; Pierre Long; Gaspare Palumbo.

Stills were furnished by courtesy of the following: *Archives:* Cineteca Nazionale; Museum of Modern Art; National Film Archive. *Producers and Distributors:* ABC Pictures Corp.; Alfred J. Hitchcock Productions, Inc.; Audio Brandon; Avco Embassy Films; Cinema V; Columbia Pictures; Compagnie Jean Renoir; Contemporary Films/McGraw-Hill; Janus Films; Les Films du Carrosse; Metro-Goldwyn-Mayer; New Yorker Films; Parc Film; Produzione Palumbo; RAI; Rizzoli Film, S.p.a.; Sandrew Teater and Film A.B.; Svensk Filmindustri; Teleciné-Italia; Times Film Corp.; Twentieth Century-Fox; United Artists; Universal Pictures, Inc.; Velde, Inc.; the Walter Reade Organization; Warner Bros., Inc. *Individuals:* René Clair; Bo-Erik Gyberg; Mario Longardi; G. B. Poletto. All stills are reproduced by permission.

The author would also like to thank those who helped in arranging or facilitating the interviews: Orin Borsten; Arthur Cohn; Mario Longardi; Françoise Longhurst; Hedy and Enzo Martinelli; Gaspare Palumbo; Beverly Walker. Acknowledgment alone hardly suffices for Nada Samuels and Lawrence Graver, who reviewed the manuscript, and Walter Betkowski, who offered kindness and help beyond the normal limits of editorial responsibility.

Research for this book was aided by a fellowship from the National Endowment for the Humanities and a grant from the Williams College 1900 Fund. I would like to express my deep appreciation for this support.

Excerpts from the interviews have appeared in the *American Scholar*, the *Atlantic Monthly*, *Film Heritage*, and *Vogue*.

Preface

The following interviews are part of my research for a forthcoming critical study of some major filmmakers in the sound era. I publish them now because I hope they will prove as illuminating to others as they have to me.

Although I agree with Federico Fellini that any artist good enough to make you want to question him has already answered you in his works, I felt that interviewing was a useful preparation for criticism. Why?

First, because the peculiarities of this art make us wonder how much any film represents a single creator. So far as I could tell, the men I chose to interview express themselves no less authentically than writers, composers, or painters. But I also realized that their form places crucial limits on dominance by a single personality. Fairness, as well as accuracy, required that I do everything possible to explore these limits so as to avoid praise that might be undeserved or blame that might be unwarranted.

Some directors are more dependent than others. We need to know why Renoir or, in certain surprising ways, Bergman is less wholly responsible for the finished film than Antonioni or Bresson if we want to describe and estimate properly the workings of each man's talent. We need to know how much freedom he permits his cinematographer, whether he allows his actors to shape their performances, and how much control—even if indirect—he exercises over the script. Distribution of responsibility can probably never be precisely established, but criticism will be more just if it acknowledges the ways in which the dominating artist is supplemented or—sometimes—opposed. Getting such information is one major motive for interviewing filmmakers.

Furthermore, film is a distinctively mechanical art. Technique, both overt and routinized, controls expression. What can you ask a writer about his working methods that might influence your understanding of the results? (The *Paris Review* interviews even try to make a joke of this irrelevancy—do you use pencil or a typewriter?) But by explaining what was unavoidable and what created, the film artist helps us map the critically significant area where choice is exercised.

Finally, commercial exigencies determine much of the outcome in this most expensive of arts. Results are rendered neither more nor less deplorable because they were forced by finances or producers, but we need to know of such factors if we want to distinguish the artist's esthetic from his moral personality.

:[11]:

For these reasons, information about a director's methods of working and collaborating can properly be regarded as antecedent to criticism. The other things I wanted to learn presume that some criticism had already taken place. Having seen the available films of each director, I had formulated a provisional notion of his style and viewpoint. I wanted to hear what he thought these were so as to corroborate or modify my presuppositions.

Though never so definitive as the image presented in his films, a director's sense of himself can supplement our understanding. Fellini is right to assert that artists speak through their art, but none does so unerringly. In telling us how he sees himself, the director reveals those needs, doubts, or confusions that he seeks to purge through art but that—humanity being always imperfect—leave behind a residue of failure. Criticism should try to investigate what it cannot admire or confidently interpret. In this endeavor, the artist's testimony has obvious pertinence.

But pertinent data aren't easily gathered. As a rule, artists don't like to explain or justify themselves. When questioned directly, they frequently become reticent or evasive. Furthermore, each of my subjects had been interviewed so frequently that he now has an "Interview" which can be regularly used to meet the requirements of publicity and the gossipy interests of journalists. I decided that if I were going to learn anything new, I should have to get below the canned response and break through the reticence or evasiveness. Candid criticism seemed the most promising strategy. Since explanations are most precisely and sincerely martialed when one is under attack, I felt it expedient to raise objections—my own and others'.

Thus, even as I quailed at my gall, I quarreled with individual choices, questioned methods and aims, tried to probe for confusions and inner motives. I knew, and hoped my questions would show, that I considered each director an outstanding artist. The trouble I had taken to review his work would prove the depth of my admiration. What I hoped to find and expose were unexpressed beliefs that nurtured and protected his talent. Insofar as I could, I wanted to encourage revelations not only about procedures, but about sensibility.

I never succeeded to my satisfaction. Despite candor to the point of abrasiveness and enticing expressions of sincere regard, I could neither provoke nor cajole all the confidences I sought. Defensive maneuvers or outright refusals could not be precluded; I would often find myself discarding my armor of questions, substituting, eliminating, even emasculating them as the circumstances required. But as Antonioni, Bresson, and others told me, when one tries to capture reality, he often succeeds by failing. What I had not intended to record proves even more interesting that what I planned. Thus, I discovered, while consecutively reading the interviews, that the consistency of my approach threw into high relief differences among my respondents. Comparisons made possible because of the presence of a common denominator themselves measure each sensibility. That is why, after having selected the verb "encounter" to indicate my interviewing style, I made it a present participle to suggest that each talk was part of a process and that none is more complete than the process itself.

As Bergman said of his films, these interviews are designed for use. How can they be used? Certainly not as definitions. An interview cannot and should not compete with more assertive modes. It isn't a statement but rather the account of a human event, in which each party conditions the other's behavior. Like any conversation, it is ambiguous and inefficient, but it is also nuanced and suggestive. Showing more than it states, it invites the reader into participation. Where so much lies between the lines, as in drama or film itself, so much more can be deduced by anyone who is resourceful in his power of inference.

Interviews are also appropriate to the job of revealing sensibility. A piece of criticism can cope with a work of art, whose contours and content are fixed; the artist himself is no more contained, hence definitely knowable, than any living being. With relevant modesty, then, an interview avoids the implicit claim of criticism to have articulated an essence. It offers data for a formulation, rather than a formulation itself. It is more like art than criticism: It asks us to discover; it does not simply tell.

For this reason, I offer an absolute minimum of interpretation. Having stage-managed these encounters through my questions—which is to say, my interests and critical position, as well as personal manner—I had no wish to further impose myself by specifying the proper inferences. I wanted to leave the reader free to draw his own conclusions, to share my privilege of making whatever use I chose of whatever facts I uncovered.

To this end, I also tried to edit as little as possible, although I decided at once that pure accuracy was out of the question. To begin with, several of these interviews were translated, and every translation distorts. Readability also demanded a degree of revision; spoken discourse inevitably rambles and sputters beyond anyone's point of tolerance. Thus, even in the Bergman talk, which is closest to the literal transcript (including a digression that, startling and irrelevant as it may seem, is also highly revealing), I only render actual speech when it is terse enough to preclude improvement. Last, there are moments in all conversations when nothing much is said, either because of misunderstanding, waywardness, or a topic's fruitlessness. Such instances, I did not hesitate to omit, nor did I hesitate to interrupt (and later excise) moments when the "Interview" started up, despite all my efforts to ensure novelty.

Although recorded by an impersonal machine, the tapes of these conversations went through the hands of a human being. Accuracy was my main goal, but readability, novelty, or pertinence sometimes dictated competing choices. I naturally assume full responsibility for these decisions, the most notable of which I indicate in the headnotes.

The headnotes also sketch the circumstances of each meeting and give a brief physical impression of the director's behavior. Such factors, of course, influenced and—if they could only be reproduced—would enhance the content. As any good film shows, a meeting is not only the words said, but also the place where they were said and the speakers' gestures. Unavoidably, these transcripts bear something of the same abstract relationship to the encounters that film scripts bear to films. In one instance—that of Fellini—the abstraction was too great to be accepted. In this case, I, therefore, depart from the single session format I use in the other interviews.

Several of them—with Clair, Olmi, Renoir, Truffaut—also took place on more than one occasion, but only the Olmi, as I explain, gains any significance from this fact. I tried to accomplish each talk in one sitting because I believed that intensity of concentration would be my greatest ally in provoking sincerity of response. Having decided to be critically assertive, I always ran the risk (nearly realized by Bergman) of being thrown out. Even more difficult than preparation for any interview was my sense that I was with each man by sufferance, that he had more important things to do, and that it was both impolite and immoral to be so contentious as I had already decided that novelty and pertinence required. I therefore relied on my subject's involvement to counteract any justifiable impulses toward reticence or refusal. In one case, I succeeded too well. Although famous for his control over interviews, Robert Bresson confided to me the nearly total disdain for other directors that logically supports the uniqueness of his own work, but that, prudentially, he never expresses in public. Months later, when he asked to see the transcript, he felt so chagrined by his inadvertency that he insisted on certain omissions. Luckily, this was my one important example of directorial second thoughts.

Within limits explained above, then, these verbal snapshots are unretouched. I offer them in the belief that they contain, in which corners the reader must decide, clues to those larger pictures made by the creators I encountered.

Michelangelo Antonioni

Rome, July 29, 1969

Feature Films: 1950 *Cronaca di un amore* (*Chronicle of a Love Affair*); 1952 *I vinti* (*The Vanquished*); 1953 *La signora senza camelie* (*The Lady Without Camellias*); 1955 *Le amiche* (*The Girl-Friends*); 1957 *Il grido* (*The Outcry*); 1959 *L'avventura* (*The Adventure*); 1960 *La notte* (*Night*); 1962 *L'eclisse* (*Eclipse*); 1964 *Il deserto rosso* (*Red Desert*); 1966 *Blow-up*; 1969 *Zabriskie Point*.

The living room of Antonioni's apartment, where this interview took place, reflects intellectual restlessness rather than a desire for comfort. Except for a plush couch, the room is sparely furnished, yet everywhere there are books, records, a wild array of bric-a-brac. One table holds a collection of arrowheads, knife blades, and other antique weaponry. Crowding the windowsills is a profusion of *objets trouvés*, including the television circuitry to which he refers during our conversation. Even the low glass coffee table is covered with an assortment of boxes, fragments of statuary, enormous ashtrays, and other items, some unidentifiable. Overwhelming the whole are striking, sometimes garish paintings, particularly the Lichtenstein he mentions and an enormous Francis Bacon of a semihuman figure installed in an easy chair but, for all that, apparently losing its innards.

We talked for four hours, despite the intense heat and his preoccupation with editing *Zabriskie Point*. My questions were posed in English, although, for speed's sake, I invited him to answer in Italian. My wife, who is fluent in that language, was present for on-the-spot explanations of anything I failed to understand. Subsequently, a full transcript was made and translated at Antonioni's expense, since he refused to let the tapes out of his hands. He explained that an uncensored conference recorded with students had been broadcast without his knowledge, thus putting at his producer's disposal certain comments he did not want publicized, including—to his later discomfort—some negative remarks about the producer. Moreover, he does not like the sound of his voice and prefers to limit its circulation.

The voice is soft and toneless, the eyes are lugubrious, and though the face and body are far younger than his sixty years, Antonioni's apparent virility is belied by an extremely austere manner and by a series of nervous tics that become more intense as he finds himself struggling for words. A week after the interview, at lunch, he showed his capacity for wit and relaxation, but as we talked now, he seemed burdened by his earnest attempt to answer my questions. Having been forewarned that he would find answering difficult, I began with something familiar and general.

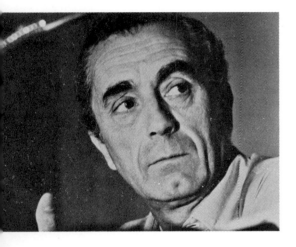

SAMUELS: You are quoted as saying, "Once one has learned the two or three basic rules of cinematographic grammar, he can do what he likes—even break these rules." What rules were you referring to?

ANTONIONI: The simplest ones: cross-cutting, making the actor enter from the right if he had previously exited to the left of the frame, etc. There are hundreds of such rules which are taught in cinema schools and which have value only until you actually begin making films. Often I have shot something simply to show myself how useless they are. You break one and no one notices, because the audience only sees the result of your "error." If that works, who cares about rules!

S: *Cronaca di un amore,* your first feature film, has more inventive and innovative camera work than your second film, *La signora senza camelie.* For example, in *La signora* you regularly track into a character when he moves toward the camera, which is certainly playing according to the rules, whereas in *Cronaca,* as in your later films, you are seldom so orthodox. Why is this so?

Lucia Bose tries to get a part in the sort of desert epic satirized by Fellini in The White Sheik, *for which Antonioni provided the subject. However, Antonioni's* La signora senza camelie *treats the matter uncomically.*

A: I can't answer that question. When I am shooting a film I never think of how I want to shoot something; I simply shoot it. My technique, which differs from film to film, is wholly instinctive and never based on a priori considerations. But I suppose you are right in saying that *La signora* seems more orthodox than the earlier *Cronaca* because when I was shooting the first film, I made very long takes, following the actors with my camera even after their scene was finished. But, you know, *Cronaca* isn't more innovative than what comes after. Later I break the rules much more often. Look at *L'avventura* and particularly *Blow-up.*

S: *Blow-up* is the most cinematographically

unorthodox of all your films. But I was interested to notice precedents for the camera work of *Blow-up* in your short documentary *L'amorosa menzogna*, which is about making *fumetti*, or live-action comic strips, and which contains almost as many trick shots as the later work. I think, for example, of the shot of a *fumetti* scene reduced to its reflection in the camera. Isn't it more than a

coincidence that the two films which contain your most complex shooting are the two that concern photography?

A: You are right to say that *Blow-up* is my most unorthodox film, but it is unorthodox in montage, as well as photography. At the Centro Sperimentale they teach you never to cut a shot during its action. Yet I continually do that in *Blow-up*. Hemmings starts walking to a phone booth—snip go a few frames—in a flash, he is there. Or take the scene in which he photographs Verushka; I cut many frames during that action, doing what the teachers at the Centro regard as utterly scandalous.

S: Is the rhythm of this scene meant to suggest the photographer's emotions?

A: Up to a point. I wanted to give the audience the same sensations as the photographer feels while shooting. However, this sort of thing is fairly common in the cinema today. I began taking liberties a long time ago; now it is standard practice for most directors to ignore the rules.

S: Your cutting in the Verushka scene has now become a sort of cliché in TV commercials.

A: Yes?

S: It doesn't disturb you, eh? Well, let's get back to this question of camera technique. Why do you so rarely use reverse cutting in dialogue scenes?

A: Because it is so banal that instinctively I find it irritating. But occasionally I do use it, even as late as *Zabriskie Point*. Normally, however, I try to avoid repetitions of any shot. It isn't easy to find one in my films. You might, I suppose, see something twice, but it would be rare. And then, you know, every line requires its own kind of shot. The American method of shooting one actor continuously, then moving to the other, then intercutting both—this method is wrong. A scene has to have a rhythm of its own, a structure of its own.

S: Progressively during your career, you seem to efface the precise moment of cutting and to avoid obvious transitions, almost as if you wish to keep the spectator from relaxing. In view of the fact that your later films tell slow, deliberate stories, aren't you trying to achieve briskness in the way you cut?

A: If so, it is instinctive. I don't do anything deliberately.

S: That's not true. You told Rex Reed that all your films were made with your stomach, except *Blow-up*, which was made with your head.

A: In *Blow-up* I used my head instinctively!

S: Checkmate. When you were interviewed by *Bianco e Nero* in 1958 you said that modern directors had eliminated the "problem of the bicycle."

A: What could I have meant by that?

S: I supposed you to mean sociological motivation for the character's behavior, and you certainly concentrate on the power of personality, of self rather than society. However, even though your characters aren't caused by society, they are embedded in a specific social context, which is what gives your films their extraordinary richness. Therefore, I think that 1958 statement indicates what is really a false distinction.

A: You know what I would like to do: make a

film with actors standing in empty space so that the spectator would have to imagine the background of the characters. Till now I have never shot a scene without taking account of what stands behind the actors because the relationship between people and their surroundings is of prime importance. I mean simply to say that I want my characters to suggest the background in themselves, even when it is not visible. I want them to be so powerfully realized that we cannot imagine them apart from their physical and social context even when we see them in empty space.

S: Because of your telling eye for detail, you do relate your characters to their background. In fact, as one goes through your films, he sees you relying less and less on dialogue and more and more on the physical environment to establish your characters.

A: Yes.

The heroine's neurosis sprayed out against the backdrop. Red Desert.

The hero moves against a backdrop of casual violence in Zabriskie Point.

S: What did you mean in the Cannes manifesto that accompanied *L'avventura* when you said that man is burdened on the threshold of space by feelings entirely unsuited to his needs?

A: I meant exactly what I said: that we are saddled with a culture that hasn't advanced as far as science. Scientific man is already on the moon, and yet we are still living with the moral concepts of Homer. Hence this upset, this disequilibrium that makes weaker people anxious and apprehensive, that makes it so difficult for them to adapt to the mechanism of modern life.

S: That much I understand, but I'm puzzled about some implications. Do you mean to imply that the old moral baggage must be thrown away? If so, is that possible? Can man conceive of a new morality?

A: Why go on using that word I loathe! We live in a society that compels us to go on using these concepts, and we no longer know what they mean. In the future—not soon, perhaps by the twenty-fifth century—these concepts will have lost their relevance. I can never understand how we have been able to follow these worn-out tracks, which have been laid down by panic in the face of nature. When man becomes reconciled to nature, when space becomes his true background, these words and concepts will have lost their meaning, and we will no longer have to use them.

S: Let me match your statement with a moment in one of your films. By the end of *L'avventura*, Sandro recognizes that his promiscuity is harmful—to Claudia, with whom he has had the one intense relationship of his life, so far as we know. Do you mean us to believe that his ensuing guilt (inspiring him to tears) is an error because what makes him feel this guilt are conceptions of romantic love and personal responsibility that have become irrelevant burdens?

A: Sandro is a character from a film shot in 1960 and is therefore entirely immersed in such moral problems. He is an Italian, a Catholic, and so he is a victim of this morality. What I said awhile ago is that such moral dilemmas will have no right to exist in a future that will be different from the present. Today we are just beginning to glimpse that future, but in 1960 we lived in a country with the Pope and the Vatican, which have always been extremely important to all of us. There isn't a school in Italy still, not a

lawcourt without its crucifix. We have Christ in our houses, and hence the problem of conscience, a problem fed to us as children that afterward we have no end of trouble getting rid of. All the characters in my films are fighting these problems, needing freedom, trying to find a way to cut themselves loose, but failing to rid themselves of conscience, a sense of sin, the whole bag of tricks.

S: I don't think you're proposing something that's only a matter of time. Would it indeed ever be good to dispense with the bag of tricks, as you call it? I wonder if we shouldn't be more proud of this tradition going back to Homer than of the trip to the moon. Speaking only for myself—no, I'm sure I speak for others, too—the ending of *L'avventura* is so powerful because Sandro has the conscience to regret what he has done. To feel such regret, one has to believe in the supreme importance of human responsibility, and I can't conceive of art without that belief.

A: I would like to make clear that I speak only of sensations. I am neither a sociologist nor a politician. All I can do is imagine for myself what the future will be like. Today we find ourselves face to face with some curious facts. For example, today's youth movement was born under the sign of anarchy. It has made anarchy point to a new society which will be more flexible, based on a system that can, by degrees, concur with contemporary events, facts, necessities. On the other hand, these youths structure themselves in mystic groups, and I must confess this rather disturbs me. I don't know what to think about it anymore. . . . I don't want what I am saying to sound like a prophecy or anything like an analysis of modern society . . . these are only feelings I have, and I am the least speculative man on earth.

S: The implication of what you've been saying as far as *Blow-up* is concerned intrigues me. Aren't you suggesting that you meant to depict the young people in that film positively?

A: Yes, *Blow-up* is favorable to the youth of that particular moment and place. I don't know how I would feel if I were to start studying certain groups in Italy, for example, about whom I must admit only the vaguest knowledge.

S: But I find the film critical, and so do others. For example, recall the peace-march scene, where the young people walk by with placards reading "Go," "On, on," "Forward." That's parody, yet you say you intended it to be favorable.

A: When a scene is being shot, it is very difficult to know what one wants it to say, and even if one does know, there is always a difference between what one has in mind and the result on film. I never think ahead of the shot I'm going to make the following day because if I did, I'd only produce a bad imitation of the original image in my mind. So what you see on the screen doesn't represent my exact meaning, but only my possibilities of expression, with all the limitations implied in that phrase. Perhaps the scene reveals my incapacity to do better; perhaps I felt subconsciously ironic toward it. But it is on film; the rest is up to you.

S: Last week I saw for the first time your documentary on the superstitions of Calabrese peasants, and I was struck by the similarities between these peasants and the hippies in whom you have such faith.

A: What similarities?

S: The hippies are also superstitious. The peasants have their magus, the hippies their guru. Hippies wear talismans, just like the Calabrese. Are they really the future? Aren't they bearing baggage even older than the moral tradition you find so burdensome?

A: I believe these similarities derive from the hippies' desire not to reform present society, but to destroy it and, in destroying it, return almost to antiquity, to a purer, more primordial life, less— less mechanical . . . not based on the same principles as present life. Therefore, they return to the original source, and their gurus resemble the wizard in *Superstizione*. But I don't believe that if they ever reach a position of power, these young people would reconstruct society along antique lines, for that would be absurd. They need to rethink society, and nobody knows the answers yet.

S: Therefore, both in *Blow-up* and *Zabriskie Point* you aren't so much admiring their present behavior as hoping that they will produce something better?

A: More or less. They believe in the possibility of life; that is what they show in their primitive communities. But I think that technology will one day shape all our actions. I don't think this can be helped, and there will be no chance to resist.

S: I'm still puzzled. You say that the future must be technologically controlled and, moreover, that you desire that. But so far as I can see, your films suggest a revulsion against technology. In *Red Desert*, for example, there's a scene where Corrado talks to Giuliana's husband in front of a factory. The noise makes it impossible to hear, and the smoke makes it impossible for them to see each other. Soon the smoke envelops them so that we don't see them either. On the other hand, you painted the factory pipes so that they become

The "love-in" from Zabriskie Point.

Daria paints an airplane with what might be regarded as Antonioni's slogan. Zabriskie Point.

rather attractive. On the one hand, you show that technological modern life is bad; on the other, you're saying it's good.

A: But I'm not saying that technology is bad, something we can do without. I'm saying that present-day people can't adapt to it. These are merely terms of a conflict: "technology" and "old-fashioned characters." I'm not passing judgment, not at all. Ravenna, near the sea, has a stretch of factories, refineries, smokestacks, etc. on one side and a pine forest on the other. Somewhere I've written that the pine forest is much the more boring feature. Look at this, for example. I find these components of a television circuit absolutely marvelous. Look! They're wonderful. So you see, I'm an admirer of technology. From an outsider's view the insides of a computer are marvelous—not just its functioning but the way it is made, which is beautiful in itself. If we pull a man apart, he is revolting; do the same thing to a computer and it remains beautiful. In *2001*, you know, the best things in the film are the machines, which are much more splendid than the idiotic humans. In *Red Desert*, I also confronted this technology and these machines with human beings who are morally and psychologically retarded and thus utterly unable to cope with modern life.

S: You mean, then, that it is man's fault and not the fault of the environment that he can't adjust, is miserable, etc.?

A: Yes. Modern life is very difficult for people who are unprepared. But this new environment will eventually facilitate more realistic relationships between people. For example, that scene, that great puff of—not smoke—steam that blasts out violently between the two characters. As I see it, that steam makes the relationship more real, because the two men have nothing to say to each other. Anything that might crop up would be hypocritical.

S: OK. But isn't it also possible to say that they can't speak to each other because their environment deprives them of an inner life to communicate?

A: No. I don't agree. In that case. . . . Wait, let me think it over a moment. I think people talk too much; that's the truth of the matter. I do. I don't believe in words. People use too many words and usually wrongly. I am sure that in the distant future people will talk much less and in a more essential way. If people talk a lot less, they will be

happier. Don't ask me why. In my films it is the men who don't function properly—not the machines.

S: That isn't what we're discussing; we're discussing the cause. Is this something unavoidable in man's soul or something located in a specific moment of history.

A: You are trying to make me into some sort of philosopher of modern life—which is something I absolutely cannot be. When we say a character in my films doesn't function, we mean he doesn't function as a person, but he does function as a character—that is, until you take him as a symbol. At that point it is you who are not functioning. Why not simply accept him as a character, without judging him? Accept him for what he is. Accept him as a character in a story, without claiming that he derives or acquires meaning from that story. There may be meanings, but they are different for all of us.

S: There is a difference between an anecdote and a story. It is interesting to hear the director whose films are most like stories and least like anecdotes asking me to take his characters as if they were anecdotal, people who are shown doing things without obvious significance.

A: I'm not saying that they have no significance. I am saying that this mustn't be extracted from the film according to a preestablished scale of values. Don't regard my characters as symbols of a determined society. See them as something that sparks a reaction within you so that they become a personal experience. The critic is a spectator and an artist insofar as he transforms the work into a personal thing of his own.

S: What if I transform the film into something wrong?

A: There is nothing in the film beyond what you feel.

S: Ah, that's Berkeley: If a tree falls and no one sees it, it didn't fall. You believe that?

A: No.

S: Then the film is an objective fact and as such can be misapprehended. Unless you're willing to grant a meaning that the film forces or should force you to understand, you've got to accept every silly thing anyone has to say.

A: What can I say? I saw a film made by a friend of mine that was panned by all the critics and withdrawn by the censor. So I wrote to the newspapers explaining why it was a good film. But I am the only one who liked it, the only person in Italy!

S: But you're talking about evaluation, which is subjective. I'm talking about objective meaning. For example, is Sandro in *L'avventura* a weak or a strong character? Sandro is a fact, and the fact equals weakness. Right?

A: No, not right. In a way, he is a strong character.

S: In what way?

A: He is capable of giving up something he had never believed he would have the power to give up. You need strength for that sort of renunciation.

S: Why does he cry at the film's end?

A: For several reasons. A man who kills people during a war—which is an act of strength and courage—can also have a crisis and break down and cry. But it doesn't last long. Ten minutes later he will probably have stopped crying. But perhaps the crying will have released him from his crisis. Who knows?

S: If you think that Sandro's crying doesn't compromise him as a courageous character, I presume that you think that others of your characters possess courage. Yet most of them cry in the final shot.

A: Where?

S: The heroine cries at the end of *Cronaca*—

A: No? Yes.

S: —and that's the way one episode ends in *I vinti*, and *Il grido* means the outcry, which is what concludes the film. . . .

A: And Nene in *Le amiche*. . . .

S: And Sandro—and Vittoria in *Eclipse*. . . .

A: No. That is a very optimistic film.

S: Optimistic? Why, the lovers don't even see one another again, or do they?

A: No. They never meet.

S: If you wanted us to be so certain of this (let's leave the question of optimism aside for the moment), why does our last glimpse of Piero indicate a change in his character? Whereas he is frantic and agitated throughout the film, at the end we see him refusing to answer his phones, leaning back in his chair and smiling, while the breeze (which has such important symbolic overtones) ruffles his hair.

Piero, before the change, at the stock market. Eclipse.

A: There are people like that living all around me, full of contradictions, with weak and strong points, etc. My characters are ambiguous. Call them that. I don't mind. I am ambiguous myself. Who isn't?

S: Well, then, what of your statement that the film is optimistic? You once said that it illustrated these sentiments of Dylan Thomas': "There must, be praised, some certainty, if not of loving, well then, at least of not loving." Isn't it stretching things to call that optimistic?

A: No. If these characters can give up an affair that is just beginning, it is because they have a certain confidence in life. Otherwise, to speak in ugly old words, if they thought they could not survive the grief of having lost love, they would not have renounced each other but would have met again.

S: But the film begins with a renunciation (when Vittoria leaves her first lover) which is one of the unhappiest scenes in your films. Why is that so unpleasant and the later renunciation a sign of optimism?

A: Because the last scene is Vittoria's refusal to relive the first. That is, she doesn't want to suffer again the pangs of love. That is more or less the sense of it—put into words.

S: What about the ending? Doesn't it symbolize the end of the world: that house which will never be finished, those bricks lying on the ground, the

Even in the midst of passion, Vittoria seems dubious . . .   *. . . or downright mocking. Eclipse.*

rainwater pouring out of the barrel, the headline "Peace is weak"?

A: That only shows the error of this way of looking at films, because if we go back there, we will see that the house was finished!

S: All right. Let's change the subject. In America, the pace and rhythm of *Blow-up* were surprising to audiences used to your previous films. Do you think, albeit subconsciously, that you made *Blow-up* a briskly paced film in response to criticism of your "slowness"?

A: Absolutely not. The film was cut that way because I felt that this story needed such a rhythm; these characters moved nervously. I never at any time thought of the critics because I rarely read them.

S: What is the function of the neon sign in *Blow-up* that can't be understood since it isn't a word?

A: I didn't want people to be able to read that sign; whether it advertised one product or another was of no importance. I placed it there because I needed a source of light in the night scenes. Furthermore, I liked having the sign near the park. It is there for an obvious reason: to break up the romantic atmosphere.

S: Are you disturbed by critics who want to go beyond that level of explanation?

A: No, because, as I've said, every object in a film is an experience of the viewer's. After all, what does the director do? He conveys what he thinks he has seen. But, good Lord, the meaning of reality, living as we do enclosed in ourselves, isn't always clear to us. We could discuss for hours an episode or even an object found on the street. And the same thing is true of a filmed episode or object. Except that I never ask explanations from what I see in real life, but with a film I ask the

director. But the director is only a man. Very often I cannot give an explanation because I see only images, and images are what I transfer to the screen. Very often these images have no explanation, no *raison d'être* beyond themselves.

S: A moment ago you said you read criticism rarely. Are there no critics who seem important to you?

A: Sometimes I pick up a magazine and read a piece of film criticism—to the end only if I like it. I don't like those which are too free with praise because their reasons seem wrong and that annoys me. Critics who attack me do so for such contradictory reasons that they confuse me, and I am afraid that if I am influenced by one, I will sin according to the standards of the other.

S: I'd like to get back to *Blow-up*. In the so-called orgy sequence one sees two men in the background behind the models. Why?

A: There is no reason for it. They are two cameramen whom I did not notice and so forgot to cut.

S: It seems to me that a statement you make in the introduction to the Italian edition of your screenplays has a particular relevance to *Blow-up*: "We know that under the image revealed there is another which is truer to reality and under this image still another and yet again still another under this last one, right down to the true image of that reality, absolute, mysterious, which no one will ever see or perhaps right down to the decomposition of any image, of any reality."

A: I would say that this applies more to the finale of *Eclipse* than to *Blow-up,* but it applies to *Blow-up* as well. In the final scene of *Eclipse,* I was trying for a sort of decomposition of things.

S: You are quoted as saying that the two main

The search for reality in a photographed image provides the central plot for Blow-up.

components of your technique are the camera and the actors.

A: I never said such a thing. Where did you read it?

S: I forget.

A: People are always misquoting me.

S: Like Rex Reed?

A: He made that whole interview up. I've never said what you report. I've always said that the actor is only an element of the image, rarely the most important. The actor is important with his dialogue, with the landscape, with a gesture—but the actor in himself is nothing.

S: Indeed, your films are vulnerable on this ground. For example, why do you use so many foreign actors whose voices need to be dubbed into Italian? Why do you use an actor like Richard Harris, who, in my opinion, is so inexpressive?

A: You must bear in mind that a director isn't a painter who takes a canvas and does what he likes with it. We are more like painters in past centuries who were ordered to paint frescoes to specific measurements. Among the people in the fresco may be a bishop, the prince's wife, etc. The fresco isn't bad simply because the painter used for models people from the court of the prince who ordered and paid for it. At the moment I made *Red Desert* the Italian actor I wanted wasn't free, or asked for too much money, or didn't have an important enough name. Harris wasn't right—but not because he was foreign. Still, I chose him, and the mistake is mine. But for the voice: Why shouldn't cinema make such a change? The voice I dubbed in suited the role better than Harris' own voice, which is soft, toneless. I needed a stronger voice to match the image of Harris' figure. But I must repeat, when we find ourselves up against practical obstacles that can't be overcome, we must go forward. You either make the film as you can or don't make it at all.

S: Let's talk about the camera now. How much independence do you give your cameraman? That is to say, does Di Venanzo or Di Palma etc. impose his style on the film he shoots?

A: No. I have always imposed my wishes on the cameraman. Moreover, I have always picked them at the outset of their careers and, to a certain extent, have formed them myself. I used Di Venanzo, for example, in my segment of *L'amore in città*. I remember that at the time he

A painterly composition with Richard Harris. Red Desert.

wasn't used to handling photofloods, photospots—that type of lighting—he was still using projected lighting. I got him to use the other sort, to shoot in reduced zones, and to use a special bulb that produced just the quality I wanted. He was using the wrong sort of film until I made him use Kodak. Now he indicates in his contracts that he will shoot only with Kodak; I had to impose that choice on him, though he went on to make it his own style. Scavarda, the man who shot *L'avventura*, has never made another film that was as well photographed. In my short documentary *N.U.* I used Ventimiglia. His photography was superb. But I chose the shots, even the moments at which they should be taken. I would say, "We will start at twelve twenty and finish at twelve thirty-two, because after that the light won't be any good." Everything depends on what you put in front of the camera, what perspectives you create, contrasts, colors. The cameraman can do great things, provided he is well grounded technically. If a person hasn't the raw material, I obviously couldn't do anything with him. But all I ask of a cameraman is technical experience. Everything else is up to me. I was amazed to find that in America cameramen are surprised that this is the way I work.

S: In the interview you had with Alberto Moravia about *Zabriskie Point* you said that America was made up of two populations: two-thirds old and awful; one-third young and fine. Is that what you feel?

Perhaps what I seek is a new kind of story. In my next films I am going to change the kinds of stories I tell and the way I tell them.

S: Do you find that being a famous director causes you to have difficulties with other people?

A: Yes. There are times when my being an

A: Well, perhaps I got the proportions wrong. Two-thirds and one-third is too absolute a statement, and I don't know the whole of America well enough to say that. Obviously, in America as elsewhere, one finds contrasts in the population, but because it is such a violent country, the contrasts stand out. That is why I have said that Wallace and the hippies are brothers: They are each children of a country that runs to extremes.

S: You once said that critics should not speak of documentary elements in your feature films but rather of narrative elements in your documentaries. If you could, would you prefer dispensing with narrative?

A: No. I always want to tell stories. But they must be stories that evolve, like our own lives.

observer changes the scene. The moment I appear, people feel a little intimidated, and that intimidates me. Because I would like to feel part of the natural atmosphere. Often I have had to resort to tricks so as to be able to see things in their natural state. But difficulties remain, and I find them very annoying.

S: Your films show a familiarity with Italian high life. Do you enter this world out of choice or to get material?

A: It is very hard to make a distinction. One doesn't enter groups of people simply because one wants or needs to. One has an infinite number of opportunities that occur for no particular reason. Sometimes you feel a sudden unexpected pleasure at being where you find yourself. The reason may be frivolous—well, why not? I'm not the cold-blooded sort who carries a little notebook around and jots down phrases from the conversations he hears. I try to live an easygoing, natural life. What remains inside me is what I'll need to draw on.

S: In an interview I had with him, John Updike said something that fascinated me: "Being an artist is dangerous because it allows one to turn one's pain too quickly to profit."

A: I couldn't use that phrase today—"being an artist"—as if that were something exceptional. And if somebody transmutes his pain into profit, very good. I find that the most wonderful way to kill pain.

S: Why do you say "today"? Could you have used the phrase "being an artist" in some other period?

A: Yes, of course. I think that during the Renaissance everything was influenced by art. Now the world is so much more important than art that I can no longer imagine a future artistic function.

S: But today what is the function?

A: I don't know.

S: You don't know?

A: Do you?

S: Yes.

A: Then tell me.

S: You want *me* to tell *you* what the function of art is! No, you tell me what you think of François Truffaut.

A: I think his films are like a river, lovely to see, to bathe in, extraordinarily refreshing and pleasant. Then the water flows and is gone. Very little of the pleasant feeling remains because I soon feel dirty again and need another bath.

S: Do you mean his films pass away because their images aren't memorable?

A: Yes, that's part of it. No. His images are as powerful as those of Resnais or Godard, but his stories are frivolous. I suppose that's what I object to.

S: But I thought you weren't too concerned about the significance of a story.

A: René Clair told light stories, too, but they touch me more. I don't know why Truffaut's leave me unmoved. I'm not trying to say that he has no significance. I only mean that the way he tells a story doesn't come to anything. Perhaps he doesn't tell my kind of story. Perhaps that's it.

S: Do you dislike his way of working because it so emphasizes tricky camera effects?

A: There is never an image that gives me a blow in the stomach. I need these punches. Godard, on the other hand, flings reality in our faces, and I'm struck by this. But never by Truffaut.

S: Let me get back to your films for a moment. At the end of *L'avventura* do you mean us to believe that Sandro and Claudia are drawn closer together by their experience?

A: No. I don't mean to say anything at that moment except what the moment itself says: Here are two people who have their own stories—rather dissimilar ones—but who are, for the moment, rather close. What their future is I don't know. I couldn't say anything about it and wouldn't be interested in the subject.

S: When I ask you about the last scene of *L'avventura*, you say you can't tell me anything beyond it. Yet earlier, when I made a statement about the end of *Eclipse*, you countered me with a fact occurring in the real world after the film was finished. In one case, you're insisting that the work of art stops and we only know so much as it tells us; in the other, you speak of the work as if its life flowed on into the life from which it came.

A: [Silence.]

S: All right. I'll go back to *L'avventura*. Let me tell you what I think the end means. Now Claudia has looked at Sandro, and she knows him completely. That's all.

A: Yes. And it has no significance, no necessary effect on their future. Time and time

again we bind ourselves to people whose limitations we know all too well, and so what? You are absolutely right. The story is over.

S: Why does Anna leave behind her the Bible and *Tender Is the Night*? Did you choose the latter simply because you like Fitzgerald, or is the book supposed to point to Anna's relationship with her father?

A: No. I merely thought that Scott Fitzgerald was an author that a girl like that would read.

S: There are a number of long shots in the film that don't seem objective, that rather suggest the perspective of an onlooker. For example, at one point Sandro's car is in a piazza. Claudia and Sandro are seen moving around. Then we cut to a distance shot taken from the end of a street leading into the piazza, and we track into them. Is this supposed to suggest that Anna may be there?

A: That is the most ambiguous shot in the film. I think it is impossible to explain. I don't know why I wanted it. I don't believe Anna was there; I shouldn't say so, at least. But it is a great effort for me to recall the mood I was in when I shot that. I felt the need for mystery, which the tracking-in produces. That's what you feel, and that's why you wonder about the way it moves. I knew that shot would create puzzlement. I don't know what mystery was created, but some mystery was what I needed.

S: Whether or not you shoot a scene instinctively—

A: I always know where I want to go.

S: Yes. You've some sense of a desired effect for the spectator. What I'm trying to get at is the effect produced. Look, the spectator is discovering in *L'avventura* that Sandro and Claudia aren't really searching for Anna, right?

A: They're searching for her at the beginning, but, little by little, they forget her.

S: Exactly. Now, if that's true, the spectator has to become aware of the widening discrepancy between their action and its ostensible purpose. We've got to keep feeling that they're not doing enough, that they're going through the motions but don't really want to find her. So in the shot we're talking of, the track-in makes us feel "Maybe Anna's there. Why don't they walk down the street and—"

A: Why should she be there?

S: Why not? We don't know where she went. She could be anywhere.

A: Somebody told me that she committed suicide, but I don't believe it.

S: I'd like to ask just one question about *La notte*. Even among critics sensitive to your work I've heard derogation of the last scene. They say they find it implausible that Mastroianni should be able to listen to so much of Moreau's reading without realizing that she is reading his own letter. Moreover, even if plausible, the point made about the marriage has already been demonstrated and the letter reading is redundant. What do you think about this?

A: Nothing at all. The letter gives a precise portrait of the writer. It's a modestly written letter, showing how correct he was to think his talent unsatisfactory. Perhaps I should have had it read so that the words could not be understood. But then one might have had the impression that it was a very beautiful letter, whereas it wasn't even a nice one. And it is needed for the rhythm of the final sequence, which ends in a squalid, unnecessary act of lovemaking. Without the letter—the emotion it provokes—without the proof that he had forgotten it, that he was so drained of feeling, the action would have been too brutal and would have had a different significance.

S: Talking about *La notte*, I'm reminded of another subject I wanted to bring up: the question

A: I don't know in what way, but I know that it is serious. I shot it seriously.

S: I'd like to get your reaction to a criticism that has been made of your films from *La notte* on. For example, Dwight Macdonald, who was one of your most devoted admirers, eventually came to feel that you show effects in characters without detailing their causes. What do you say about this?

A: Is it important to show why a character is what he is? No. He is. That's all.

S: I agree with that for all of your films except *Red Desert*. In the others we see normal characters at a certain moment, and all our questions are about that moment. But Giuliana is sick, and sick people always make us want to know how they got that way.

A: To answer that question, I should have had to make another film. How someone becomes neurotic is a long, complicated story.

S: But doesn't the film show that her ambience is, in some sense, the cause of her neurosis?

A: Yes, but nobody becomes neurotic if they haven't a—I mean, neurosis attaches itself to a fertile ground where it can flourish. There is always a physical basis so that the environment

of repeated moments in your films. At the end of *La notte* the camera leaves the couple in the sand trap and pans to a new day dawning, with obvious irony. The same effect occurs in your first feature film, *Cronaca di un amore*, when the lovers meet in the planetarium. At precisely the moment when we first realize the hopelessness of their relationship, the lights go on, signaling a new day.

A: Not at all. It is only the light going on because the performance is finished.

S: What about ending both *Blow-up* and the English episode of *I vinti* with a tennis court?

A: People play tennis all over England. The two scenes have different purposes.

S: Why did you use the tennis court in *I vinti*?

A: Because it was near the courthouse and because I wanted to show this sort of life continuing while a man was condemned to death. A frivolous game.

S: But you've just pointed to a similarity of meaning. In both cases a murder has occurred, and yet we end up with a frivolous game.

A: It's not frivolous. The game is serious.

S: Without a ball?

A: Yes, in a way.

S: In what way?

plays its part only to the degree that the physical makeup of the person is susceptible to its influence. It doesn't interest me to go into the origins of neurosis, only its effects.

S: But there are characters in *Red Desert* who resist their environment and don't become neurotic. What typifies their makeup and is absent from Giuliana's?

A: I don't know, but Giuliana was more important to me than the others because she represents an extreme version of them. When I was searching locations for *Red Desert* I found myself among whole families of neurotics. One of them, for example, lives near an electric works whose turbines were going day and night. I found that noise almost unbearable, so that by the end of the day I thought I was losing my mind. However, the woman of that family never complained. Yet when we started up our generators, she came to the door and began to scream at us. Our generators were nothing compared to the turbines, but you see, they produced a new noise. That woman was a neurotic without knowing it. One day she will explode, just like Giuliana. In her, there is that basis for the environment to work on. Who knows why? Hereditary defects, maternal or paternal? There are a thousand reasons why a person is neurotic. Then one day the neurosis explodes. That explosion is what interests me.

S: In this film, am I right in thinking that the color represents Giuliana's state of mind?

A: Yes. It is transfigured from the point of view of a neurotic.

S: But there are problems. For example, in the hotel scene, the plants etc. are white before she enters the lobby. That is, we see color distortions that don't seem to be the result of her perspective.

A: It strikes me as an oversimplification to claim that all the shots from her point of view must be transfigured and those from anybody else's not. The whole world around her is transfigured.

S: For us as well?

A: Not for us. I mean that she is aware of the whole world crowding in around her.

S: Let me pose a similar question about another shot. In your interview with Godard, he asked you about the sequence when Corrado is telling the workers about Patagonia. Suddenly we cut from him to the wall, and the camera pans, tilts up, etc. You said this was Corrado's mind wandering to Giuliana. I find this difficult to accept. There is no other shot in the film from his perspective, and there is no reference to Giuliana made in his dialogue. How can the audience know that he is thinking of her just from seeing the shot of the wall?

A: I only said that he was distracted as he spoke and that he might have been thinking of Giuliana. Later he exits; what for? It seems likely that he is thinking of this love affair that has only just begun. After all, what does a man in love think about? It goes without saying that I could not insert a cut to Giuliana. Godard might have done that. I never could.

S: Why does the ceiling change colors in the seduction scene?

A: You mustn't ask me to explain everything I do. I can't. That's that. How can I say why at a certain moment I needed this. How can I explain why I needed a confusion of colors?

S: Recalling the end of *Il grido*, *Red Desert* opens with a strike. Why did you start the film this way?

A: Perhaps because I wanted to show that when a man is absorbed in his personal problems, he can ignore everything else.

S: But you're talking about *Il grido*. I asked you about *Red Desert*.

A: They are totally different.

S: But the strike—

A: There is no strike in *Red Desert.*

S: Yes. At the beginning.

A: Ah, at the beginning. But the situation is different. She isn't a person from the factory; she's only the wife of one. These problems are far from her concern.

S: That's what I've said. In both cases a strike is going on so that we can see how little concerned with it the central character is.

A: Well, so what! [We all laugh.]

S: Well, you are right in a way. Because the scene in *Red Desert* contains one implication missing from *Il grido*: a contrast between workers and the bourgeoisie. Because Giuliana is not only a neurotic, but also a bourgeoise. In your film both seem forms of incapacity.

A: Okay. But I would never be able to make this comparison.

S: There is so much evidence for it in the film.

Remember the woman whose apartment Giuliana and Corrado visit. They offer her husband a well-paying job, but she won't let him leave her. That scene depicts an obvious contrast between the familial feelings of the workers and the bourgeois characters who have already embarked on the road to adultery. Or remember that worker to whom Giuliana talks near the antennas.

A: [Silence.]

S: In the preface to the Italian edition of your screenplays you say, "The greatest danger for those working in the cinema is the extraordinary possibility it offers for lying." What did you mean?

A: To give an interpretation that we know is untrue to life. Because at that moment it is more interesting or amusing to put something in, to forget the real sense of what we are doing in our amusement with the medium.

S: Here you are speaking of a standard outside yourself; usually you say your only standard is what pleases you.

A: Whenever I make a film, I have inside me a certain truth—"truth" is a bad word. Here inside, rather, I have a confusion in the pit of my stomach, a sort of tumor I cure by making the film. If I forget that tumor, I lie. It is easy to forget, even if I subconsciously realize I am forgetting. Very easy.

S: Do you mean lying so as to please the audience?

A: No. Suppose I have to film a character coming down those stairs. I want to focus on his face because his expression while seeing a second character is very important in this moment. So I make him come down, but then my fancy is caught by that Lichtenstein. I like that, too. So I make the character stand for a moment before the Lichtenstein, with its glowing greens and whites. I like that. I'm tempted by it, but it is a mistake. It means making the painting important at the very moment that the only important thing is the character.

S: You've been quoted as saying that Aldo in *Il grido* is an admirable character because he seeks to break out of his unhappiness. Is that what you believe?

A: No.

S: So far as I can see, he's a sort of egoist of grief. All the women he meets are much braver than he.

A: I agree.

Aldo beats his mistress, Irma, when she tells him she is leaving him . . .

. . .uses various women in an attempt to forget her . . .

and, after adding their pain to his own, goes to the factory where he had worked and kills himself.

S: Am I correct in believing that you did not write the commentary that introduces *I vinti*?

A: I had a fight with my producers, and because of that, I was helpless. They insisted on an introduction and conclusion. I worked on it a little, but it isn't mine.

S: Did you learn anything of value from your apprenticeship to Carné?

A: I was in general disagreement with him for temperamental reasons and because we came from such different backgrounds. His poetic world never interested me. Perhaps what he taught me was a certain method of framing in which he was especially good. But I think time has dealt badly with his films.

S: I was surprised to read that you like Andy Warhol's films. Could you tell me why?

A: I can't say I like his films—some yes, the others no. I like his freedom. He does what he wants to and is fundamentally contemptuous toward cinema, which is usually taken too seriously. But I don't mean to say that he is contemptuous toward his own films. He makes more films than paintings now, so he must like his films. What I admire are his means: His characters do and say what they want to and are, therefore, wholly original in contemporary films.

S: Who are your favorite Italian directors?

A: Fellini and Visconti. The only young man who seems very promising to me at the moment is Bellocchio. There are others who have possibilities—Maselli, for one—but they haven't yet realized them. But I know all these men personally and so prefer not to discuss them.

S: Do you think any American directors belong in the front rank?

A: I don't have any favorite directors, in truth. My taste changes according to my current interests. I was, however, very impressed by *Easy Rider*. There are many young men today who are breaking the rules of American cinema, and they interest me. I've noticed in their work the influence of underground films; this shows how fruitful that movement has been.

S: With the exception of *Blow-up* each of your films is about a woman who loses something for having placed her faith in some man. Why do you keep returning to this plot?

A: You are making me think of this just now. It's very difficult to explain what I do. It is much more instinctive than you realize; much, much more. For example, I was amused by the articles I read about Joseph Losey, for I know how he works. He reads a book; if he likes it, he makes a film. But if a producer says, "Make another film," he drops his own choice. For me, of course, it is different, but even for me, the reasons that make me interested in a subject are, how shall I say, fickle. Many times I have chosen, among three stories, one for reasons that are entirely accidental: I get up and think this one will be stupendous because the night before I had a certain dream. Or perhaps I put it better by saying that I had found inside myself reasons why this particular story seems more valid.

S: Joseph Losey is a dreadful director. You see this in *Accident*, which is a veritable parody of Antonioni, in which he does things you do but for no discernible reason. Now are you trying to tell me—leave the selection of stories aside—that when you film a story, you are as unconscious of motives as he seems to be? Or is it simply that you don't wish to explain your motives?

A: I always have motives, but I forget them.

S: Sometimes you'll explain something in your films and at other times you refuse.

A: You make me look for a reason. I had none.

S: But in some cases. . . .

A: Maybe what I told you so far is completely wrong.

S: Sometimes you are willing—

A: I am never willing.

S: But you do.

A: Only when I am forced. Otherwise, I would prefer not to.

François Truffaut

Paris, September 1 and 3, 1970

Feature Films: 1959 *Les Quatre Cents Coups* (*The 400 Blows*); 1960 *Tirez sur le pianiste* (*Shoot the Piano Player*); 1961 *Jules et Jim* (*Jules and Jim*); 1963 *La Peau douce* (*The Soft Skin*); 1966 *Fahrenheit 451*; 1967 *La Mariée était en noir* (*The Bride Wore Black*); 1968 *Baisers volés* (*Stolen Kisses*); 1969 *La Sirène du Mississipi* (*Mississippi Mermaid*), *L'Enfant sauvage* (*The Wild Child*); 1970 *Domicile conjugal* (*Bed and Board*); 1971 *Les Deux Anglaises et le continent* (*Two English Girls and the Continent*).

The image presented when François Truffaut played the principal role in *The Wild Child*—that of a short, compactly built, but expressionless and ordinary-looking young man in his late thirties—leaves out his most striking features: a smile no less charming than his most charming films and the continuous glint of risible interest in his eyes. Truffaut's quick lucidity made him the ideal interview subject. Even when he had to interrupt an answer to await translation (he speaks no English), he never lost the thread. Nor did he ever hesitate or appear to find any question unexpected.

The interview took place in two sessions at Les Films du Carrosse, the production company he founded and runs. In his private office and throughout a small suite in the same building where *Bed and Board* was filmed, the atmosphere is literally one of "quiet elegance." The firm is clearly busy, but the employees seem to be running a doctors' consortium rather than a movie company.

During the period when I met Truffaut, he was attending to every detail of the press premiere of *Bed and Board*, prior to attending the Lincoln Center opening of *The Wild Child*. He invited me to the screening, where he greeted each guest personally. When, on the next day, I arrived for the interview, Truffaut was equally hospitable to me and particularly to my friend, Mme. Françoise Longhurst, who acted as translator.

During the conversation, growing rapport made translation progressively dispensable. Eventually, we began to respond to each other directly, joking away an occasional contretemps in our mutual involvement in the give-and-take.

The smile captured in a publicity photo for Bed and Board.

SAMUELS: You began your career as a critic. What effect has this had on you as a director?

TRUFFAUT: It is difficult to say, because one looks at films differently when one is a director or a critic. For example, though I have always loved *Citizen Kane,* I loved it in different ways at different stages of my career. When I saw it as a critic, I particularly admired the way the story is told: the fact that one is rarely permitted to see the person who interviews all the characters, the fact that chronology is not respected, things like that. As a director I cared more about technique: All the scenes are shot in a single take and do not use reverse cutting; in most scenes you hear the soundtrack before you see the corresponding image—that reflects Orson Welles' radio training—etc. Behaving like the ordinary spectator, one uses a film as if it were a drug; he is dazed by the motion and doesn't try to analyze. A critic, on the other hand (particularly one who works for a weekly, as I did), is forced to write summaries of films in fifteen lines. That forces one both to apprehend the structure of a film and to rationalize his liking for it.

S: Are there any critics you particularly admire or, as a director, have found particularly useful?

T: No filmmaker likes critics, no matter how nice they are to him. Always, he feels that they

didn't say enough about him, or that they didn't say nice things in an interesting way, or that they said too many of their nice things about other directors. Since I was a critic, I am perhaps less hostile to critics than other directors are. Nevertheless, I never consider the critic more than a single element in the reception of my films. The attitude of the public, publicity material, post-premiere ads: all these things are as important as critics.

S: There are two traditions in film. One, ultimately derived from silent film, emphasizes editing and camera movement. The other—which André Bazin seems to have preferred (and which he exemplified with a film like William Wyler's *The Little Foxes*)—is more theatrical, depends on staging. Now your closeness to Bazin is well known. However, I think that you are not only less theatrical than the directors he professed to admire but that, indeed, your camera work and editing are more varied than that of any director of equal stature. If this is so, *did* Bazin have the influence on you which he is widely assumed to have had?

T: I don't agree with the distinction you've made. Furthermore, Bazin overestimated *The Little Foxes,* which was just photographed theater—though it gave *him* a pretext for some interesting observations on the cinema. I would rather see a distinction made between filmmakers who attempt to keep the camera invisible—as John Ford did—and those who make it evident to the spectator.

S: All right. But your camera was once extremely visible and now is becoming less so. Why?

T: Because it became more visible in everyone else. No, I have a better reason: I have become more interested in my characters, in their situations, and in what they say.

S: As a critic, you attacked vigorously the films made by French directors during the period before the so-called New Wave. What made them so hateful to you?

T: I attacked them because they didn't have either a personal vision of life or of cinema.

S: But some of them created great films. Isn't that admirable? Or do you deny the greatness of a film like Carné's *Children of Paradise* or Clément's *Forbidden Games*?

T: I first became interested in films during the

war, and therefore the first films I saw were native. I liked *Children of Paradise*, all the Carné-Prévert films—I even liked *The Night Visitors*, though I don't anymore. I liked the films of Becker, Clouzot's *The Raven*, and, of course, above all, the films of Renoir. Then there was the shock of the American films after the liberation. I saw them when I was thirteen or fourteen and in random order, without knowing which were made during and which after the war. I found them all richer than French films—except the best of ours, like *Children of Paradise* and the films of Renoir.

S: I share your enthusiasm for six or seven Renoir films, but I've always been surprised at the extent of your admiration for him because though Renoir certainly made several first-rate films, it seems to me that some of his are even faultier than Carné's. They are even more theatrical—I think of a film like *Chotard and Company*. And then there is that awful sentimentality toward the French peasants, as in *Toni*.

T: No, I adore *Toni*; it is a very important film for me.

S: Why?

T: Because a filmmaker always thinks that his films aren't close enough to real life, and *Toni* shows how to attain that closeness. It is like a news item; its atmosphere is so real; there is a sort of madness in its events that one does not find in a novel or short story but only in something from real life. Because, you know, even when you start with something from real life, it gets theatrical when translated into a scenario, and then the reality is gone.

S: Precisely. Reality is what I find gone in *Toni*. Let me give you one example: In order to seduce Toni, the heroine pretends to have been bitten by a bee and asks him to suck the stinger out. Naturally, while doing so, his passion rises. That seems to me a theatrical cliché—perhaps not in all its details, but in its essentials.

T: It is a cliché of love, not a cliché of drama. Perhaps you would find this banal if you merely read the script. But the way it's done, the way the actors play it, makes it real.

S: You agree that the scene is banal in conception, but you think it's redeemed by the acting. That raises an interesting parallel to your own films. For example, in *Mississippi Mermaid*, when

Deneuve and Belmondo leave a movie theater where they have just seen *Johnny Guitar*, they agree that the reality of the performances transformed that horse opera into a story of real people. Wasn't that your intention in *Mississippi Mermaid* and many other films: to take a banal idea and cause the actors to give it real life?

T: Yes. Yes. Certainly.

S: Do you think Deneuve and Belmondo did save the story?

T: Yes. Whatever is wrong with that film is my fault and not the fault of my stars.

S: Like many American critics, I'm surprised by your admiration for Howard Hawks and John Ford. Would you explain why you like them?

T: Originally, I didn't like Ford—because of his

A typical Truffaut homage: Jean-Pierre Léaud meets a friend in front of a John Ford movie in Bed and Board.

material: for example, the comic secondary characters, the brutality, the male-female relationships typified by the man's slapping the woman on the backside. But eventually I came to understand that he had achieved an absolute uniformity of technical expertise. And his technique is the more admirable for being unobtrusive: His camera is invisible; his staging is perfect; he maintains a smoothness of surface in which no one scene is allowed to become more important than any other. Such mastery is possible only after one has made an enormous number of films. Questions of quality aside, John Ford is the Simenon of directors. Hawks, on the other hand, is the greatest cinematic intelligence among American directors. He isn't a cinema addict, nor is he anguished or obsessed. Rather, he loves life in all its manifestations, and because of this harmony with life in general, he was able to make the two or three greatest examples of every genre of film (except perhaps comedy, in which you have Lubitsch etc.). To be specific: Hawks made the three best Westerns (*Red River*, *The Big Sky*, and *Rio Bravo*), the two best aviation films (*Only Angels Have Wings* and *Air Force*), and the three best thrillers (*The Big Sleep*, *To Have and Have Not*, and *Scarface*).

S: M. Truffaut, Hawks' very versatility might be called an indication that he lacks a single vision of life or of cinema. Yet it is precisely that lack which you condemn in your French predecessors.

T: But Hawks does have a vision of life and cinema! For example, he is the first American director to show women as equal to men (think of his handling of Lauren Bacall vis-à-vis Humphrey Bogart in *The Big Sleep*). He always knows what he is doing. When he decided to make *Scarface*, realizing the danger of a film about sordid mobsters, he instructed his scriptwriter, Ben Hecht, to join him in constantly thinking about the history of the Borgias so as to give the film some tragic stature. It is to this that we owe the nearly incestuous love between George Raft and his sister in the film.

S: With the exception of *Jules and Jim* you usually adapt trash novels to the screen. Why?

T: I have often been asked to direct great novels, like Camus' *L'Étranger*, Fournier's *Le Grand Meaulnes*, Céline's *Voyage au bout de la nuit*, and *Du côté de chez Swann*. In each case my admiration for the book prevented me from making it into a film. *Jules and Jim* was an exception because it was so little known, and I wanted to increase its popularity by calling it to the attention of a large audience. However, despite what you say, I have never used a trash novel or a book I did not admire. Writers like David Goodis [author of *Down There*, the basis for *Shoot the Piano Player*] and William Irish [source for *The Bride Wore Black* and *Mississippi Mermaid*] have special value, and they have no counterparts in France. Here detective story writers are rotten, whereas in America writers as great as Hemingway work in that field. But because so many books appear each year in the States, these detective story writers are usually ignored. Ironically, this liberates them. Made humble by their neglect, they are free to experiment because they think no one is paying attention anyway. Not expecting to be analyzed, they put into their books anything they choose.

S: I hadn't thought of that. Therefore, they reflect life as a muddle—incomprehensible variety. You see life that way, too, don't you?

T: Yes. But let me tell you something. After seeing *Shoot the Piano Player* and liking it, Henry Miller was asked to write an introduction for a new edition of *Down There* and therefore had to read the book. He then phoned me to say that he suddenly realized that whereas my film was good, the book was even better. So you see, I don't film trash.

S: In an interview you gave Louis Marcorelles, you said that people shouldn't distinguish art films from the more commercial product, that the only true distinction was between good films and bad. Is that a correct quotation?

T: Yes.

S: But don't some directors force one to make the distinction that you deplore? In France, one thinks of Bresson, who is a great artist but whose films fail at the box office.

T: Commercial success is a result, never an intention. For example, Orson Welles never succeeded either, only one out of every two films Buñuel makes earns much money, etc.

S: Well, then. . . .

T: Well, in America I still think that you simplify this issue. You say that Hollywood films are commercial and New York films are artistic. That is wrong.

S: No doubt! There is a fascinating tension in

your films. In most of them, the hero yearns for and searches after security while your technique keeps showing us that nothing in the world is safe or permanent. Am I right?

T: Exactly. In fact, I said much the same thing in *Le Figaro* apropos my latest film, *Bed and Board*.

S: Leave *Bed and Board* out of it for a moment. It also seems to me that your technique hasn't been so redolent of insecurity lately.

T: Perhaps. But then for me life lately hasn't been so cruel!

S: Another constant in your films has been the subject of love. I'm not asking you to be a philosopher, but are you aware of some settled notion about love that recurs in your thinking or feeling about it and that you reflect in your work?

T: I have no ideas on this subject, only sensations, nothing more than I put in my films.

S: Whenever you treat erotic passion, you keep it distant, never allowing us to see it closely. Why?

T: I don't know.

S: Music is terribly important in your films. How do you choose a composer? After you've chosen him, how much control do you exercise over his work?

T: Actually, I am moving away from music in my films, like other directors (consider Buñuel and Bergman), who no longer use it at all. Still, it's not always possible to do without music completely, and I don't always like what I have. I like the music in *The 400 Blows* and *Shoot the Piano Player* but am not crazy about the music in *Jules and Jim*. The music in *The Soft Skin* and *Fahrenheit 451* is excellent, less so in *The Bride Wore Black*. *Stolen Kisses* has a wonderful score, as does *The Wild Child*. But the score of *Mississippi Mermaid* isn't very good, and that in *Bed and Board* is simply awful.

S: Now that you have made this rundown, can you generalize about the qualities that appeal to you in movie music?

T: It's very difficult to say. I like music to flow as uninterruptedly as the images. No, it's too difficult to express. Well, I suppose I can say that music shouldn't stop a film, which is what happens when the score is nonmelodic. For example, if you use jazz or pop music, the effect is antinarrative.

S: You've said that you never completely plan a film in advance and therefore improvise a good deal. What do you rely on to discipline your improvisations?

T: The dialogue and the actors. I try to create units of emotion. That's why, for example, I filmed each scene of *Bed and Board* in a single take.

S: Don't you also try to play each unit of emotion off against the next one?

T: Exactly. Yes, that's absolutely true. For example, one of my favorite moments in *Bed and Board* is when Antoine enters the apartment after a visit to his Japanese girlfriend and the camera cuts from his astonished face to his wife, who is dressed and seated in traditional Japanese style. The audience laughs. But when the camera closes in on her face, we see her tears, and this shocks the spectator. It is precisely this kind of emotional contrast that I love.

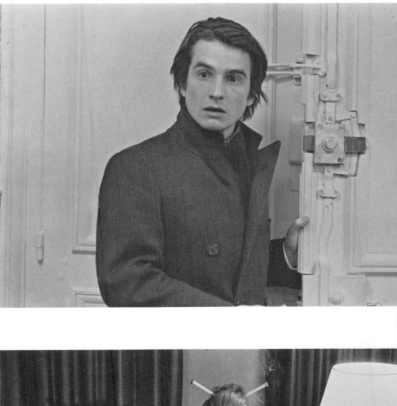

S: The acting in your films is usually extremely natural, but the situations in which the people find themselves are very formulaic. Is this a deliberate goal?

T: Yes . . . how shall I answer this? One proceeds always by contrasts. If the situation is extraordinary, then one must force the actors to be naturalistic, and vice versa. But this is something one cannot reflect upon; it is completely instinctive.

S: *The 400 Blows* is often compared to *Zero for Conduct.* Do you think this film or its director, Jean Vigo, influenced you?

T: Jean Vigo went further than anyone—even than Renoir—in achieving real, crude, natural images. For that reason, we French directors speak of a secret that Vigo possessed and that we long to fathom. In my opinion, the one who has fathomed it most completely is Godard, and *Breathless* is the closest in spirit to Vigo of any recent French film. The only reason Vigo was invoked so often apropos of *The 400 Blows* is that there are so few French films dealing with children that whenever one appears people are immediately reminded of *Zero for Conduct.* I was equally influenced, as a matter of fact, by the films of Rossellini and above all by *Germany: Year Zero,* which I greatly admire.

S: *The 400 Blows* is very episodic. Were any of the episodes introduced during shooting?

T: No. We followed the script without deviation.

S: Why did you include in *The 400 Blows* that little "guest" scene between Jean-Claude Brialy and Jeanne Moreau?

T: Brialy was a good friend of mine and offered to pass through the film, bringing Moreau with him. Since I knew and admired her work as a stage actress, I was very happy to agree.

S: This sort of thing occurs very often in your films. For example, one of your colleagues from your film company appears both in *Mississippi Mermaid* (where he plays Belmondo's business partner) and in *Bed and Board.* In the latter film Helen Scott, who was your interpreter with Hitchcock, makes a brief appearance. And I could go on. Why do you do this?

T: Why not?

S: Very funny! How about giving me a more serious answer. You realize that you've been greatly criticized for this. Critics have said you're playing a childish game, rubbing the noses of your viewers in their ignorance of your life, private tastes, etc. Do you just say *merde* to this criticism, or do you have some defense of this practice?

T: It's ridiculous to criticize this. The public isn't aware that I am putting my friends into my films. Only the few people who are aware question what I am doing. Moreover, I would never do it if I thought it might harm my story in any way. On the contrary, while writing I sometimes think, "This character is just like X. Why not have X play the role?"

S: But it isn't only putting your friends into your films; it's all the references to other films—like having Belmondo in *Mississippi Mermaid* recuperate at a clinic named Heurtebise, which alludes to Cocteau's *Orpheus*.

T: What difference does it make to the public if the clinic is called Heurtebise or Smee. It doesn't detract for anyone ignorant of the allusion, and it adds for someone who recognizes it. But those who know how I operate and perceive ten allusions in one of my films are so terrified that they've missed ten others that out of their own vanity they condemn this whole game—which, by the way, is not unique to me.

S: In *The 400 Blows* how do you want us to react to the scene in which Antoine whirls in the centrifuge? That scene has inspired sharply contrasting interpretations.

T: I didn't think of the reaction the public was going to have. I simply wanted to show a child in a situation that was new to him and because I wanted to avoid clichés—say, showing him on a roller coaster—I chose the centrifuge.

S: In *The 400 Blows*, during that marvelous interview with Antoine and the psychologist, why don't you show the psychologist?

T: The scene had to be improvised. I began by filming a 16 mm version in which I asked Léaud [who plays Antoine] questions, and he replied spontaneously. When we reached this scene in the actual shooting, I decided that what we were getting was inferior to my 16 mm trial, which had been so fresh. To regain that freshness, I adopted a peculiar method of working. I told everyone to leave the set except Léaud and the cameraman. Then I read out the scripted psychologist's questions, asking Léaud to answer on the spot with whatever came into his mind. During post-

synchronization, I had my questions read over by the actress who played the psychologist. However, since I wanted a woman with a very soft voice, who by this time was very pregnant and therefore reluctant to be filmed, I had only her voice but not her person, so you hear and don't see her.

S: Is this why the scene is full of interior dissolves?

T: Exactly. Since when I originally filmed the scene, I had banished the script girl and clapper boy from the set, I had no one to mark the precise moments of cutting and thus had to use the relatively imprecise dissolve to mark all connections between the pieces of Léaud's response that I decided to retain.

S: *The 400 Blows* ends with the famous freeze shot of Antoine, but that freeze is frequently anticipated in the film. For example, there are freezes of Antoine when the mother comes to school and learns that Antoine had said she was dead, when Antoine is being photographed by the police, when he is looking after his retreating friend in the reformatory sequence, etc. Was this motif intentional? If so, it indicates that, as it were, Antoine's end was fated.

T: I had no such plan. Moreover, a freeze like the one at the police station is simply the result of showing a still photograph. And the final freeze was an accident. I told Léaud to look into the camera. He did, but quickly turned his eyes away. Since I wanted that brief look he gave me the moment before he turned, I had no choice but to hold on it: hence the freeze.

S: The opening scene in *Shoot the Piano Player* tells us that the film will shift back and forth between lighter and darker emotions. Isn't it also an introduction to your theme?

T: I don't know. No, it comes from Goodis.

When I make a film by a writer, I like to read all his books. That scene you refer to occurs in another Goodis novel. I just thought it belonged there.

S: Why?

T: It's lifelike and striking. It establishes the film's tone.

S: As I said. But in it the two characters discuss the definition of love, which points to your subject. Without that scene the audience could feel they were seeing a mere gangster story.

T: I suppose so. You know when I film a gangster story, I feel safe: I know that the images will create the plot so that the dialogue can concentrate on love. On the other hand, when I take a story that is about love, I have to force it into a detective story mold. This is what I pushed to an extreme in *The Bride Wore Black*. We know that the heroine has to kill five men, so there is no plot suspense. Instead, I create suspense about character by not having the heroine ever discuss her motives. She goes to each place, says nothing, and the man courts her.

S: I'm happy to hear you say that. I never thought this film was properly understood. I always thought it was about the meaning of love.

T: It is a film that illustrates five different ways of comporting oneself with a woman.

S: All of them bad, which is why she becomes a sort of avenging angel striking men down in behalf of her sex.

T: Exactly.

S: That is why each murder reflects the victim. For example, victim number one has no capacity for fidelity. On the day of his wedding, he is capable of being drawn to a balcony, where he has no business being, because he wants to flirt with Moreau, who is standing there. This allows her to push him off. The third victim, whose wife is away, wants to be closeted with her so they can make love, but he first has to get rid of his son. Therefore, she can persuade him to play hide-and-seek and, during the game, can wall him in a closet.

T: Yes, but all those details are in the novel. Only the characterization originates with me.

S: In that first murder, when we have a shot of her scarf floating down, did you mean thereby to block our disapproval of her, since the shot is so lyrical and makes the audience feel pleasant?

T: No. It was completely accidental. I had

Victim No. 2 (Michel Bouquet).

thought the scarf would fall very quickly. By chance that day the air current caused it to fall very slowly and in gentle movements. I liked that, and so I followed it all the way to the ground.

Victim No. 4 (Charles Denner) will be killed by the arrow he arranges picturesquely for his murderess.

S: Did you mean the character played by Charles Denner to be a latent homosexual?

T: I don't know.

S: In *Shoot the Piano Player* when Charlie and Lena are walking together for the first time and he is trying to decide whether to make a pass, you

have his conscience speak in a voice different from his own. Why?

T: Because Charles Aznavour's voice is too authoritative to be appropriate at that moment.

S: Another odd effect: When the owner of the bar informs on Charlie, you show him in three oval frames, panning across them. Why?

T: I don't think that worked. Maybe it could be taken out.

S: I don't understand the editing in the love scene between Lena and Charlie. The pattern of cuts and dissolves is obscure.

T: I wanted to give the impression of passing time and, again, because Aznavour's voice is too authoritative, I didn't want him to speak in the scene. So I took bits of Lena speaking and used the transitions you mention to unite them.

S: Yes, but there are elisions in the time sequence, which is also, unless I'm mistaken, sometimes scrambled.

T: Now I remember. I wanted to give the impression that they sleep, get up, talk, go back to sleep, get up, etc. etc. That's why it seems as you say.

S: If you had to give an account of the meaning of this film, what would you say?

T: I made *Shoot the Piano Player* completely without reflection. When people first saw it, they said, "Why did you make a film about such a disgusting lowlife?" but I never posed this question to myself. You see, I love *Down There* very much. I am always drawn by the fairy tale aura of the American detective novel—as I also was in *The Bride Wore Black*. Both films are like Cocteau films, mixing elements that are typically American and typically French and thus achieving an effect that is timeless, without country. . . .

S: Not of this world.

T: Exactly. Well put. Not of this world. That's what I want. When Godard saw *Shoot the Piano Player*, he said this is the first film laid in a country of the imagination. I don't think one should say at the beginning of a film, "This takes place in a purely imaginary world," because then the audience will certainly feel let down since they will expect too much. But the audience should be made to feel gradually, while watching the film, that they are in no certain place.

S: In *Jules and Jim*, what do you think of Catherine?

T: She is totally fabulous. If you met such a woman in real life, you would see in her only faults—which the film ignores.

S: Not at all. In fact, many critics—at least in America—asserted that Catherine was a witch, a neurotic, a man-eater.

T: You know what a French psychiatrist said: "*Jules and Jim* is about two children in love with their mother."

S: As far as you're concerned, why does Catherine kill Jim?

T: Because it happens in the last pages of the novel. Even the casket in the flames comes from the book. Everything I show is from the novel. I can't say why she killed him because the book doesn't say. It isn't a psychological novel. It is simply a love story that started and finished. If there is one difference between film and book, it is that the film is more puritanical. You see I was under thirty when I made it, whereas the novel's author was a man of seventy-three.

S: Why did you put in the book-burning sequence?

T: Because Jim is German, and that is the Reichstag fire. So far as I was concerned, that marks the end of an epoch—an epoch of artists and dilettantes. Moreover, it prepares us for the burning of Jim and Catherine which ends the film.

S: Yes. This historical dimension is very important in the film. Isn't that why each successive scene includes a Picasso from a later period? Isn't that the way you mark time?

T: Yes.

S: This film is full of photographs, this story is full of stories. Why?

T: *Jules and Jim* was an autobiographical novel, written fifty years after the events reported in it. What I admired about the book was not only the story, but the temporal distance, which I had somehow to render on film. Thus I rarely shot the characters in close-up, and when I did, I tried to give full-length views. I wanted the film to look like an album of old photographs.

S: You so often answer my questions about your intentions by saying you do what you do to be faithful to the novel you are adapting. What about *Fahrenheit 451*, which is very untrue to the spirit of its source? Ray Bradbury's novel is an allegory about the McCarthy era, highly political in its theme. Were you aware of this? In any case, why doesn't the political dimension appear in your film?

T: It is not the sort of thing that interests me. I usually make films from books I admire, as I've told you. *Fahrenheit 451* was different. One day I was having a conversation with a friend about science fiction, which I told him I didn't like because it is too far from reality, too arbitrary in its events, incapable of rousing any emotions in me. In rebuttal, my friend told me of the plot of Bradbury's book, describing a society in which books were forbidden, in which firemen did not put out fires but set them in order to burn books, in which men who wanted to read were forced to commit the text to memory. When I heard all this, I instantly decided to make the film, but I had not actually read the novel.

S: Do you have a special feeling for books?

T: No. I love them and films equally, but how I love them! When I first saw *Citizen Kane*, I was certain that never in my life had I loved a person the way I loved that film. My feeling is expressed in that scene in *The 400 Blows* where Antoine lights a candle before the picture of Balzac.

S: You say that politics didn't interest you as a theme for *Fahrenheit 451*. But though the reference is different from Bradbury's, your film does have a slight suggestion of political allegory. The firemen wear quasi-Nazi uniforms, Oskar Werner has a thick German accent, and anyone who comes to the film after seeing *Jules and Jim* sees in the earlier film's newsreel sequence about the Reichstag fire a sort of model for *Fahrenheit 451*.

T: Originally, *Fahrenheit 451* was to have been made in France with Jean-Paul Belmondo. I couldn't find financing here and so had to shoot the film in England with Oskar Werner, who had

not been my first choice for the starring role. I did want an actor of his type—one more poetic than psychological—but I did *not* want an actor with a German accent. During the shooting I kept telling him to play Montag gently; *he* decided to play the man as a Nazi.

S: Beginning with *Fahrenheit*, the influence of Hitchcock seems to make itself felt. Is that why you made a studio film and used back projection in the Hitchcock manner?

T: That has nothing to do with Hitchcock. We were in England, yet I wanted to show the French countryside. Consequently, I had to shoot in a studio and project the French countryside on a screen behind the action.

S: I have the impression that this film began to bore you while you were making it. The first fifteen minutes are utterly successful: tense and moving. Later you dissipate the tension by little jokes that seem to subvert the film's seriousness. For example, when Cyril Cusack (the chief) leads the firemen in a book search in a park, he finds a minuscule book in a baby's pram and wags a finger at the child. Later, when Montag has begun to read and is rejected by the firepole (which the men go up rather than down), Cusack turns to him and says, "What's this, Montag, something wrong between you and that pole?" At the end of the film, when we meet the book people who have

"become" books, a set of twins appears, one named Pride, the other Prejudice. And so on.

T: Ha-ha. You know it is oppressive for me to make a film on a "big subject." I found this film lacking in humor and so put in those jokes you mention. But perhaps some of them are wrong. You see, if I had done the film in French, I would have had complete control of the language; in English, I never quite knew if a line was right. Making *Fahrenheit* is what taught me that dialogue was more important in a film than I had realized. It is, in fact, the *most* important thing. With images, if they are good, one attains seventy percent of possible satisfaction; with good dialogue, one attains perhaps ninety percent. The most personal of attributes is one's fingerprint; dialogue is the fingerprint of a film. In *Fahrenheit 451* I was blocked by my imperfect control over the dialogue, and therefore, I was frustrated. Since then, you will note, all my films have a lot of dialogue in them.

S: Since you like dialogue so much, why don't you write plays?

T: I am bothered by the theater. The performance is not the same every night. Beside, I hate to talk to several people at once.

S: I can't find any significance in *The Soft Skin*. It seems almost a documentary.

T: But a documentary powerfully dramatized!

S: I wonder about that and about numerous implausibilities. Why should so lovely a girl be attracted by the middle-aged hero, Lachenay?

Jean Dessailly (Lachenay) and Françoise Dorleac (his mistress) in The Soft Skin.

Montag having trouble with the pole.

T: But that is very normal. In life one never stops wondering what someone sees in someone else.

S: All right. I accept the fact that she falls in love with him, but can I believe that she spends all those hours sitting in a restaurant listening to him lecture about Balzac?

T: Even an unappealing man becomes appealing when he discusses his work. That's why I made him discuss Balzac not in a scholarly way but as if he were describing a football match. His profound involvement in his subject moves her.

S: Do you think Françoise Dorlèac listens in that way?

T: She needn't show her interest. She is a girl of the twentieth century impressed by a man of the nineteenth.

S: The film is full of uneventful shots of objects. Were you trying to establish a certain style with this mute realism?

T: That didn't give a style to the film; it *is* its style.

S: *Stolen Kisses* seems more improvisational than your other films.

T: It was.

S: How did the improvisations take place? Were you or Léaud their guiding spirit?

T: The improvisations were forced on both of us because of the desperate state I was in when the film was made. Nothing worked. I had already written *The Wild Child* and *Mississippi Mermaid*, yet I was shackled to a rotten project. I got into it because I had wanted to make another film with Léaud but couldn't find any material. We began with a vacuum that had to be filled. We said, "Let him have a sweetheart, let him have an affair with a married woman, let him work for a detective agency, etc."

S: What did you rely on to hold it all together?

T: Léaud. There are actors who are interesting even if they merely stand in front of a door; Léaud is one of them.

S: One of the best scenes in *Stolen Kisses* occurs when the homosexual comes to the detective in search of his missing boyfriend. One hand, which is gloved, caresses the other, suggesting subtly but brilliantly the nature of the man.

T: The gesture was improvised. We hit on it naturally because everything about that character needed to be bizarre.

S: It's particularly interesting because the homosexual's love is both more powerful and more moving than the normal affairs of Antoine.

T: But this is a true story which a friend learned while interviewing a detective. The dentist in the film is also taken from real life. Everything in that film is true.

S: One of the film's most striking scenes shows Antoine looking into the mirror and chanting the names of the two women in his life. How did you hit on this idea?

T: I needed to show that Antoine was torn between them, but there was no other character in the film whom he could talk to. Therefore, I had him talk to himself.

S: It is very charming. But, you know, many people hold that sort of charm against you. They say you calculate such effects simply to please, with one eye cocked at the audience.

T: But the scene isn't charming. It is long and makes people uneasy. In Germany, they cut it.

S: But what about the general point?

T: The role of Antoine is so close both to me and to Jean-Pierre Léaud that we never think of other people. For example, Antoine never quarrels with anyone in the films because I am the same way. If a quarrel begins, I simply leave.

S: Is that why you won't correct misinterpretations of your work?

Truffaut (top); Léaud (bottom).

T: In *The 400 Blows* I thought I had presented the parents and Antoine very neutrally. The parents were guilty of showing so little love, but, after all, Antoine was very difficult. Then, to my surprise, I found that audiences thought the film slanted in the child's favor. But one learns to live with misunderstanding. Once the film is finished, that's all I care about.

S: Did you feel that way as a critic?

T: I never understood the meaning of a film. I am very concrete. I only understand what is on the screen. In my whole life, I have never understood a single symbol.

S: I would like to talk about *Mississippi Mermaid* for a while. Andrew Sarris pointed out that the film was cut in New York.

T: Though the film wasn't very expensive, United Artists considered it a major project, and because of the stars, they had high hopes for its success. But the film was a big flop in Paris. The critics didn't like it, nor did the public—perhaps because Deneuve and Belmondo didn't appear in their usual sort of roles. Owing to the Paris reception, United Artists asked me to let them cut about eight minutes out of the film when it opened in New York. I could have refused, but in this business I hate to see people losing money on my account. I should have held out, though, because when the film opened in Japan, it proved a smash: my greatest success and the greatest success either Deneuve or Belmondo had ever experienced.

S: Are you now able to control the cuts producers wish to make?

T: One never has that power. Frequently, one simply doesn't know what has been done. For example, I only learned about the cuts in *Stolen Kisses* because a journalist who had seen the film in an art house supported by the government complained that it was shocking to see cuts in films presented under such auspices. The journalist's article forced the cinema distributor to replace the scenes. But, of course, that doesn't always happen, much less get reported.

S: Many people in the States thought the stars implausible in their roles.

T: Implausibility is not a crime in all films. *Mississippi Mermaid* is a fairy tale for adults.

S: Don't you rather overemphasize that fact—so much so that your serious ideas get compromised? For example, why did you superimpose that colored map of Réunion every time Belmondo took a trip there? I felt the need for more authenticity and fewer tricks to prepare the audience for your final statement about love.

T: It's possible.

S: It seemed to me that footage from *Fahrenheit 451* gets reused when Belmondo has his dream at the clinic.

T: It seems that way to me, too. Actually, the scene was shot with a monorail in *Fahrenheit*, whereas in *Mermaid* a road and trees were used. It is, you are quite right, the same effect with different means, but I think it works better in *Fahrenheit*.

S: Why did you include that shot in which Belmondo climbs Deneuve's balcony? It seems to me only an opportunity for Belmondo to show off his athleticism.

T: Not at all. I did it for myself. First, I set the scene in that square because it is named after Jacques Audiberti, a French writer for whom I have the deepest admiration and whom I always think of when making my films. I wanted it to be very hard for Belmondo to get into Deneuve's room, but also unusual. So I couldn't have him wait for the concierge to leave or somehow steal the key. When I got to the square, I noticed this

house with many balconies. First, I had a sign hung, turning it into a hotel (the sign says "Hotel Monorail" because *Monorail* is the title of one of Audiberti's novels). Then I thought that I would shoot the whole scene of Deneuve leaving the hotel and entering the cabaret and then of Belmondo going to the hotel and climbing from one balcony to the other in one single movement of the camera. That was a fascinating shot. He climbs so I could take it.

S: Does the film's last scene take place in the cabin from *Shoot the Piano Player?*

T: The very one.

S: I was struck by the number of long shots in *The Wild Child.* Was this an attempt at detachment?

T: As in the case of *Jules and Jim,* I was telling a period story and I wanted some suggestion of historical distance. Furthermore, the child star couldn't understand the exigencies of cutting and couldn't recapture his rhythm from one take to the next, so I had to shoot him from a distance.

S: Did you have eighteenth-century painters in mind when you shot this film? Many scenes reminded me of them.

T: I know little about painting and always think in terms of prints. I dislike paintings and hate going to museums.

Compositions from The Wild Child.

S: You're right. The shots are more like engravings than paintings. Is the frequent use of iris shots meant to recall the cameo or oval engravings of the period?

T: In the last twenty minutes of *Mississippi Mermaid* I experimented with fades produced not by countering the negative but by shutting off the camera. But the camera we used for *The Wild Child* didn't permit this method. So Nestor Almendros, who is a brilliant technician, offered to use the iris shot.

S: How autobiographical is the film?

T: Some people have said that Dr. Itard is Truffaut and the child Léaud; I think that Itard is André Bazin and the child Truffaut.

S: Both seem true.

T: In any case, I think this film matured me. Previously, I always identified with the young men in my films; here I identified with an adult for the first time. On the other hand, I went back to the time of *The 400 Blows* because once again I was directing a thirteen-year-old boy. According to the *Cahiers du Cinéma*, the film isn't about a doctor but about a director. I didn't think of that when I was working, but it is true nonetheless because there are obvious similarities between the doctor who teaches the boy to be civilized and a director who teaches an actor to be a character in his film.

S: I agree that this film is especially mature: sober, restrained, serious.

T: This is a responsible film where I didn't make any jokes.

S: It is your *Émile*, isn't it, in which you most fully express your typical belief in the perfectibility of man?

T: Yes.

S: I am also impressed by the implied political assertion in Victor's ultimate refusal to accept injustice.

T: That is the scene in the report that determined me on making the film.

S: Here, at last, politics enters the world of Truffaut.

T: Possibly.

S: Before *The Wild Child* you seem to be avoiding politics. When it enters, you make fun of it. For example, in *Bed and Board* it's the prostitute who is political.

T: That wasn't a joke. Usually politics are forced into a film because artists, in order to please their friends, make obligatory references. Yesterday it was the Algerian War; today, Vietnam. But this is not artificial. This shows politics as it affects the people. So she says formerly her customers stopped coming by the twenty-third of the month, whereas now they stop by the fifteenth.

S: In short, they run out of money more quickly because of inflation.

T: Exactly. But, you know, there are other references to politics in the film. For instance, when the concierge changes all the garbage cans from metal to plastic, he says the new ones signify the new society. The "new society" is a slogan borrowed from you Americans by Chaban-Delmas.

S: While we are on the subject of films and politics, would you please tell me what you think of *Z*?

T: I think it's a good film which is more important politically than artistically. It was politically efficient because it reached people who were not already convinced. After seeing *Z*, the average man leaves the theater thinking that it isn't good for a country to be run by the military. Although the authors never claimed this, I believe the film had an influence on French politics. In an interview, I said that it contributed to the referendum which brought down de Gaulle. A pity it wasn't stronger; then we might have also avoided Pompidou!

S: I hated *Z* because it was so cartoonlike. I wish you would make a political film. It would be sure to have a lifelike ambiguity.

T: But then it would be politically useless.

S: What about a book like Dostoyevsky's *The Possessed*?

T: I never read it. But for an example think of *La Marseillaise*, which Renoir made when he was a Communist. That film fails because it is ambiguous politically. The most interesting characters turn out to be Louis XIV, Marie Antoinette, and the Swiss Guards, rather than the people who should have been the heroes. Still it is a beautiful film. On the other hand, Brecht, whose plays are effective politically, always relied on tricks and bad faith.

S: To get back to *The Wild Child*—I noticed that the sound track was especially careful. The sound of footsteps, for example, fully created the reality of those old rooms.

T: This is a story of sound because the child is originally deaf. As a result, I was more scrupulous than usual, reshooting when I was dissatisfied with the sound and not—as I usually do—only when I was dissatisfied with the image.

S: When I saw *The Wild Child*, I immediately thought of *The Miracle Worker*. Is there a connection between these films?

T: Yes. In 1962 I saw the play performed in its French version: *Miracle in Alabama* by Marguerite Duras. The play's little star was prodigious; I cried throughout the performance. The next day I wired New York for the film rights, but I was told that a movie was in progress, directed by Arthur Penn. I was terribly disappointed, but I was consoled by the fact that I had liked Penn's *The Left-handed Gun* and so thought he would do the play justice. A few months later I went to New York, and the first night of my visit they screened *The Miracle Worker* for me. I also met Penn then, who had just come from the hospital where his wife had given birth.

Sometime later I read Helen Keller's autobiography, and only then did I realize that the film was inferior to its source because it had manipulated what was more powerful in its original state. But I don't think it was Penn's fault. You see, William Gibson, the play's author, also produced and wrote the film, so Penn was translating another man's idea.

When I came across Dr. Itard's report, which had been out of print for a long time, I instantly felt the emotion I had felt when first seeing *Miracle in Alabama*. I tried to analyze my reasons for finding the story so powerful. Itard's situation is the most heroic in the world because he is doing bad things to another human being in order to save him. I have had this experience myself: the first time I took one of my daughters to the dentist.

S: Your career and Penn's have crossed since then, haven't they? Weren't you supposed to direct *Bonnie and Clyde*?

T: Benton and Newman wrote the script for me. But I refused to direct it because the story took place in Texas and was thus too purely American for me. However, I did spend two days in New York with them trying to tighten what they'd written. Later, when it seemed that I'd never find money to make *Fahrenheit 451*, I told Benton and Newman that I had changed my mind and would

direct their film. This time the studio said no, so I went on to London to make *Fahrenheit 451*. When I got to London, I met my old friend Leslie Caron, who was looking for a film to make with Warren Beatty. Out of my friendship for her, I gave her Benton and Newman's scenario. Eventually she no longer wanted to join Beatty in a film, but Beatty decided that he wanted to make *Bonnie and Clyde*. He requested the rights from Benton and Newman for two months, during which they refused him, but in the third month they gave in, because when Warren Beatty wants something, he gets it. Leslie Caron, as you know, was replaced by Faye Dunaway.

S: You've told me you don't like the music in *Bed and Board*. Why didn't you replace it?

T: Had I made the film for United Artists, I would have thrown it out and reused the music from *Stolen Kisses*, but since the two films were made for different companies, I couldn't do that. Anyway, once music is recorded, there isn't much you can do. You can discard what you don't like, repeat certain phrases, not much more. The music is what it is in *Bed and Board* because Albert Duhamel, the composer—I say this without laughing at him—is one of those artists who believes that since the May Revolution of 1968, art can never again be what it was.

S: But the music is secondhand Darius Milhaud!

T: No. Stravinsky.

S: There are several other problems in the film. I don't, for example, like the satire of the American businessman.

T: Helen Scott said the same thing.

S: But not because I'm a superpatriot. On the contrary, I don't think it's sharp enough.

T: I was hoping to find an actor as subtle as Michael Lonsdale for the part. I failed.

S: And the plot is so predictable. All the events are so familiar.

T: Yes, and I suppose that makes *Bed and Board* weaker than *Stolen Kisses*. But in the earlier film there was no set subject, which made for unpredictability. Here, it is the reactions of the characters within a set framework that remain unpredictable.

S: Antoine is a writer in *Bed and Board*. Did you ever want to be one?

T: A little, but not much. Anyway, that scene wasn't in the original script. I introduced it during shooting.

S: In general, do you write most of your scripts?

T: Always.

S: In this day of women's lib do you anticipate criticism for making a film that seems to support the double standard and the wife's permissive attitude toward her husband?

T: No. I think the film is more likely to be criticized because the heroine is an old-fashioned bourgeoise, but the type hasn't been sufficiently presented.

S: One scene in the film seems to contain two jokes, and I'm wondering if the latter was intentional. When Antoine sees the Japanese girl and her roommate under the door, we are obviously to laugh at how long it's taking to get rid of the roommate, who then comes out saying she has to visit her sick mother. But visually the scene is funny in its suggestion of fetishism—all those boots and chains.

T: I dressed Kiriko by chance, only asking her not to wear Oriental clothes that morning. Homosexuality never enters my films.

S: I predict that the American audience will see it here.

T: Not the public, the American critics!

S: *Touché!*

T: When I go to New York I'm also sure they shall demand my sign of the zodiac. I've been warned about it!

S: You're famous. What does that feel like?

T: One is never famous. He is known by certain people and not by others.

S: A profile in the *Times* said that you are interested in nothing but films. How can that be when your films show extraordinary sensitivity to other people? I'd like to give you the opportunity of correcting the impression presented in the *Times*.

T: You are right in saying that the legend is a bit false, but I let it stand. You can't count on my cooperation in correcting it.

S: Are there any directors whom you feel people underestimate?

T: Howard Hawks and Hitchcock among Americans; Claude Berri in France; Rossellini; no English director is underestimated.

S: Let's talk about Hitchcock. Although I admire him, I do so in a very different way from you.

T: Write a book then.

S: Don't you think you overcomplicate Hitchcock? You said, for example, that you've never

understood a symbol, yet you are forever understanding symbols in your book on Hitchcock, and I don't think they exist. Take *The Birds*. *The Birds* is a disaster, yet—

T: A disaster?

S: If you want to know why, I'll explain.

T: No. I can guess.

S: All right. Then, please, you explain why you hate Antonioni so.

T: First, for his lack of humor. He is so terribly solemn, so terribly pompous. I don't like the image he projects of himself as *the* psychologist of the feminine soul. When De Gaulle was trying to restore the confidence of the French in Algeria, he said, "French men and women, I have understood you." Antonioni stands like that and says, "Women of the world, I have understood you." And he follows the fashion. That's why he was arrested the other day at the London airport with hashish in his shoe.

S: No, marijuana, and it happened months ago.

T: All right. But look, it is first of all unnecessary to put marijuana in your shoe because you can get it just as easily in London as in America. And more important is the fact that four years ago he wasn't smoking marijuana, but now he is. That shows his childish need to keep up with youth.

In fact, my hostility to Antonioni helped me make *The Wild Child*. One of the big themes today is the difficulty of human communication. This is very nice; it makes for good conversation among intellectuals. But when you come in contact with a family that includes a deaf-mute child, only then do you realize what lack of communication means. I wanted to show a real lack of communication in my film, not the modish variety that involves Antonioni.

S: In an interview you gave the *Cahiers du Cinéma* you denigrate the deliberately difficult or subtle, but many of your films (above all, *Jules and Jim*) are both difficult and subtle. Were you misquoted, or would you now modify this assertion?

T: No. The interviewers and I cooperated in that oversimplification. What I should do is distinguish between intention and execution. Take, for example, Joseph Strick who decides to film *Tropic of Cancer*, *Ulysses*, and Genet's *The Balcony* without being cinematically armed for the job. Were he more honest, he would attempt things for which he is better prepared: simple things. *The Rules of the Game* and *The Golden Coach* are very subtle films, but Renoir didn't, like Strick, set out to be subtle; subtlety was an attribute of his character. When simple people attempt to bring subtle writers to the screen, the discrepancy between source and adapter always spoils the result. I much prefer Godard, who takes small novels and treats them in the manner of a great novelist. I have tried this, too. Both *Shoot the Piano Player* and Godard's *Band of Outsiders* try to give cinematic equivalents of a novel by Raymond Queneau, but neither of us would actually dare to adapt one of Queneau's novels.

S: In the same interview you made your famous analogy between film and a circus. That analogy implies something that people have criticized you for: a streak of P. T. Barnum, a desire to give thrills without caring about their meaning.

T: I made the analogy simply to remind people who come to film from literature that a director must always be aware that he is performing before a crowd. Men like Orson Welles, Nicholas Ray, and Elia Kazan—men who have been actors, who have lived the realities of the theater, who have worried that the public might be bored, that the play must move forward, that a progression must occur which will hold the public's attention—such men would understand my point. Even Bergman would understand. He is afraid to be boring; that is why he never goes beyond an hour and a half. One is always influenced by what he did before becoming a director. Welles was an actor. Fellini was a caricaturist; he makes caricatures in film. Buñuel was an administrator. That is why all his films finish shooting on time, use only twelve thousand meters of stock, and are edited in ten days.

S: You are particularly good with your actors, though you are said to be very gentle on the set. How then do you get such marvelous performances?

T: By gentleness. And I proceed always by contradiction.

S: Can you give me an example?

T: Yes. In *Jules and Jim* the danger was that Catherine would be too beautiful. I told Jeanne Moreau to remember Scarlett O'Hara for capriciousness but also to bring something sad to her caprices. It was important that the constant shifts in mood not make her resemble a comedian:

as we say in French, *une belle emmerdeuse.* Therefore, I asked for gravity where there was lightness and vice versa. This is the method I follow in everything I do, even though it confuses the public. For example, at the end of *The Soft Skin*, when the woman has just killed her husband, I have her smile. I had great difficulty getting that expression, which is not quite a smile but the woman getting ready to smile. In real life, I suppose the woman would fall on the ground, screaming, but that would never do in my film. Her first reaction is relief. After that, perhaps something else will come. I had to get just the right amount of smiling, however, as you see, for otherwise the audience would think she had lost her mind.

S: But in the preceding scene where the wife gets her rifle ready to kill her unfaithful husband, don't you think you go on awfully long? I found it boring. Moreover, I laughed where I shouldn't have. Do you remember when she puts her rifle under her coat to hide it and then walks out as if she has hidden it, whereas the audience sees it sticking out under her hemline?

T: The audience in the theater broke up at that moment.

The protruding gun (of which Truffaut made understandably few stills) is circled in white.

S: So it was a mistake?

T: A technical defect. After making many films, one learns that in such a scene you must first photograph the weapon and later show the woman carrying—perhaps a piece of wood under her coat. Here you have in a nutshell the difference between Hollywood and France. In *Psycho* when Anthony Perkins wraps Janet Leigh's body in the shower curtain, I am sure there is no body there—not even a double's. But when Claude Chabrol shot a similar scene in *The Unfaithful Wife*, he actually left the "dead" actor in the sack. As a result, the actor who plays the assassin has a terrible time carrying the load. I'll give you an even more disturbing example of our lack of expertise. It concerns a film made by a director who had previously done only four or five movies. In them, he had never shot a love scene and was distraught at the prospect of having to shoot one in his next film. He was so frightened, in fact, that when he came to the scene all he could do was tell the actors actually to make love. And do you know how the audience reacted to the fornication? "Not bad," they said, "but the scene is nothing special."

Robert Bresson

Paris, September 2, 1970

Feature Films: 1943 *Les Anges du péché* (*Angels of Sin*); 1944 *Les Dames du Bois de Boulogne* (*Ladies of the Park*); 1950 *Le Journal d'un curé de campagne* (*Diary of a Country Priest*); 1956 *Un Condamné à mort s'est échappé* (*A Man Escaped*); 1959 *Pickpocket*; 1961 *Le Procès de Jeanne d'Arc* (*The Trial of Joan of Arc*); 1966 *Au hasard, Balthazar*; *Mouchette*; 1969 *Une Femme douce* (*A Gentle Creature*); 1971 *Quatre nuits d'un reveur* (*Four Nights of a Dreamer*).

Bresson's living room, where this interview took place, is almost too appropriate for the most uncompromisingly austere director in film history: white walls, tan curtains and upholstery, worn wooden floors, and one spot of color coming from a frayed patterned rug that must have been reticent even in its heyday but was now positively attenuated in contradicting the general pallor.

In his mid-sixties, Bresson shows few signs of age (a slight suggestion of arthritis in the hands) but many of vigor and even of modishness (he wears his white hair long and dresses in American-style sports clothes). His most imposing features are icy blue eyes that flash with impatience, even when he smiles, at the apparent bidding of some inner voice that seems always to be in competition with the voice of his interlocutor. At one moment he drums his fingers nervously on his chair; at another, he seems totally absorbed in the conversation. All shifts are reflected in his eyes, which never leave your face, no matter how distracted he may seem.

Our conversation took up an entire afternoon during the period when Bresson was shooting *Four Nights of a Dreamer* through the night, waking up around midday, and devoting his afternoons to preparation. Despite this grueling schedule and the rustiness of his English (a language, as he apologized, that he rarely used but adopted for my comfort), Bresson proved responsive and articulate. As the length of the interview shows, there were no lulls in the conversation.

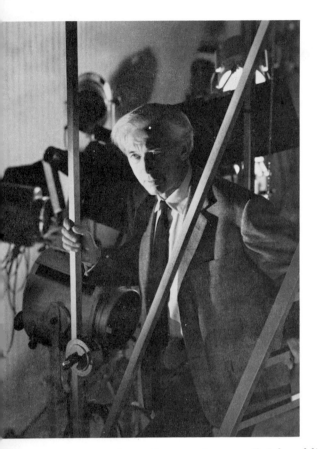

Robert Bresson in an official publicity photograph taken a number of years ago.

SAMUELS: You've said you don't want to be called a *metteur en scène* but rather a *metteur en ordre.* Does this mean that you think the essence of film is editing rather than staging?

BRESSON: For me, filmmaking is combining images and sounds of real things in an order that makes them effective. What I disapprove of is photographing with that extraordinary instrument—the camera—things that are not real. Sets and actors are not real.

S: That puts you in the tradition of the silent film, which could not rely on dialogue and therefore created its effects through editing. Do you agree that you are more like a silent than a sound film director?

B: The silent directors usually employed actors. When the cinema became vocal, actors were also used, because at that time they were thought the only ones able to speak. A rather difficult part of my work is to make my nonactors speak normally. I don't want to eliminate dialogue (as in silent films), but my dialogue must be very special—not like the speeches heard in a theater. Voice, for me, is something very important, and I couldn't do without it. Now, when I choose someone to appear in one of my films, I select him by means of the telephone, before I see him. Because in general, when you meet a person, your eyes and ears work together rather badly. The voice tells more about anyone than his physical presence.

S: But in your films all the people speak with a single, a Bressonian voice.

B: No. I think that in other films actors speak as if they were onstage. As a result, the audience is used to theatrical inflections. That makes my nonactors appear unique, and thus, they seem to be speaking in a single new way. I want the essence of my films to be not the words my people say or even the gestures they perform, but what these words and gestures provoke in them. What I tell them to do or say must bring to light something they had not realized they contained. The camera catches it; neither they nor I really know it before it happens. The unknown is what I wish to capture.

S: If it is true that your goal is the mystery you draw out of your nonactors, can anyone besides you and them fully appreciate the result?

B: I hope so. There are so many things our eyes don't see. But the camera sees everything. We are *too* clever, and our cleverness plays us false. We should trust mainly our feelings and those senses that never lie to us. Our intelligence disturbs our proper vision of things.

S: You say you discover your mysteries in the process of shooting. . . .

B: Yes. Because what I've just told you was not something I had planned for. Amazingly, however, I discovered it during my first moments behind the camera. My first film was made with professional actors, and when we had our first rehearsal, I said, "If you go on acting and speaking like this, I am leaving."

S: On your second film, you had many quarrels with Maria Casarès. But, you know, I think her performance in *Les Dames du Bois de Boulogne* is one of the greatest on film. Don't you think you conquered her usual hamminess just a bit?

B: A friend told me that in Julien Green's *South* she had to appear on the stage saying, "It's raining"; in French, *il pleut*. Despite the simplicity of these words, her tragedian's temperament made her shout emphatically: *"I . . . l . . . pl . . . eut!"* Because *Les Dames* was not a tragedy, she was worried at the beginning. To get courage, she used to drink a little glass of cognac before acting. When I chanced to discover this, I asked her to take a sedative instead, which she willingly did. Then things started to go better.

S: Your major characteristic as an editor is ellipsis. Do you leave more and more out in each version of a given scene, or do you instinctively elide things while shooting?

B: I always shoot on the dangerous line between showing too much and not showing enough. I try to work as if I were on a tightrope with a precipice at either side.

S: What I want to know, however, is whether you consciously eliminate things during editing or instinctively eliminate things as you go along. Put this another way: Did you eliminate as much in your earlier films?

B: I have always been the same. I don't create ellipsis; it is there from the beginning. One day I said, "Cinema is the art of showing nothing." I want to express things with a minimum of means, showing nothing that is not absolutely essential.

S: Doesn't that make your films too difficult? I'm not even thinking of the average viewer. Doesn't your extremely elliptical manner baffle even the educated viewer? Can anyone get all the things you merely sketch in?

B: Many do.

S: Aren't you worried about being too rarefied?

B: No. Here is the problem: The public is educated to a certain kind of film. Therefore, when they see what you call my elliptical films, they are disturbed. Bad critics say I am inhuman and cold. Why? Because they are used to acting; since they find none in my films, they say I am empty.

S: Let me ask you about your actors now. Jules Roy wrote an article about *A Man Escaped* in which he said that you never paid attention to your associates, that you were always locked into yourself, and that whenever you faced simple and difficult means toward a given end, you always chose the difficult.

B: Things are always difficult. And I lock myself into myself because often it seems that some of the others are against me. I find that when I don't concentrate, I make mistakes.

S: I noticed when I saw you shooting *Four Nights of a Dreamer* on the Pont Neuf that you were walking around, ignoring everyone, and continuously peering at the shooting area between two fingers. I also noticed that you make use of accidents. For example, a passerby walked behind your actors while they were performing, yet you did not instruct the cameraman to stop shooting.

B: It's possible.

S: You would use such an accident, wouldn't you?

B: Yes. In *Pickpocket* I deliberately shot the long sequence at the railroad station during rush hour so as to be able to capture all the accidental occurrences. I courted the reality of the crowd through the impediments they placed before my camera.

S: It is said that you shoot every scene many times. How do the actors respond?

B: Sometimes they react badly, so I stop; sometimes the third shot is the best, sometimes the first. Sometimes the shot I think the best is the worst; sometimes the shot that seems worst when I film I later learn is exactly what I wanted. I require from a shot something I am not fully conscious of when photographing. When we are

editing, I tell my editor to search for what I remember as having been the most successful take, and as he is running the film through the machine, I discover that what I had not sought is in fact what I had always wanted. I must add that lately I don't shoot so many takes.

S: A common criticism of *Pickpocket* is that Martin Lassalle fails because he isn't enough of an actor.

B: No, I think he is marvelous. Extraordinarily, he identified exactly with the hero of the film: somehow a little lost in the world but very sensitive and clever, with an incredible manual talent. As a result, he became nearly as good a pickpocket as the professional I employed to teach him. The only difficulty I had with him is that he had a Uruguayan accent, which we succeeded in correcting.

S: According to one of your interviews, in *A Man Escaped* you helped Leterrier to give a good performance through mechanical means. What were they?

B: By "mechanical" I mean, as I said before, words and gestures. Because I tell my actors to speak and move mechanically. For I am using these gestures and words—which they do not interpret—to draw out of them what I want to appear on screen.

S: For you, the nonactor is raw material—like paint.

B: But precious raw material.

S: You've said you don't even let him see the rushes.

B: That is true, and for the same reason I never use the same person twice, because the second time he would try deliberately to give me what he thought I wanted. I don't even permit the husband of a nonactress to see rushes because he would evaluate her performance and then she would try to improve it. Anyway, mechanics are essential. Our gestures, nine times out of ten, are automatic. The ways you are crossing your legs and holding your head are not voluntary gestures. Montaigne has a marvelous chapter on hands in which he says that hands go where their owner does not send them. I don't want my nonactors to think of what they do. Years ago, without realizing any program, I told my nonactors, "Don't think of what you are saying or doing," and that moment was the beginning of my style.

S: This is very interesting. You seem to be talking about what is now known as body language. Scientists are now writing books about the meaning of involuntary gestures.

B: Even as early as *Les Dames du Bois de Boulogne* I told the actors to think about anything they wanted except their performances. Only then did I hear in their voices that inflection (so unlike theatrical inflection): the inflection of a real human voice. In three-quarters of a person's activities, his mind does not participate, and that is what I am trying to capture.

S: You once said you choose your actors only after talking to them for a long time.

B: It used to be true, but it isn't anymore. Perhaps I have grown lazy. And imprudently, as I told you, I sometimes choose my nonactors as a result of a phone call. A voice calls me up and says, "I hear you are looking for a girl to star in your film," I listen to that voice, and I say to myself, "The role is hers." That's the way I chose Dominique Sanda for *Une Femme douce*.

S: Do you work this way now because you are so sure of yourself that you can get what you want out of anyone?

B: Yes, I am sure of myself, but, you know, a human being has so many contradictions and oddities that I can never be entirely sure that I've chosen the right person.

S: You have often expressed contempt for psychology. Yet you keep talking about the mystery of personality in ways that sound psychological. What's the difference between what you want to understand and what the psychologist wants to understand?

B: The psychologist discovers only what he can explain. I explain nothing.

S: You are a person with no preconceptions.

B: None at all.

S: Whereas psychology is a closed system, whose premises dictate its method. Therefore, it discovers evidence in support of a preexisting theory of human behavior.

B: If I succeed at all, I suppose some of what I show on the screen will be psychologically valid, even though I am not quite aware of it. But of course, I don't always succeed. In any case, I never want to explain anything. The trouble with most films is that they explain everything.

S: That's why one can go back to your films.

B: If there is something good in a film, one must see it at least twice. A film doesn't give its best the first time.

S: I think that many of your ideas are a consequence of your Christianity. Am I right in saying that you pursue mystery without worrying that the audience will be baffled because you believe that we all partake of one essential soul?

B: Of course. Of course.

S: So that every viewer is fundamentally the same viewer.

B: Of course. What I am very pretentiously trying to capture is this essential soul, as you call it.

S: Do you believe that there is anybody that does not partake in this essential soul. For example, is an atheist outside your audience?

B: No, he is not. Besides, there are no real atheists.

S: What attracted you to Bernanos?

B: I was attracted by the same thing, on a different scale, that attracts me in Dostoyevsky. Both writers are searching for the soul. In fact, I don't share Bernanos' faith and style. But in every book of his there are sparks, remarkable insights, that are very peculiar and that you do not find in other writers. In *Diary of a Country Priest* there are many such sparks.

S: Most of your films are adaptations. Why did you create both story and script for *Pickpocket* and *Au hasard, Balthazar?*

B: In the latter case, I can answer the question simply. One day I saw very clearly a donkey as the center of a film, but the next day that image faded away. I had to wait a long time for it to return, but I always wanted to make this film. You may recall that in Dostoyevsky's *The Idiot* Prince Myshkin says he recovered his good spirits by seeing a donkey in the marketplace. *Pickpocket* is another matter. I have always liked manual dexterity and, when young, made balancing toys, juggled, etc. I've never understood intellectuals who put dexterity aside.

S: Everything you say points to your belief that the human mind isn't enough.

B: Our senses tell us more than our intelligence.

S: Isn't it ironic that you are known as an intellectual director? I have always thought you profoundly emotional.

B: Most of what is said about me is wrong and is repeated eternally. Once somebody said that I worked as an assistant director to René Clair, which is not true, and that I studied painting at the École des Beaux-Arts—also not true—but this kind of error appears in nearly every account of my career. Of course, the worst mistakes concern my ideas and my way of working.

S: You've said that your films are sometimes solutions to technical problems. For example, you made *The Trial of Joan of Arc* to see if one could make a film that was only questions and answers.

B: I like exercise for its own sake. That is why I regard my films as attempts rather than accomplishments. People always ask me about the motivation of my characters, never about the arrangement of shots.

S: You seem more interested in putting shots together than in moving the camera.

B: No. My camera is never stationary; it simply doesn't move around in a blatant manner. It is too easy, when you want, for instance, to describe a room, to pan across it—or to show you are in church by tilting upward in a spiraling fashion. All that is artificial; our eye doesn't proceed like that.

S: You told Godard that you prefer as often as possible to replace image by sound. Why?

B: Because the ear is profound, whereas the eye is frivolous, too easily satisfied. The ear is active, imaginative, whereas the eye is passive. When you hear a noise at night, instantly you imagine its cause. The sound of a train whistle conjures up the whole station. The eye can perceive only what is presented to it.

S: Would you prefer working in a medium where you could eliminate images?

B: No, I want both image and sound.

S: You just want to give the latter predominance?

B: Yes.

S: How do you prepare your sound tracks?

B: There are two kinds of sound in my films: sounds which occur during shooting and those I add later. What I add is more important, because I treat these sounds as if they were actors. For example, when you go into the street and hear a hundred cars passing, what you think you hear is not what you hear, because if you recorded it by means of a magnetophone, you would find that the sound was a mere jumble. So when I have to record the sound of cars, I go to the country and record every single car in pure silence. Then I mix all these sounds in a way that creates not what I hear in the street, but what I think I hear.

S: In this way you can reflect the mind of the character. For example, in *A Man Escaped* the amplified sounds of keys and trams etc. reflect the supersensitive hearing of a man in prison.

B: Yes. In that film freedom is represented by the sounds of life outside.

S: In view of your emphasis on sound, why do you avoid music?

B: Because music takes you into another realm. I am always astonished when I see a film in which after the characters are finished speaking the music begins. You know, this sort of music saves many films, but if you want your film to be true, you must avoid it. I confess that I too made mistakes with music in my early films. But now I use music, as in *Mouchette*, only at the end, because I want to take the audience out of the film into another realm; that is the reason for Monteverdi's *Magnificat*.

S: Why did you suddenly move to color in *Une Femme douce*?

B: Because suddenly I had money for it.

S: Did the new technique produce any special problems?

B: Yes. Since the first rule of art is unity, color threatens you because its effects are too various. However, if you can control and unify the color, you produce more powerful shots in it than are possible in black and white. In *Une Femme douce* I started with the color of Dominique Sanda's skin and harmonized everything to it.

S: The sight of her nude flesh is one of the most important in the film.

B: I am also using nudity in *Four Nights of a Dreamer*. I am not at all against nudity so long as the body is beautiful; only when the body is ugly is its nudity obscene. It is like kissing. I can't bear to see people kissing on the screen. Can you?

S: That's why you sometimes have your characters kiss each other's hands?

B: Yes. Perhaps.

S: It happens in *Au hasard, Balthazar*. I wanted to ask a question about that. In those many beautiful shots in which Marie embraces the head of the donkey, were you thinking of the common figure that appears in Renaissance tapestries of the Virgin and the unicorn?

B: No. The resemblance is accidental.

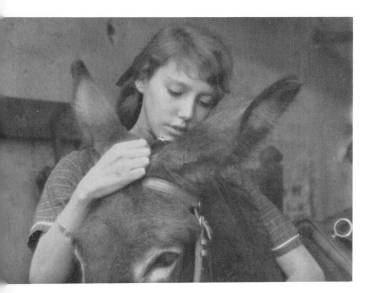

S: You've said that the whole universe is Christian and that no story is more Christian than any other. What do you think is the Christian element in *Les Dames du Bois de Boulogne*?

B: I never look for a Christian meaning. If it comes, it comes.

S: But this is the only one of your films that seems wholly secular.

B: I never thought about it much, but I suppose you are right.

S: Did you and Cocteau agree completely when you were working on the script?

B: You know, Cocteau did very little. I initially wrote all the dialogue myself, retaining as much of Diderot as I could, but inventing the story of the two women whom Hélène uses. Their behavior and what happens to them in my film aren't in Diderot. What I needed Cocteau for was to help me blend Diderot's dialogue with my own. This he did magnificently in ten minutes, out of friendship for me. And since he was Cocteau and I was not known as a writer, I asked him to take credit for the dialogue.

S: Actually, as is well known, your adaptation of Diderot changes the spirit of the tale completely. Diderot's story is comic and emphasizes class distinctions. Why did you want to film this if you didn't intend to film it as written?

B: It was my second film, and I needed an adaptation because producers are more difficult about original scripts. I admired the story of Madame de la Pommeraye from *Jacques le fataliste* because it was well constructed and dramatic, not comic as you seem to think. I merely used his basic situation and much of his dialogue, adding characters, scenes, and so forth to make a film about things that did interest me.

S: Why did you change the period and bring the story up to date?

B: Because I think that costume drama violates the essence of cinema, which is immediacy. The period I was able to change because feelings— unlike clothes—don't change from century to century.

S: You say always that you're a demon for truth, yet this film is obviously stylized.

B: But style goes very well with truth.

S: I find symbolism in this film. Was it deliberate? For example, when Jean comes to ask Hélène to arrange a meeting with Agnès, Hélène stands in front of the fireplace suppressing her jealousy, but we see it reflected in the raging fire at her side.

B: I don't remember if I meant it that way. I never look for symbolism.

S: Take another instance. Hélène is frequently seen in front of mirrors, suggesting what is true: that there are two Hélènes, the self she pretends and the one she really is.

B: That wasn't deliberate, but you teach me now what I ought to have done or what I did without realizing it. Because you see, luckily, everything important is instinctive. One mustn't plan every detail in advance. I agree with Valéry: One works to surprise oneself.

S: There are many more fades in *Diary of a Country Priest* than in *Les Dames du Bois de Boulogne*. Are you deliberate about the number and kind of transitions? In *Une Femme douce* there are no fades at all.

B: Because more and more I try to be quick. Moreover, to produce a fade in a color film, you have to superimpose one negative over another, and that destroys the quality of the shot. As I have always said, a film is not its shots, but the way they have been joined. As a general once told me, a battle occurs very often at the point where two maps touch.

S: You often said that you don't like spectacle. However, *Diary of a Country Priest* is spectacular. For example: Chantal's white face hovering in the blackness of the confessional or

the priest passing beside that magnificent tree. If you remade the film now, would you eliminate such shots?

B: Absolutely. Those things attracted me at the time. One needs much more experience than I had to eliminate such nonessentials. The most important shots for me in that film were those in which you see the priest writing in the diary. At those moments one sees the contact between his soul and, if you like, the world of matter, as he pronounces the very words that he is writing down.

S: On other occasions, when he is speaking but not writing, you obtain marvelous effects. For example, we see him dipping bread into wine as he says, "I am able to take some bread with wine because I am feeling better." But his face shows that he is dying. As a result, we see how humble he is, how unaware of his own suffering.

B: Let me tell you something. What you saw in that shot you invented. The less the nonactor does, the more he suggests. The combination of the wine and the bread and the nonactor's face (with a minimum of gesture) suggests that he is going to die. He does not have to say so. If he

acted "I am going to die," it would be awful.

S: You said I "invented" it. I didn't invent it.

B: No, you felt it.

S: Don't you see, "invent" is the wrong word?

B: A book, a painting, or a piece of music— none of these things has an absolute value. The value is what the viewer, the reader, the listener bring to it.

S: There is a difference between value and meaning. We can disagree about the value of a film and still agree on what it means.

B: There are people who when seeing *Diary of a Country Priest* feel nothing.

S: But that's their fault. That's not the fault of the film. There is a German proverb: "If a jackass stares into a mirror, a philosopher can't look back."

B: Unfortunately, the public is used to easy films. More and more this is true.

S: Then you are suffering from lack of comrades. If there were more directors making suggestive films like yours, the public would be able to understand better.

B: I have always said that the world of cinema ought to be organized like the world of painting during the Renaissance, so that apprentices might learn their craft. Today a man assists now this, now that director, and learns nothing.

S: In *Diary of a Country Priest* for the first time—

B: You are right; this is the first film in which I started to understand what I was doing.

S: I had in mind something more specific that one also sees in *Une Femme douce*, but above all in *Pickpocket*. Before a character enters a place or after he exits from it, the camera holds on the set.

B: Where? What do you mean?

S: In *Diary of a Country Priest* he rides his bicycle to the house of the Bishop of Torcey. He enters the house, and you hold outside the house. It happens repeatedly in *Pickpocket*.

B: I don't remember.

S: I'll give a more recent example. In *Une Femme douce* the couple comes into the house, and the camera remains on the door. Then they walk upstairs, and the camera holds on the landing. We see the door to their apartment before they open it and after they close it etc. You weren't conscious of this?

B: Of course, I was conscious, but I never

remember what I have done later. Let me tell you something about doors. Critics say, "Bresson is impossible: He shows fifty doors opening and closing"; but you must understand that the door of the apartment is where all the drama occurs. The door either says, "I am going away or I am coming to you." When I made *Les Dames du Bois de Boulogne*, I was also accused of showing too many doors. And Cocteau said I was criticized for being too precise. "In other films you see a door because it just happens to be there," he said, "whereas in your films it is there on purpose. For that reason each door is seen, whereas in other films the door is scarcely noticed."

S: You say that you first discovered yourself in *Diary of a Country Priest*. Was part of that discovery the use of commentary?

B: Perhaps. But you know, I shouldn't have used commentary in my next film, *A Man Escaped*. Since it was virtually a silent film and since it required some rhythm, I depended on commentary.

S: I want to ask some questions about *A Man Escaped*, which, by the way, seems to me your greatest film. Incidentally, does that judgment upset you?

B: I don't know how to make such comparisons. But there may be something in what you say.

When I finished it, I had no idea about its value. Yet I had, for the first time in my life, an impulse to write down everything I felt about the art of filmmaking, and for that reason *A Man Escaped* is precious to me.

S: You have been working on this book for a long time. When will it be published?

B: I haven't worked at it much. I have no time to finish it. It is principally a gathering of notes on little pieces of paper, on cigarette wrappers; things I wrote down while shooting or on some other occasion.

S: *A Man Escaped* shares with *The Trial of Joan of Arc* an implication of French nationalism. Did you want that?

B: No, the prisoner could have been a young American or a Vietnamese. I was interested only in the mind of someone who wishes to escape without outside help.

S: The problem is more serious in *The Trial of Joan of Arc*, in which you use certain historical facts and ignore others. For example, in one tradition, the soldier who offered Joan a crucifix at the stake was British. But you don't show that. Moreover, you make the British characters particularly stupid.

B: Not stupid but rather brutal. Indeed, the English bishop is intelligent and refined.

S: Your films are the fastest films made, but people say that you are slow.

B: Because my characters don't jump about and scream.

S: The most serious criticism that can be made against you is that you are too fast. For example, I can't imagine anyone catching everything in *Au hasard, Balthazar*. Consider the inquisition of Gérard at the police station. I have seen the film twice, and I still can't understand what happens in that scene.

B: I only wanted to show that a crime had occurred and that the boy was questioned by the police. The scene shows the stupidity and vanity of the boy and of his comrades. The police captain says, "In prison for stupidity!" It is also important because in the next scene the boy tries to make Arsène think that Arsène, who is a tramp, is also the murderer that the police are looking for.

S: To return to *A Man Escaped*: Though you create very well the experience of being in prison, you never show the brutality. For example, you don't show Fontaine being beaten. You only show him afterward. Why?

B: Because it would be false to show the beating since the audience knows that the actor isn't really being beaten, and such falsity would stop the film. Moreover, this is what it was like

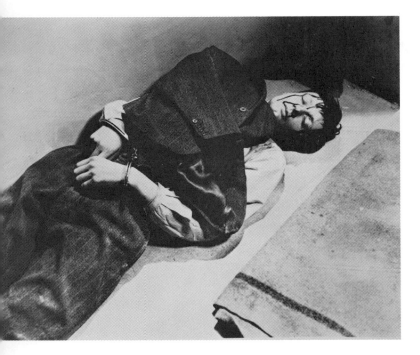

when I was a prisoner of the Germans. Once I heard someone being whipped through a door, and then I heard the body fall. That was ten times worse than if I had seen the whipping. When you see Fontaine with his bloody face being brought back to the cell, you are forced to imagine the awfulness of the beating—which makes it very powerful. Furthermore, if I showed him being taken from his cell, being beaten, then being returned, it would take much too long.

S: There is another wonderful effect of concentration in this scene: Fontaine says, "After three days I was able to move again," although only a few seconds of film time have passed. This suggests how quickly he restores himself and how much courage he has.

B: That is very important. His will to go on establishes a rhythm of inexorability that touches the public. When men go to war, military music is necessary, because music has a rhythm and rhythm implants ideas.

S: Whenever we see the window in Fontaine's cell, it glows like a jewel. Was that a special effect?

B: No, but I do remember that I worked with my cinematographer to obtain just the right degree of light from both window and door.

S: There is one thing in the film that seems uncharacteristic in its patness. When Fontaine is sentenced, the scene takes place at the Hotel Terminus. . . .

B: Every city in France had such a hotel where the Gestapo stayed during the occupation.

S: You didn't desire the pun?

B: Of course not. Everything in this film is absolutely factual. I had no trouble inventing details and was familiar with the history of the place. All of the characters' actions take place exactly where they occurred in real life.

S: You search for mystery in your films. It seems to me that here you really attain it because although the title tells us that he will escape, the film is very suspenseful.

B: The important thing is not "if" but "how." Here is another mystery: Although every detail of the film came from the report of André Devigny, I invented the dialogue with the young boy who is finally brought to Fontaine's cell. When I read it to Devigny, I was very worried about his reaction. Do you know what he said? "How true!" This shows that truth can be different from reality, because in the actual event, as Devigny told me, he behaved as if the boy were a woman he needed to seduce in order to make good his escape. In my film, on the other hand, I show Fontaine dominating the boy. You know, I wanted to call the film "Help Yourself," and that's why I showed Devigny as dominating in the last scenes. Help yourself and God will help you.

S: There are other great moments in the film. For example, when Fontaine tells the old man in the next cell that his own attempt to escape is being made for the old man, too, or the moments when a community is achieved by means of men tapping on the walls. I could go on. This film is your greatest, I think, not because it is technically superior to the others but because it is richer in content.

B: *Mouchette* is rich, too!

S: I would place *Mouchette* with *A Man Escaped* among your greatest films.

B: But it seems to me there is a little too much spectacle in *Mouchette.*

S: You added a lot to the Bernanos novel in *Mouchette.* Conversely, *Pickpocket*, which is an original, appears to be inspired by *Crime and Punishment.* For the viewer aware of this parallel, there is a problem in *Pickpocket.* In *Crime and Punishment*, whether justifiably or not, Raskolnikov thinks of his crime as benefiting humanity and thus earns a measure of sympathy. Your hero has no excuse for the crime and thus

seems a little pretentious in his desire to be taken as a superior being.

B: Yes, but he is aware that pickpocketing is very difficult and dangerous. He is taken with the thrill of that. He is pretentious perhaps, like Raskolnikov, but on quite a lesser scale. Like Raskolnikov, he hates organized society. And I am sure you know that Dostoyevsky took the idea of his novel from Max Stirner's *Der Einzige und sein Eigentum*, though that is perhaps not the actual title of the book. The French version, at any rate, which is called *L'Unique et sa propriété*, contains sentences like these: "What am I legitimately allowed to do? All that I am able to" and "My rights, so far as I'm concerned, extend as far as I can extend my arm." These are a good encouragement to pickpocketing, especially the latter sentence.

S: What I am trying to explore with you is the emotional problem for the spectator.

B: I never think of the spectator.

S: But you can see that your hero might appear unsympathetic.

B: He *is* unsympathetic. Why not?

S: I am also puzzled, in view of your uninterest in psychology, at the heavy psychological emphasis in this film. Let me explain. As we see the hero stealing, we don't know his motive, but toward the end of the film we find out that he previously stole from his mother. We then realize his psychological motivation; he stole from his mother, felt guilty about that, was ashamed to confess to her, and, therefore, commits crimes so as to be punished and fulfill his need for penitence.

B: Perhaps, but only a psychiatrist would explain it like that. As Dostoyevsky frequently does, I present the effect before the cause. I think this is a good idea because it increases the mystery; to witness events without knowing why they are occurring makes you desire to find out the reason.

S: But this doesn't answer my question. Here, in the first of your films from an original story, you, who profess to dislike psychology, are at your most psychological. Why?

B: You think it's psychological? I didn't mean it to be. I simply showed a man picking pockets until he was arrested. I included the fact that he stole from his mother simply to provide evidence the police needed in order to be put on his track.

S: In other words, you didn't put it in as explanation but rather as plot device?

B: Yes. It is only to make the chief of police certain that Martin is a thief. What interested me is the power this gave the inspector, because the inspector liked to torture him—as in that long scene, where the hero doesn't know how much the inspector knows. In fact, I originally wanted to call the film "Incertitude."

S: There is something else I rather doubt you wanted in the film. The hero of your film is a criminal in two ways: He is a thief, and he denies God.

B: On the contrary, I make him aware of the presence of God for three minutes. Few people can say they were aware of God even that long. This line of dialogue is very personal; it shows that although influenced by Dostoyevsky, I made my story benefit from my own experiences. At his mother's funeral, a singer sings the *Dies Irae* in exactly the same simple way another singer sang it at my mother's funeral in the Cathedral of Nantes, where, apart from ten nuns, my wife and I attended the service alone. Somehow this *Dies Irae* made a strange impression on me; I could have said then, like my pickpocket, "I felt God during three minutes."

S: This raises another question. You are famous for maintaining your privacy. I didn't even know you were married, and it was a great surprise when your wife came to the door. Isn't *Pickpocket* a game of hide-and-seek since, according to you, it reflects so much of your personal experience, although if you hadn't told me, I wouldn't have known it?

B: I hate publicity. One should be known for what he does, not for what he is. Nowadays a painter paints a bad painting, but he talks about it until it becomes famous. He paints for five minutes and talks about it on television for five years.

S: That reminds me of Godard. He makes bad films, but he defends them so interestingly.

B: His films *are* interesting. He upsets the official cinema, which cares only for profits. He taught films how to use disorder.

S: Don't you think his purpose is more important than the individual results—which aren't very good?

B: When he uses professional actors, I don't like his films, but when he doesn't, he makes the best that can be seen.

S: On this matter of your zeal for truth: There are moments in *Pickpocket* which seem to me to be true only to your peculiar style. For example, in the opening scene where the hero steals the purse, the people at the racetrack are preternaturally calm. I can't believe that people watch a race so impassively.

B: But not every part of a racetrack crowd reacts in the same way. There are always certain people who watch impassively. I didn't want him to commit his theft when people were shouting; I wanted it to happen in silence, so that one could hear the crescendo of the horses' galloping.

S: But such a scene, even among sympathetic viewers, raises the question of whether we are seeing truth in your films or the reflection of a very deliberate and personal style. I ask myself that question occasionally in *Pickpocket* and almost always in *The Trial of Joan of Arc*.

B: If that happens, it is my fault. My style is natural to me. You see, I want to make things so concentrated and so unified that the spectator feels as if he has seen one single moment. I control all speech and gesture so as to produce an object that is indivisible. Because I believe that one moves an audience only through rhythm, concentration, and unity.

S: When I watched *The Trial of Joan of Arc*, however, I found myself interested—moved, if you will—not by the dialogue and characters but by your subtle method of crosscutting: the way, for example, you indicate that Joan has scored a point by keeping the camera on her when Cauchon is responding. Aiding this, of course, was the great familiarity of the trial itself.

B: It's a pity you didn't hear it in your own language.

S: Even so, my French is good enough so that I got most of it.

B: But, you know, her words are very subtle.

S: Even so, they seemed to me less subtle than your editing, which began to replace the words as my object of interest.

B: Look, I am even surprised that you were able to sit through the film. Its effect depends so much on subtlety of dialogue, which is said so rapidly, that if you were sufficiently caught by the rhythms to like the film even when you couldn't fully follow the dialogue, I'm very pleased.

S: Yes, but I think that interest in the editing rhythms conflicts with interest in the dialogue— that is, interest in technique replaces interest in content. I think here your interest in technique is subverting the story. In any case, you once said what impressed you most about Joan was her youth. Since she is a famous figure of rebellion, were you thinking of any analogies between her and contemporary youth?

B: Not exactly, but I wanted to make her seem as similar to young girls now as I could, which is why she is dressed as she is.

S: I have always been put off Joan by her fanaticism. I mean, what if a fanatic believes in something you find terrible?

B: I understand this feeling, but I don't share it. Joan of Arc was not a fanatic. She wanted to save her country. For me, she is the most extraordinary person who ever lived. I made the film to see what would happen when I had a young girl say the words Joan actually said.

S: I wondered about that. This story is so familiar, so often told. How did you think you were correcting your predecessors?

B: The legend, which the public is used to, of a poor and ignorant little shepherdess commanding the army and saving her king and France is known now to be false. Besides, we have her exact words and those of her questioners at the trial. I wanted to be very simple and only insist, without prejudice, on what she said.

S: What does she mean to you?

B: Renaissance painters frequently depict the world with a level above it, on which sit God and the angels. Joan lived her whole life with one foot on earth and the other on that higher level. And the typical drama of her trial, with everyone

against her! The French were as bad as the English, but they were hypocrites, which is why I don't show Cauchon as a total villain.

S: We talked before about your speed. There are signs in *Au hasard, Balthazar* of excess speed. You once said, for example, that you wanted Arsène to be gentle when sober so that the audience could feel Balthazar's bafflement at the total change wrought in his master by a simple bottle. But you never show us enough of the gentle Arsène to make the contrast felt.

Arsène, the drunkard.

B: I don't remember, but you quote me accurately. I had two ideas in this film. First, to see an analogy between the different stages of the life of a donkey and the life of a human being; second, to see the donkey suffering for all human vices. Drunkenness is, of course, one vice.

S: Something new enters your films in *Balthazar.*

B: Eroticism.

S: Something else, too. Until now, all your films take place, as it were, without spatial or temporal particularity. Here, for the first time, contemporary mores are unmistakable: the *blousons noirs*, jazz, etc. Was this conscious and deliberate?

B: No.

S: It just happened? Yet it happens again in *Mouchette* and in *Une Femme douce*. For example, in each film jazz enters with such volume and cacophony that it becomes hateful. Am I not correct, then, in sensing, beginning with *Balthazar*, your hatred for the modern world?

B: Perhaps not hatred, but rather distrust for some kinds of modern society. I am starting to write a script about the forces that dominate modern man.

S: What causes this recent interest of yours in contemporary life?

B: This interest is not recent. Since my films have become simpler and simpler, I want to attach myself to some material that is resistant and that will make my work tougher.

S: Do you think it is a reflection of your time of life: the impulse to judge the age?

B: No. I don't judge; I only show. Or rather, I show how the world makes me feel now.

S: You say that Balthazar must pass among the vices of man. But Gérard, because of the very accuracy with which he is portrayed as a contemporary juvenile deliquent, seems to me to be too banal to represent vice.

B: Since six years have passed, he may seem banal. In any case, he is imbecility and violence, which go well together, the one producing the other.

S: Some of the editing in *Balthazar* is brilliant, like the montage of the donkey's work life. Why,

Gérard taunting Balthazar.

however, did you superimpose the subtitle "the years pass" in that scene? It isn't necessary.

B: You know, I'm also using titles in my new film—"first night," "second night," "story of Jacques," "story of Marthe," etc.—not to amuse myself but to make the distinctions among the various parts of the film sharper.

S: That's okay, because it will emphasize the fact that you are shooting a four-part story. But the title to which I refer is the only title in *Balthazar*, and it only makes clear what is already clear from the editing.

B: You are quite right. You see, you teach me many things about my films.

S: No.

B: Yes.

S: One thing I want to criticize in this film—

B: One thing more!

S: One thing more. Certain objectionable coincidences. Let me give you an example. After the violent scene in which Gérard beats Arsène while the other boys watch, Marie just happens to come by on the motorcycle when the beating is finished, which permits a scene between her and Gérard that makes an obvious point about her susceptibility to evil. Even more serious is Arsène's death scene. I understand that it is meant to be ironic, but when Arsène falls off the donkey at the precise moment that, having just won a fortune, he says good-bye to this country in which he has suffered so, it is too pat.

B: It is, as you said, the irony of life. Like bad things, good things never happen at the right time.

S: That is another sign of life's mysteriousness?

B: Yes. But you didn't like this scene?

S: I'll tell you why.

B: But Arsène is a drunkard, so it is quite natural that he would fall off the donkey. Moreover, the others pushed him. They place him on the donkey and kick it so that it goes too fast and he falls off.

S: If I had shot this, I would have allowed thirty seconds more of him riding.

B: Yes: in a state of happiness. You are right.

S: Because, you see, the cuts from the kick, to him saying good-bye, to the road market, to him falling off the donkey are too quick and make the sequence seem contrived, so that the irony seems rather the result of your artificial manipulation.

B: What you don't know is that I work with very

little money, and when I shot that scene in the south at night in the mountains, I couldn't reshoot anything. I even lacked the time to imagine that anything might be reshot. I begin by improvising, but when I see that money is running out, I shoot whatever stage we have arrived at. But your criticism is exactly right, as I now see. I should have made him gallop happily before the fall, so that it would be more shocking. Perhaps. Perhaps. I'm not sure.

S: Your working conditions make repeated takes difficult.

B: Yes. I never approach what I want to do. Many things that I see and want to include in my films I am prevented from including by lack of funds. But too much money can also be a handicap.

S: Why did you include in *Au hasard, Balthazar* that short scene with the action painter?

B: He sits on a clever donkey; I make him speak nonsense.

S: Do you know how this has been interpreted?

B: That I like action painters?

S: Yes. Not only that, but that he symbolizes your method as a director because he says that his paintings catch the essence of a thought. But that is obviously wrong.

B: Originally, I had three other people talk in that scene, but I cut them out while editing because the scene was too long.

S: Another question: In the scene where Arsène comes to the circus at which Balthazar is performing, I think Balthazar is moving away from Arsène, but critics have said that he is moving toward him. Who is right?

B: He is going away.

S: He must be; he's frightened.

B: He's frightened because he sees the bottle; he expects that Arsène will beat him. It's obvious.

S: Do you know that everyone I've discussed this with says the opposite. Some critics have even written that Balthazar moves toward Arsène in a gesture of Christian forgiveness. When people cannot see what they see, what do you do?

B: What can I do?

S: Every day you become more difficult for your audience. So, you only shrug! You're a hard man.

B: No, I am simply someone who likes exercise. You know that "ascetic" comes from the Greek word for practice of exercise. You know where the title of the film comes from? In the south in Les

Beaux there is an aristocratic family that pretends to be the descendants of the Magus Balthazar, and so on their crest they wrote "Au Hasard Balthazar." I found it by accident, and the whole story of Balthazar is his chance involvement in the lives of others, so I decided to use this title, which, besides, has a very beautiful rhyme.

S: But to get back to this question of coincidence: Just before she seems to be going off to be married, Marie feels she must visit Gérard one last time. Why does she feel she must see him?

B: Because although she is a lost girl, she still has something straight left in her character. She wants to exorcise Gérard from her life; because she wants to make her life better, it is made worse.

S: But once again the thematic meaning is clearer than the personal motivation. If only we saw thirty seconds more of her expression so that we could see the force of her compulsion to return to Gérard. It is all done simply and beautifully: Out of shame, she kisses her fiancé's hand before leaving him.

B: But your thirty seconds of expression would mean that the nonactor acts!

S: I want to move from *Balthazar* to *Mouchette*, which is very easy because they resemble each other more than any other two of your films. Indeed, the latter seems a new version of the former. Do you agree?

B: Perhaps it is because this was the first time that I shot two films in successive years.

S: Mouchette is like the donkey: stubborn, sordid, long-suffering.

B: Both are victims.

S: One difference between Bernanos' novel and your film is that Bernanos explains Mouchette's motives. . . .

B: All the time! But how can he know what goes on in a little girl's mind!

S: Oddly enough, though, I understand her suicide more in the film than in the novel.

B: Because his explanation is wrong, like his description of her suicide; you don't jump in the water the way you put your head on a pillow. When I was reading the novel, I thought at once that she had to die as she does in the film.

S: So heartbreakingly, for it is a game, the only game she ever plays in the film.

B: You know death is like a magic trick: In a

flash, the person vanishes. That is why I don't show her falling in the water. We see her rolling down the bank, there is a cut, and she is gone; we know she is dead only from the sound and the circles growing in the water.

S: Obviously, you must show Mouchette's suicide because that is the conclusion of Bernanos' novel, but as a Christian how do you feel about it? You seem to celebrate suicide—the blast of the *Magnificat* at her death—but isn't this heretical?

B: Yes, but I confess that more and more suicide loses its sinfulness to me. Killing oneself can be courageous; not killing oneself, because you wish to lose nothing, even the worst that life has to offer, can also be courageous. Since I live near the Seine, I have seen many people jump into the river in front of my windows. It's remarkable that more don't do it. There are so many reasons for suicide, good and bad. I believe that the church has become less rigorous against it. Sometimes it is inevitable, and not always because of madness. To be aware of a certain emptiness can make life impossible.

S: On the surface it seems that Mouchette kills herself because life is so terrible, but I think the real reason is that she is so ashamed of herself for what has happened to her. Do you agree?

B: There are so many motives, which is why this film isn't too bad. I explain nothing, and you can understand it any way you like. Still, you must feel that no single explanation will suffice. One is the wall placed before her by other people after the rape. She can't live in the village; she can't live in the house. Then too, she has been abused by a man whom she started to love.

S: Not only does she love him, but she forgives him his crime. She blames herself.

Arsène and Mouchette before the rape.

B: You must have noticed that in the film there is not one word about what her experience means.

S: Why did you include the prologue in which the mother is in church lamenting her tuberculosis?

B: To introduce this sick woman early so that I can pick her up later without having to make elaborate preparations. Later we see what her illness has done to her faith.

S: Here and in *Balthazar* one senses a new fascination with pain.

B: Yes?

S: Why?

B: Perhaps because I feel that pain must be acknowledged no less than happiness.

B: But not like a symbol! It shows the sort of world in which she lives. If you like, she is caught, just as the partridges are caught, in a trap.

S: I love also the amusement park sequence, which is so poignant, since it shows Mouchette having her one moment of pleasure by being hit in bump cars. Even pleasure involves being hit for her. But I was curious why you shot it as you did, with the stationary camera that misses some of the action.

B: Only a stationary camera permits you to show real movement—there is no other way.

S: The constricted framing is marvelous; it keeps us from feeling released. It prepares us for that horrible slap with which the father, inevitably, concludes Mouchette's one moment of

S: The opening of *Mouchette* seems to me the greatest in your films. . . .

B: When I was young, I hunted small animals in exactly this way. It is not exactly a symbol, but it provides the right atmosphere.

S: It introduces Mouchette.

enjoyment.

B: Perhaps; at least at the time I had no sense that my shot was mistaken.

S: Why does that unidentified woman give Mouchette the money to take the ride?

B: Why not? Life is very often like that. It is the

same in *A Man Escaped*, when the man, whom Fontaine doesn't really know, knocks at the door of his cell. Can you imagine if I had to explain: "My little girl, you are so poor, I will let you take this ride"?

S: Why do you start *Une Femme douce* with a floating scarf?

B: To avoid the cliché of showing her falling to the pavement. And that is worse than a cliché. Since I try never to show anything that is impossible and since, of course, Dominique Sanda does not actually hit the ground, I used the scarf to indicate what was happening. Furthermore, when she is putting the scarf on her shoulders, because you have seen it floating in the air at the beginning, it tells you she is going to commit suicide.

S: It's also emotionally effective: this beautifully floating scarf and then the blood. Did you intend that?

B: Of course.

S: Several people have called the film necrophiliac in its constant focusing on the corpse.

B: I want to understand death, and I hate flashbacks. There are no flashbacks in the film: it is all the live husband now confronting his dead wife. Walking around the corpse, he says, "I had only desired her body," and there it is: dead. People saw the film as a series of flashbacks, but it is all life in the face of death.

The proposal occurs at a zoo, so that Bresson can shoot toward the actors through a cage.

S: This film has a background of car sounds, and there is that harsh cut to the modern sculpture when they go to the Museum of Modern Art. Does this too reflect your suspicion of the modern world?

B: On the contrary, I think that sculpture is pretty.

S: Why does the wife like it?

B: Probably to spite her husband. He likes the old, she the new. She is much cleverer than he, which is the opposite of Dostoyevsky, in which the girl is an innocent stupid waif.

S: Doesn't she marry him to try to escape her past?

B: Many girls marry to escape their homes, but I didn't even try to explain her action to myself. I only wanted to show that marriage wasn't enough to her, that it disappointed her. As Goethe says, marriage has something awkward about it.

S: Isn't the problem in the marriage her fault, too? In some sense, she shows the prison of original sin. She reads in a book, at the end, that birds all repeat the song of their parents, and her dressing gown has a bird pattern on it. She says she comes from a sinister home, and she can never throw off its influence. Aren't you showing

that she wants to but cannot get rid of her bad upbringing?

B: No. I only made her say that she wants marriage to be more than marriage.

S: Another interesting relationship in the film is that between the husband and the maid. Isn't the maid a kind of confessor for the husband?

B: Perhaps.

S: The horror of the film is that they kill each other. She saves him from liking only money; he saves her from a difficult life. As a result, they destroy each other.

B: It seemed to me that many people couldn't

understand her true motive for killing herself. There are many motives here, too, but principally it is obvious she will never know whether or not her husband saw her attempt to kill him.

S: And the more he loves and forgives her, the more difficult he makes things for her. His love kills her.

B: Yes. Yes. One often hurts most the person one loves most.

S: I think you do have a scene in the film which is a clue to your meaning: when the husband and wife discuss Mephistopheles' speech in *Faust*.

B: I like these words of Mephistopheles. They are in Dostoyevsky's story.

S: This is the first of your films containing allusions to other works: *Faust*, *Hamlet*, etc.

B: *Hamlet* I included because I hate such theatrical shouting. I have myself seen it performed by a French company that omitted Hamlet's advice to the players because it contradicted their style.

S: But I think there is a mistake here. When she goes back to the apartment and reads Hamlet's speech. . . .

B: I included this to show that she is utterly unconcerned with her husband's feelings and only wishes to annoy him.

S: But doesn't the whole business about *Hamlet* stop your film to provide an essay about your theory of acting?

B: No, I don't think so. Perhaps it is too long, but I simply couldn't cut it.

S: It's not that it's boring, but I begin to be puzzled about its function.

B: It prepares the following scene, as I told you.

S: Why do they always see races and machines on television?

B: The auto race excites them sexually in the scene after the wedding, and the noise of the airplanes goes with his anxious awaiting of her at night.

S: The wife is a terrible person in a way.

B: Of course, the title is ironic.

S: Her suicide is a hostile act, dooming him to an eternity of grief unmitigated by understanding.

B: Of course.

S: There is one other group of directors that shares your feeling about professional actors: the Italian neorealists. Do you feel any affinity for them?

B: I don't know their films well. But although they use nonactors, I understand they sometimes dub their voices with professionals. That is wrong, because the voice sums a person up as nothing else can.

S: Why do so many of your actors walk about with their eyes cast downward?

B: They are looking at the chalk marks.

S: You've made several films from works of fiction. Do you think it's possible for a film to be faithful to its source?

B: Yes. For example, in *Diary of a Country Priest* I wasn't faithful to the style of Bernanos, and I omitted details which I disliked. But I was faithful to the spirit of the book and to what it inspired in me as I read it. Of course, I included as many things as I could from my own experience.

S: Why did you give up painting?

B: For reasons of health. The doctor made me stop because it was making me too nervous.

S: How were you enabled to break into films?

B: I first made a short film which I called *Affaires Publiques.* After that, for six or seven years, no one would give me a job. In 1939, I was a prisoner of war, but I succeeded in coming back to France after a year. Since there were few people in Paris when I returned and since the film industry was just starting up again, I was able to find work. Pathé signed a contract with me, but they threatened to break it. I needed to use Giraudoux as a collaborator on *Les Anges du péché*; without him, I wouldn't have received money to make the film. Nevertheless, even with Giraudoux, I had to find another producer.

S: Cocteau helped you, too, didn't he?

B: Yes, but Cocteau was my choice.

S: What influence does your being a painter have on your films?

B: Painting freed me from the desire to make paintings with each frame and freed me from the need to worry about beautiful photography. It helped me make every shot a *necessary* shot.

S: Why was there such a long gap between your first two films?

B: I couldn't find any money. Two or three contracts were signed, but all were broken.

S: How did you occupy yourself in those days?

B: With waiting in producers' offices and with teaching myself to write. You see, I believe that I cannot make my own films if I have collaborators on the script.

René Clair

Paris, April 9 and 10, 1971

Feature Films:1923 *Paris qui dort* (*The Crazy Ray*); 1924 *Entr'acte, Le Fantôme du Moulin Rouge* (*The Phantom of the Moulin Rouge*); 1925 *Le Voyage imaginaire* (*The Imaginary Voyage*); 1926 *La Proie du vent*; 1927 *Un Chapeau de paille d'Italie* (*The Italian Straw Hat*); 1928 *Les Deux Timides* (*Two Timid People*); 1930 *Sous les toits de Paris* (*Under the Roofs of Paris*); 1931 *Le Million* (*The Million*), *À nous la liberté* (*Freedom for Us*); 1932 *Quatorze juillet* (*July 14th*); 1934 *Le Dernier Milliardaire* (*The Last Millionaire*); 1935 *The Ghost Goes West*; 1937 *Break the News*; 1940 *The Flame of New Orleans*; 1942 *I Married a Witch*; 1943 *It Happened Tomorrow*; 1945 *And Then There Were None*; 1947 *Le Silence est d'or* (*Silence Is Golden*); 1949 *La Beauté du diable* (*The Beauty of the Devil*); 1952 *Les Belles de nuit* (Beauties of the Night); 1955 *Les Grandes Maneuvres* (The Grand Maneuvres); 1957. *Porte des Lilas* (*Gates of Paris*); 1961 *Tout l'or du monde* (*All the Gold in the World*); 1965 *Les Fêtes galantes.*

To meet René Clair is to experience the rejuvenating effects of intelligence and urbanity. Although in his seventies, Clair is totally alert, undimmed in memory, quick, and candid. He speaks fluent, if accented, English and obviously enjoys punctuating his utterances with slang.

The interview occurred in two sessions in a living room crowded with signs of his distinguished career and with pictures (including Picassos, Braques, a sketch of Clair by Cocteau) that express both connoisseurship and the luck of having lived through this century's renaissance. At our first meeting, Clair was turned out in a manner befitting his surroundings: with a black smoking jacket piped in red braid, a yellow foulard of small red diamond pattern, and gray flannel trousers. At our second meeting, which took place in his study, he was even more imposingly dressed in the gray pinstripe of the classic *boulevardier*; still the dashing figure of the early photographs, with only a slight hunching of one shoulder to qualify the appearance of ageless elegance.

The study is crowded with books and leather-bound boxes (to which he had recourse at one moment), containing scripts and documents for each of his films. Although he has been relatively inactive for seven years, everything seems ready for some new project. Indeed, at the conclusion of our talk, he informed me that he had not stopped writing and was now trying to adapt a comedy by the Elizabethan Thomas Middleton. When I mentioned a Middleton play that I preferred and that he had not heard of, he seemed as anxious for information as if he had been a scholar on the point of discovering a lost text.

Coincidentally, we began our talk with the problem of lost films, since I had been unable to locate prints of Clair's *Fantôme du Moulin Rouge, Proie du vent,* and *Break the News.*

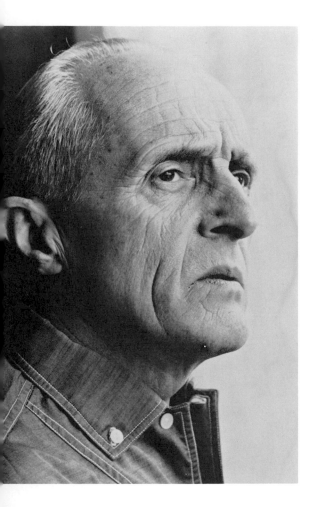

SAMUELS: I've been amazed at how difficult it is to locate prints of a given director's films. How is it that a man of your stature doesn't possess copies of his work? It's as if a famous writer didn't own any copies of his books.

CLAIR: It's very easy to keep a book; films are different. The object itself doesn't belong to you. However, although I don't own my films, I sometimes have control over their distribution.

S: Don't producers feel, even though they own the film, that you, the creator, ought to have a copy?

C: Producers have no such feeling, but you could get a print by making it a clause in your contract. I never tried.

S: In *Reflections on the Cinema,* you say that cinema is what can't be expressed in words, yet as your career progresses, you increasingly use dialogue. Was this by choice or necessity?

C: Like all aspects of show business, a film is made in collaboration with the public. I have always maintained that if the Elizabethan public had not been gifted with genius, we would have no Shakespeare or Marlowe. Theoretically, I believe that films should be expressed more by images than sound, but I don't believe that the public today would understand a completely silent picture.

S: Don't you think many directors today—Antonioni, for example—depend more on gesture than on dialogue and that avant-garde cinema is advancing by going back to silent film technique?

C: If you're right, I'm glad. But most pictures today owe more to radio than to film technique. You could black out the images and nothing would be lost.

S: You've said that the script is the most important element in a film. What then did you mean by "script"?

C: Everything: ideas, inventions . . . everything that you must plan before you begin shooting. Of course, this mustn't keep you from having new ideas during the filming, but the basis must be firm.

S: You've said that at the beginning of your career you improvised less than later on. Is that true?

C: No. I meant to say that I prepared my films very carefully at the beginning because I wasn't sure of myself. But now my scripts have very few technical indications. I describe what image must accompany the dialogue, but never how the shot is to be taken. I have that worked out in my mind because, since I write my scripts myself, I always know how I want things to look.

S: Yes, you are one of cinema's most important writers. Being so fundamentally that, why did you choose to make films rather than plays?

C: Pure accident. I was a journalist who aspired to be a writer; I would have written plays had I not happened into the motion-picture world. I played a few parts in some amateur films and then was asked to act in others. You see, I am a kind of prostitute: I discovered that I could make more money in films. But since I was such a bad actor, I quickly realized that my future lay behind the camera. Bit by bit, I became fascinated with the medium. Then I began writing scripts. I don't know why they call me a director; I have never directed anything I didn't write.

S: Isn't that the only way to be a great director?

C: No, there are great directors in Hollywood who have never written a line: John Ford, George Cukor.

S: I don't agree. Carol Reed is a great director without writing his own scripts, but I can't think of anyone else. Even Hitchcock, though he doesn't write the dialogue, effectively creates his scenarios.

C: Yes, I suppose that most important directors collaborate on the scripts, but direction itself is a separate thing.

S: What are the gifts that can ensure greatness for a director who doesn't work on his scripts?

C: I don't know. But let me give you an example, which I discuss in my latest book, of the difference between writing and directing. In Howard Hawks' *Scarface* there is a brilliant scene when the young scarface discovers his first machine gun. He is in a room full of billiard cues; he takes up the gun and "kills" them all in a row.

S: We'd say "mows them down."

C: Exactly. It's a splendid image. Well now, who is its author? When I went to New York and met Ben Hecht and Charlie MacArthur, who had written the script, I asked them whose idea that was. The answer is not the man who staged the scene but the writers who placed it in the scenario.

S: That's a problem in judging a director, isn't it? Finding out just how much of his brilliance really is his.

C: That's why it's stupid to write, as they do in Europe, a film by so-and-so. The English or American terminology is much better: written by——, from a play by——, adapted by——, produced by——, directed by——. Then you know—approximately—who did what. In my case, the film is really mine. And I must also admit that most of the young interesting directors in France today write, as well as direct, their films. But in Hollywood . . . I remember when I was at Paramount discussing scripts with a producer—a very nice man, by the way—and he presented me with a subject Paramount owned, saying, "René, would you be interested in filming this?" I replied, "Let me write it first and then I will tell you if it is suitable." He said, "René, I don't understand you: Are you a director or a writer?" That typified the Hollywood mentality.

S: In fact, you've called the Hollywood system of filmmaking the Irving Thalberg School. But unlike most European directors, you don't hate Hollywood. What did you like about it?

C: The technical facilities. The great difficulty was agreeing on a subject, but once you got past that hurdle, everything was a dream because of the wonderful technicians.

S: A friend of Antonioni's explained the failure of *Zabriskie Point* by saying that MGM gave him too much money. The facilities worked against him, almost paralyzing his imagination.

C: You can always turn money down. The greater difficulty is getting it.

S: Although you don't hate Hollywood, you've deplored the fragmentation of control. How did you manage to make René Clair films there?

C: I never did. Everything was a compromise between what I wanted to do and what I could do. My system of self-protection, however, was very simple. I saw some of my American colleagues selling themselves body and soul until nothing was left, so I simply turned down offers. I lost money; that was the only way.

S: Which of your American films do you think most characteristic?

C: It's difficult to say. Probably, that little picture, *I Married a Witch*.

S: I'd say *The Flame of New Orleans*.

C: That was a terrific flop!

S: But it has wonderful things in it, though Marlene Dietrich didn't seem right for you.

C: One American critic wrote that I had

contrived to parody her. But she understood this. I didn't do it against her will. When Norman Krasna and I wrote the script, we intended that it be ironic: a romance with a sense of humor. Perhaps that's what surprised the public; they didn't know quite how to take it.

S: Why did you go to Hollywood in the first place?

C: On account of a certain man called Hitler. I was in France preparing a picture when the country was invaded. Between Hitler and Hollywood, I decided to choose Hollywood.

S: Was Dietrich your original choice for the part?

C: I was her choice. She was under contract to Universal, when I approached them because I wanted to make a picture with Deanna Durbin and W. C. Fields. Joe Pasternak, who was the producer, said, "Look, I'd like to work with you, but Deanna is not free now. Why don't you make a picture with Marlene Dietrich?" I said, "I don't think she's my type of actress." "Why don't you talk to the writer?" Pasternak said, so I did. In front of Pasternak, Norman Krasna, whom I did not know at the time, began outlining the story. I nodded approval, but when I got home, I called Krasna and said, "Your idea is very interesting, but it is what I call a producer's synopsis. You have no idea how to shoot it." Then Krasna, who was very charming, said, "Mr. Clair, I see that you're someone who understands motion pictures." He then called Pasternak and told him to hire me.

S: I have another idea why the film failed. It breaks in the middle. It starts out as an ironic comedy about sexual opportunism and then becomes a stock Hollywood romance.

C: Probably.

S: Was this forced on you?

C: Nothing was forced on me. Norman and I were completely free.

S: In general, you treat sex distantly and tenderly. But in *The Flame of New Orleans* it is treated in a typically American way: with lots of leering double entendre. Was this conscious on your part?

C: No, it was a result of my collaboration with Norman. It was his style, and of course, whenever I worked outside of France I relied on my collaborators. That's why I never attempted, in England or America, a naturalistic film.

S: Because you felt that you didn't understand the mores?

C: I had seen so many foreign directors make pictures in France that I felt to be completely false that I was very careful not to do the same thing elsewhere.

S: Perhaps that's why there are unconsciously insulting portrayals of blacks in both *The Flame of New Orleans* and *The Ghost Goes West*. For example, in *The Ghost*, when they have a party and the blacks come out playing calypso. . . .

C: That wasn't an insult. It was intended to show the contrast between the old romantic castle and the modern millionaire who celebrates his possession of it with jazz.

S: The maid in *The Flame of New Orleans* is a cliché.

C: Just the opposite. The professionals were shocked because in American films at that time one always showed a black maid as a fat woman. Instead, we picked a lovely young girl; everyone on the film fell in love with her. We were considered too pro-Negro.

S: Wouldn't her subjugation to Marlene Dietrich now be thought condescending?

C: She was a maid! We had trouble with the Hays Office over her character. When the old woman gives Marlene sexual advice before her

wedding, the maid gives a look saying how little the advice is needed. The Hays Office wanted me to cut that.

S: Did you often encounter censorship troubles?

C: Once or twice.

S: The other problem in the film is Bruce Cabot. Why did you use him?

C: That was a mistake made by me and my agent. Hollywood at that time was a machine for producing films; they wouldn't wait until someone else was available for the part. I made a test of

Cabot that was rather good, but no doubt he wasn't a good choice; he lacked subtlety.

S: Did he follow your directions?

C: Yes, but as William Wyler told Norman, "René is a great director, but there are certain things even a great director cannot do."

S: You've said that audiences have collective genius, that when they cough, they show a problem that must be corrected. This suggests that you accept the masses as arbiters, but it seems to me that some of your finest effects can be appreciated only by the connoisseur.

C: The role of art is to be accepted by the masses while being appreciated by the connoisseur. Consider the great masterpieces of the motion pictures: *The Gold Rush, Potemkin.* Many things in those films are not seen the same way by the public and also by the connoisseurs, but both audiences see that the films are great.

S: What about great films that don't have a mass appeal?

C: Von Stroheim?

S: I was thinking of more recent works, like *Diary of a Country Priest* or *L'avventura.* Do you think it's a shortcoming that they lack mass appeal?

C: Not a shortcoming. Probably they are too literary for the masses. If they were closer to the older style, they would be more popular.

S: But these films do emphasize action over words. For example, remember that scene in *L'avventura* where Ferzetti is inquiring in the hotel while Monica Vitti stands outside and is surrounded by an ogling crowd of men? This is all action, but the meaning isn't explicit. You see, I think the problem is subtlety of meaning, whereas you and Chaplin and Eisenstein worked to make things completely clear.

C: Always! I always considered film a mass art. If you included something for the connoisseur, that was fine, but first the film must be understood by the masses. In the history of films practically every cinematic landmark was also a popular success.

S: Do you think that sound films are less suited than silent films for comedy?

C: It all depends on what you call comedy. If you mean the sophisticated genre one associates with a director like Lubitsch, then sound is all right. But the true comic art disappeared when sound came in.

S: I'm interested in your opinion of certain recent comedies.

C: I'm no critic.

S: You don't have to answer. What do you think of *Smiles of a Summer Night?*

C: I don't give opinions about contemporaries. Let me tell you, it's not just a matter of tact. I don't see enough pictures, and it is unfair to offer a judgment based on fewer films than are seen by a professional critic.

S: Every director I meet tells me he doesn't go to the movies.

C: I don't either.

S: Why not?

C: You ask the question at the wrong time because I saw three films last week. But usually I don't go. Before I see a film, I want to be practically certain that it will be good, because when I see a bad picture, it discourages me so that I never want to make another film. But when I see a good film, I think, "For God's sake, I wouldn't have thought of that! How I wish I could do something like that." And then I want to get to work again.

S: I hope you'll give me an opinion on one contemporary because I'm puzzled about him. All the directors I've interviewed have nothing good to say about one another, but they all say good things about Godard.

C: I never answer about contemporaries. They all like Godard?

S: They hate one another, but they like Godard.

C: I don't hate anyone.

S: In *Reflections on the Cinema,* you said that Vittorio De Sica was Chaplin's most authentic successor. What did you mean by that?

C: I was not speaking of the comic Chaplin; I was speaking of that singular emotion that you find in him and in the early De Sica. There is a good example in *Umberto D.* that I have often cited to show the difference between dialogue and visual invention. The old professor who has no money and sees a beggar in the street realizes that he could make some money in this way. Then we have a five-minute sequence in which there is no speech. We see that he is ashamed to beg because when a man comes by, he removes his outstretched hand and pretends to be searching for something in his pocket. The same quality you find in the last scene of *City Lights,* when the girl is blind.

S: What about De Sica's latest films?

C: Ah, Vittorio makes too many pictures. They are well directed, but one does not see the genius of De Sica in them.

S: I am interested in your condescension toward suspense films. That genre and yours are so similar in their musicality. Why do you find it unimportant?

C: Not unimportant, facile. I don't want to speak of others, so let me give you a personal example. I made a picture a few years ago called *The Grand Maneuvers*, which was very difficult to write because it's a love story. When two people are in love, if they go to bed, it's the end of the picture; if they don't, what the hell are they waiting for! So I had to find a lot of complications, and the script took me almost a year to write. My next picture was *Gates of Paris*, which I made from a novel I had bought. A gangster is hidden in the cellar with a machine gun under his jacket, and two innocent people are playing cards upstairs, though they know he is down there. Four weeks to write!

S: There's a problem in that film. Henri Vidal is so convincing in his love for Dany Carel that I can't believe it when the plot shows he lied.

C: For me, he isn't convincing.

S: He acts out his love so well.

C: In order to trick her.

S: There's a difference between convincing another character of what you don't believe and convincing the audience.

C: Vidal was too practiced a lover.

S: Did your early work as an actor teach you anything about directing them?

C: A little. First, you should never get angry, because if you do you paralyze the actor. You should always try to be as kind as possible, even when you are furious. You say, "That was very good; now let's try to do it a little better." That's about all; the rest I learned while directing. When you write, you have an ideal of what the character is going to be like, and then one day you meet the actor who will incarnate him. You should never force the actor to match that original image, because he cannot. The greatest law of directing is never to force an actor to do what he cannot; you must collaborate with his abilities.

S: You often remind me of Hitchcock when you speak of editing, of your control over shot length and sequence, as the essence of directing. Don't you think this idea differentiates those who came to cinema in the silent era from those whose background is theatrical?

C: It's possible. When I was in Hollywood, a head producer would see rushes of six or seven films a day, and the average director shot five thousand feet, whereas I only shot five hundred. The producers thought I was crazy. One day, without telling me, one of them went to my cutter and asked if I had a film, because it was considered phenomenal in those days to produce one without shooting much more than was necessary. Most Hollywood directors shot everything from every conceivable angle. As a result, the producer could put the film together as he wanted to. But I always knew exactly how much I needed and how it would be assembled. That's why I wasn't interfered with, because there was nothing left over from which they could choose. Lubitsch worked the same way.

S: Hitchcock uses a jigsaw method of editing that keeps anyone but him from knowing how to put the film together.

C: You need something like that in Hollywood.

S: It is well known that asynchronism—contradiction between image and sound track—is fundamental to your style. But why have you said that it should never go to the extreme we find in a commentary?

C: First, because I invented the trick, and it was a dangerous invention since it makes things too easy for a director lacking in imagination. He can have the voice-over say, "And since then he fell in love," when he should find the means to show this.

S: You told Bernard Pastor that cinema was in a period of stagnation. What would you like to see happen in the future?

C: I've discussed that in my newest book. It's amazing that an industry which has existed for seventy-five years still maintains its original methods at a time when everything else is changing. Cinema remains a machine, a light, and a white sheet. But this, which might be called a crisis, is really a phase in the medium's evolution. As I say in my book, cinema resembles that other powerful, though more lucrative, industry: the automobile. They both were born at the same time, and neither has adapted to the pace of invention. After all, the automobile is still based on that stupid internal-combustion machine which has proved a disaster for mankind.

To take the simplest example: distribution. By using videotape, we can send the same film to a thousand theaters at the same time. In our stupidity, we are still carrying those cans of film from theater to theater.

S: There's even been talk of computerized transmission. But I take it you are speaking of the industry and not of the art.

C: In the mass media, art is wholly dependent on technical possibilities. Forty years ago we couldn't talk about television. Even now, some other invention is on the way that we cannot foresee.

S: While we are on the subject of distribution— why haven't some of your films been distributed in the United States? I think, for example, of *Les Fêtes galantes*.

C: *Les Fêtes galantes* came at a time when all the distributors wanted to see was ass. In *Les Fêtes galantes*, which is by no means my best picture, at the very beginning there is a scene where the hero takes the princess, who is disguised as a shepherdess, and lays her down on the straw. At that point, I cut away. If I had just waited three minutes longer, the picture would have been sold.

S: There's your television! Movie producers feel they have to seduce people away from their sets, and the main difference between movies now and TV is nudity!

C: That won't be true for long.

S: How do you feel about criticism of your films?

C: I am glad when the reviews are good. When they are bad, either it is my fault or the reviewer was in a bad mood. For the most part, I think I've been well treated by critics and historians.

S: Your films are defined as much by what they exclude as include. There are political sentiments expressed by your characters, but not politics or contemporary problems; there are love affairs, but no graphic sex; people fight, but there are no wars, etc. Are these exclusions dictated by temperament or by your artistic goals?

C: That's for someone else to decide. I don't think an artist can analyze his own choices.

S: Do you disagree with my statement?

C: Not at all.

S: You've usually avoided location shooting except—

C: If I were a historian of the cinema, I would say, "M. Clair likes to invent everything"— speaking as a historian, mind you. "It was probably unconscious, but it gave all his films a certain style." Even in a naturalistic work, like *Under the Roofs of Paris*, sets provide an atmosphere that could never be obtained if I had shot in the streets. They compose reality, and that is my definition of art.

S: Do you think that contemporary audiences can accept painted sets?

C: Anything will be accepted if it is well done.

S: I find you very candid in self-criticism. For example, you included in your volume of four screenplays strictures against each of the films. Why is that so easy for you?

C: Probably because I am never satisfied with what I do. In fact, I don't like to see my old pictures. I always think, "Why wasn't that better done?" "My God, that's too slow." I even think I get a sort of sadistic pleasure out of criticizing my old films.

S: Do you think that the cameraman has a crucial effect on the style of the film that he shoots for you?

C: The camerman, the art director, all the chief collaborators influence a film. Film is a collaborative art.

S: What are the disadvantages and advantages of working in color?

C: First of all, I don't think that black and white will completely disappear. In art, color engravings never made black and white obsolete. However, for some technical or economic reason, color may win out in films.

S: I think producers are now forcing directors to shoot in color because they think that this novelty value is necessary to combat TV.

C: It's true that a public accustomed to color will find black and white dull. But black and white contains gradations of shading impossible in color. It is also a more artistic method because it transforms reality and requires more invention in lighting.

S: But it's easier to do well, isn't it? I've seen very few successful color films. When I look at the colors in this room, they harmonize because my eye naturally selects among them. On screen, colors usually seem to clash. Color is almost too powerful a genie to be contained within the movie frame.

C: That's why I try to control it very carefully. I made two color films. In *The Grand Maneuvers* we tried to obtain a general impression of gray, which is very difficult because there is no gray in the color band. Gray is a sort of equilibrium between two other colors.

S: Did you instinctively choose gray because it is closest to black and white?

C: No. I had thought a good deal before I started working in color. Consider that painting over there. The painter's problem was to place a certain quantity of color in a certain space, but in the movies you must think not only of space, but also of time. In the painting, that pink is interesting because it works with that bit of green near the bottom of the frame. But in a film, where images follow one another, a brilliant yellow can become a problem because it is followed ten seconds later by a blue. Therefore, when I made my first color film, I depended on gray to give unity and preclude shocks. But I must say neither the public nor the critics gave a damn. Maybe two or three people noticed that there had been an effort to control color in that film. In *Les Fêtes Galantes* my art director and I based our colors on the palette of Braque: brown, gray, a little yellow, occasionally a pink. That was rather well done, but nobody noticed it either.

S: Isn't that because artists discover things long before the public or critics realize what has happened?

C: Maybe. But you know, neither of them understands photography. If you show them a camel flying in the sky—which is an absolute cinch to produce—they say, "What a wonderful piece of photography!" But if you show them a low-lighted picture with all the details distinct—something very difficult—they aren't impressed. This isn't important, though, because sets and photography shouldn't be noticed; it's the action that counts!

S: There's a growing tendency among directors to dispense with music. Music is essential in your films. What do you think of this tendency?

C: I myself use music less and less. In a naturalistic film I never use music unless it's coming from something like characters singing. But in a work like *Beauties of the Night* music is my language.

S: Your use of music is as significant as your asynchronism, though it has received less attention. I think, for example, of *Under the Roofs of Paris*, where the music at the beginning is the

Paolo Stoppa singing his dialogue to Gérard Philipe and Martine Carol in Beauties of the Night.

sound of the rain. You seem always to want to rationalize music.

C: You saw that little scene at the beginning where people are running in the rain and the boys approach the girl? I thought that had disappeared from all copies of the film.

S: It's available in America.

C: In most places, the film starts with that long tracking in to the set.

S: But that's terrible. . . .

C: You don't have to tell me! Probably it was cut somewhere and someone saw it that way, and so when he sent the film on, he forgot to send the first reel. This is a crazy business!

S: Are you planning to make any more films?

C: I have no ideas and no money.

S: I hope you get both soon. But can we review your career now?

C: Please.

S: How did you get the opportunity to shoot *The Crazy Ray*?

C: First, let me tell you that you didn't see that film. There is not a true print of it anywhere in the world. When the film was made, it was developed in small reels, one by one. When I saw the film at the Museum of Modern Art, it was clear to me that some of these reels had got lost and others were mixed up. At the beginning of the film, the hero is supposed to be alone in Paris, but when he looks down, he sees a cab. I don't know where the hell that came from.

S: I'm glad you've told me that because when I saw the film, I thought the editing was dreadful.

C: I was so disgusted, because my original picture lasted thirty minutes.

S: The print I saw was longer.

C: Much longer. I recently reassembled the film in its original form. I hope it will be shown in the United States.

S: Let's return to my question: How did you get to shoot your first film?

C: I wrote the idea and gave it to Jacques de Baroncelli, my mentor. He gave it to someone else, who provided the little money on which the film was made.

S: You made it only to experiment with stop-motion photography?

C: Of course.

S: It's a theoretical film; the plot is merely a pretext.

C: It was purely an experiment. I wanted to

recall the first slapstick French films made before Mack Sennett. I think also that I had a vague recollection of a film I'd seen when I was still a child. It showed a woman who loses her wig and has to chase it to the top of the Eiffel Tower.

S: Don't you think you show too many views of the tower?

C: Maybe. I love the Eiffel Tower; I even made a short documentary about it.

S: Why did you include the cartoon sequence?

C: To show how the sleep ray moved through the city. There was no other way to explain that.

Irreverent moment from a funeral procession full of bounding mourners.

S: *Entr'acte* was created for the intermission of a ballet.

C: The Ballet Suèdois asked Picabia to create a program for them. On a napkin at Maxim's he wrote out some ideas, and from these I created a script.

S: What was your purpose in making the film?

C: Experimentation, because since it was not a commercial film, I was given a free hand. Picabia wanted a film for the intermission so as to recall the method of a music hall. By luck, I was around when he needed me.

S: What did you think was the central line holding the film's improvisations together?

C: I really don't know. I took Picabia's notions and tried to give them some development. For example, Picabia wanted to show a funeral procession that included a camel. From this, I developed the long sequence that ends the film.

S: The film links up to your later work mainly through its satire of the bourgeoisie.

C: The funeral procession was also meant to travesty the idea of death.

S: Why did you want to film Labiche's play *The Italian Straw Hat*?

C: He is one of my favorite playwrights, and I love the play, which is a classic model of chase farce. I use that motif also in *The Million*, which is nothing more than a long chase that allows me to enter different milieux. Incidentally, this structure also underlies *The Bicycle Thief*.

S: *The Italian Straw Hat* shows what is characteristic of your work: You mock things, but you are never strongly against them.

C: Because I am never strongly against anything.

S: I am not too fond of the staging of the scene in which the horse bolts after eating the hat. Did the horse give you trouble?

C: No, he was a very nice horse, but I had difficulty convincing him to eat the hat.

As the lawyer "talks," the content of his speech appears through superimposition.

S: I am puzzled that you wanted to make *Two Timid People* because its script takes such a long time to be funny.

C: I don't like that film. It's taken from another play by Labiche, but an inferior one.

S: What drew you to it?

C: I really don't know. As a matter of fact, I wrote the first version and gave it up, turning instead to what probably would have been the first neorealist film. But for some reason, that film could not be made, and so I was forced to return to this idea I had rejected. I shot the film without enthusiasm. The only thing that amused me was the opportunity the script offered to render speech through images rather than sound—because it was precisely at this time that the silent era was coming to an end.

S: Why did you make occasional use of a split screen?

C: Abel Gance had at that time used the split screen for *Napoleon*. My use of it was a gag between professionals.

S: Was it also to interest yourself in a project that you found boring?

C: Yes. I was playing technical games.

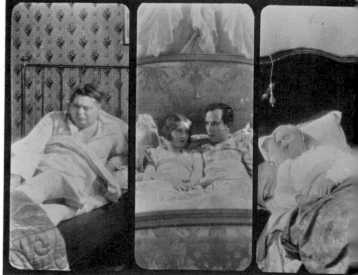

S: *Under the Roofs of Paris* is an exception in your career because of its stylistic realism and seriousness of subject. Why did you suddenly turn to this mode?

C: While I was shooting one of my silent films, I walked out of the studio one day and saw a crowd that turned out to have gathered around a street singer. The scene was so moving, so charming, so typically Parisian that I wanted to make a film on the subject, but since we were in the silent era, it was not possible. As soon as sound came in, I did it.

S: The film is obviously an experiment in sound. I think, for example, of the wonderful scene in which the street singer warns the heroine that her purse will be stolen simply by raising his volume. As always, you do things to prove a technical point, but it doesn't interrupt the flow of the story.

C: I wanted to show people that you could make a sound film without forgetting the old lessons.

S: How did you manage that magnificent tracking shot that begins the street scenes?

C: I wanted that to get the effect of coming gradually closer to the singing, but it was very

difficult to produce. Even in America, where they had unparalleled technical resources, I was asked how we did this. We built a primitive railway—it was very dangerous—which the camera slid down, until it reached the ground, where it pivoted to shoot the girl. At the bottom, we hid the tracks with a piece of the set. The only trouble was stopping the vibration of the descending camera, so we mounted it on wood and tennis balls to muffle the movement. We tried it ten times before we got it right.

S: It glides. Had it been faster, it wouldn't have created the right effect. Tell me, why didn't you shoot this realistic film on location?

C: Because it was impossible at that time. What we now call New Cinema is based on something the critics never write about because they don't know these things: high-sensitivity film stock! When film wasn't so sensitive, we had always to use lots of lamps, electricians, and equipment that could not be mobilized in the street. Today film stock permits you to go into a railway station and shoot without any lamps.

S: If you could redo the film now, would you shoot it outdoors?

C: It wouldn't be so good. You know, realism isn't realistic. It is simply a different convention. You aren't shooting reality; you are shooting things that you have arranged in the streets.

S: When the hero hides the thief's sack on top of his armoire, is it meant to be suspenseful or funny?

C: Neither. I simply needed to motivate his subsequent arrest.

S: I understand that, but the scene baffles me emotionally. I can't feel suspense because he picks such a dumb place to hide it.

C: When I was young and living in a small room in Paris, a girlfriend of mine asked me to hide something for her. It turned out to be drugs. I kept it for her for two weeks, but I could easily have suffered the same fate as Albert.

S: But if you expected the police, you wouldn't hide it on top of your armoire, where it could easily be seen.

C: As a matter of fact, I never even thought of hiding it.

S: But you see the problem it poses the audience?

C: Yes. I never thought of it.

S: There is another scene that is emotionally puzzling, though clever cinematically: when you show the passing of time by what happens to the things that fell on Albert's floor. For example, it seems to take months for the mice to eat the bread.

C: Maybe it was only a small mouse.

S: Why did you include that funny drunk in the last scene?

C: Because when a scene is in danger of becoming sentimental, I always like to include a comic touch.

S: Aside from the technical experiments, the film is daring because of its open ending. How did the audience take that?

C: Well. The hero is singing in the street. Probably he will meet another girl. That's life!

S: Most people, myself included, regard *The Million* as your masterpiece. Would you agree?

C: From the point of view of invention, I suppose it's my most important contribution to the cinema. A young man can't appreciate the little revolution made by this film in its use of music. Because by now you have seen thousands of musicals inspired by my film and others like it made in the first days of sound.

S: If you could change anything in the film, what would that be?

C: Many things. For example, in those days I never cared if dialogue was thrown away under the music. Today this shocks me when I see the film. It's not an ambitious picture, but perhaps for that reason, it's probably my most successful.

S: Was the film a response to the Depression?

C: It hadn't begun yet in France.

S: Nor by the time of *À nous la liberté*?

C: No, because that film was still a satire of the consumer society. You know, I saw it recently and realized that it was a hippie picture. The conclusion tells us to go off into the country and do whatever we like.

S: The ending has been criticized. You've been accused of treating a large social problem and presenting a frivolous conclusion to it.

C: That's why I treated it in operetta style: because I knew the subject was so serious. The film was violently attacked by the Communist Party, which, up until that time, I had been on good terms with. They correctly perceived "anarchist tendencies."

S: Here's where a hostile critic can say, "Clair gets so close to the facts but then runs away."

C: It wasn't my business. But you know, one always gets his reward. The film was attacked by the party in Germany and Russia, as well as France. Last year, however, the Communists asked me to lend them a copy for the Moscow Film Festival.

S: How much of *The Million* is copied from the original play?

C: Very little. For example, all the scenes at the opera are original. All I retained from the play were the characters and the idea of a lost lottery ticket. I did the same thing in *The Italian Straw Hat*, where I used only the first and last of five acts.

S: Do you remember this film as the one that was most fun to make?

C: Yes, certainly. I remember that when we first dressed the actors for the opera scene, we nearly died laughing.

S: Did you make the set of the roofs deliberately heavy so as to produce a great contrast when the camera looks down the skylight?

C: I must tell you that this wasn't in the original script. Originally, it started with a knock at the door and the entrance into the painter's studio. When I saw the final print, I realized that this was terrible. The film was completed before I got the idea of the opening traveling shot.

S: That's amazing. Because the beginning now repeats the end and so gives the film perfect roundness of form.

C: That's right . . . how could I have done it? It's very strange what you say just now. I don't remember.

S: I don't want to put words in your mouth, but could you have got the idea for the beginning because you made this particular ending?

C: I must look at my original script. [Does so.] Ah, I see there is no indication of the rewriting. That's very strange. But I remember that I was shooting the rooftop scene at the very moment that my producer was showing the film to a German distributor. I remember that because my collaborators and I were so angry that he was exhibiting the print without our permission that we shot the scene over and over again in order to waste money.

S: I am puzzled by what you say because the film now begins with a cut from the scene of people dancing in the room to Michel's studio. The cut comes exactly on the downbeat of the music which coincides with Prospero's dropping a bowl. It seems all too perfect to have been an afterthought.

C: I can't remember . . . I am looking, but I can't solve the mystery. Yet I'm sure the scene was added.

S: I can't ask you any more questions about *The Million*. I've discovered that the better a film, the fewer the questions I can usually ask its director. As a work of art approaches perfection, it answers your questions itself.

C: Of course.

S: So let's move on to *À nous la liberté*, which, though first-rate, presents more problems. One of the things that was first in evidence in *Under the Roofs of Paris* is very striking both in *The Million* and in *À nous la liberté*: the theme of male friendship. How do you account for this?

C: You are perfectly right, but I can't account

for it. I remember that St.-Exupéry also said that my best films were on this subject. As I told you before, I'm not a critic or historian of myself. But it is very true that friendship has always played an important part in my life. And it's also true that the drama of friendship is less banal than that of love.

S: Because less often treated.

C: Yes, and because love is egotistical but friendship is more interesting.

S: That underlies one of the best scenes in the film: when Émile comes to Louis out of friendship but Louis can only think that he wants money.

C: That's a scene I would like to remake. The acting is poor.

S: You wouldn't alter the sequence of shots?

C: I'd alter everything. I should like to have a second life in which I could reshoot all my pictures. No, not all. Some are not worth reshooting.

S: But not *The Million!*

C: Oh, I could do that much better. Many times I was asked to remake it, but that's something one should never do. People will then say that the original was better. Also, I could never recapture that original joy in making the film.

S: Let me tell you what I think is wrong with *À nous la liberté*. The brilliance decreases as the romance becomes more prominent.

C: The romance was nothing.

S: Why did you put it in?

C: Out of superstition, because even the best films—like those of Chaplin—were thought to require romance. In fact, my romance is a typical Chaplin romance, only lacking his genius.

S: Your romances aren't all bad. Look at the one in *Silence Is Golden!*

C: But *Silence Is Golden* is a film about love, whereas *À nous la liberté* is about modern times. I needed the romance for the plot. It was a way of arranging the story; it wasn't the story.

S: It seems to me that you indicate your discomfort with it by the way you introduce the heroine. We think she is singing, but it turns out she's posing while a record is playing. This makes fun of her.

C: I didn't intend that. People at that time were terribly worried about perfect lip synchronization. I was simply playing a technical joke.

The heroine seems to be singing in a bower until the record is turned off and her father appears.

S: Did you use any special methods of staging to produce the impression of regimentation at the factory?

C: It's very simple in a country like France to get people to march in a line.

S: Why did you include the scene in which Louis' butler accidentally drops baked Alaska on all his guests?

C: Because I wanted a scandal to interrupt the social event and because the week before I shot that scene I had been to a large dinner party where the hostess was splashed by some red sauce from a lobster. She remained sitting quietly throughout the dinner. Later she came into the room wearing a new dress.

S: But in the film it doesn't seem plausible that the guests would sit there so long without noticing it.

C: Probably I was too influenced by that episode I've just told you.

S: I think the plot lurches forward in the second half of the film. Was it completely written or improvised?

C: Completely written. That's the film I would most like to remake because it is the best idea that I ever had, but I didn't spend enough time on it.

S: I think your genius is done an injustice by the widespread emphasis on this as your best film.

C: Because it has a serious theme. People are never willing to admire farce as much as something serious.

S: Nor art as much as content.

C: Another old superstition!

S: There is an interesting theme in the film that never gets quite developed: capitalism using sex to manage its workers. I'm thinking, for example, of the scene where Émile tells Louis he's in love with a worker, who is promptly produced for him.

C: That's simply to show how organized things were and that in the factory every worker is just a number.

S: I am being presumptuous to offer a suggestion. . . .

C: Not at all. What you say is interesting.

S: The romance might have worked better had it been seen as a creation of the factory.

C: Probably. By the way, did you see the version with the café scene?

S: Yes.

C: A whole reel is missing in most prints of the film.

S: That's a fantastic problem. How can anyone seriously interested in films study them when he can't even be sure he's seeing what was actually the film?

C: It's maddening. Nothing has been done about film preservation.

S: Isn't that the job of film archives?

C: They can't, poor people. Usually they make their copies from corrupt prints.

S: Can't producers and distributors be convinced to help out? It seems clear to me that the current student mania for all sorts of film would make it worth their while.

C: Years ago I tried to promote such an idea, but there is a problem of money, and no one listened to me. Since we cannot know now what will later be considered the great films of the day, you need to preserve everything. My idea was to require every producer to deposit a print of his film in the country where it was made. In that way, without too much cost to any single country, you could eventually build up a cooperative *cinémathèque* that would be the best in the world.

S: Do you think that will ever happen?

C: You know the world! Simpler and more important things can't get done.

S: Why wasn't *The Last Millionaire* a success?

C: It was a bad film; the idea was amusing, but it wasn't well executed. Some people said that the film flopped for political reasons, and that isn't totally false either. It appeared at a time when Fascist sentiments were surfacing. When it opened in Paris, the scene in which the banker banished the government was applauded, but when he was hit on the head by the falling chandelier, the public was so disappointed they began tearing things up. However, that doesn't explain the failure; any theme will be accepted if it is well done.

S: As far as I'm concerned, the film is terribly acted, especially by Marthe Mellot, who plays the queen.

C: You're right; she's terrible. She had been a singer rather than an actress. I selected her because she fit my physical image of the role.

S: Did you realize she was bad while you were making the film?

C: No, only afterward. I didn't even realize that the picture was bad while I was making it. Pathé, for whom the film was made, offered me Elvira Popesco, but I foolishly turned her down because she had been trained in the theater.

S: Another thing that bothers me in the film is the really stupid slapstick: people tripping or knocking their heads together.

C: That was one of the many occasions when I was trying to change my style. I had been very impressed by the new slapstick coming from America—W. C. Fields and the Marx Brothers—but I did not realize that this is an Anglo-American style of acting that the French can't imitate. I also made the mistake of not putting anyone in the film with whom the audience could sympathize.

S: Let's turn to a better film: *July 14th*.

C: I made that before *The Last Millionaire*.

S: Of course. I've got them out of order. *The Last Millionaire* was the last film you made before leaving France.

C: It's what made me leave the country!

S: Ah, that and Hitler sent you to Hollywood.

C: No, Hitler sent me to Hollywood; *The Last Millionaire* sent me to England. I made *July 14th* because after *The Million* and *À nous la liberté* I wanted to return to my favorite style: that of *Under the Roofs of Paris*. Moreover, July 14 is an important French holiday. But I must say that the film is better in parts than as a whole.

S: As in *À nous la liberté*, the film starts

Holiday celebration in July 14.

marvelously but then falls off. The romance isn't at fault here; I just can't believe it when the hero falls in with the crooks.

C: He goes with them because of his former lover.

S: I can understand him going back to her out of lust, but he isn't the sort of person to turn criminal.

C: You're right. The film is mostly a series of sketches. As I was writing it, I felt the need of a plot, but I didn't create a very good one. I wanted to make a feature out of little sketches. Had I succeeded, it would have been quite a trick.

S: In this film the heroine is blond, the villainess brunette. Was that deliberate?

C: That's a Hollywood convention that I wasn't using. The heroine was played by Annabella, whom I had used in *The Million* and wanted again, although I discovered she was much more gifted for comedy than for romance. The other girl was a Rumanian actress I had used in *Under the Roofs of Paris* but who was now out of work. She could have had a great career if she hadn't been so lazy. She wouldn't even read the script! One day I asked her what sort of dress she thought she should wear in the modiste scene, and she answered. But there was no such scene in the film!

S: Some directors, like Bresson, have told me they won't let their actors read the scripts or even see the rushes. What do you think of that?

C: That's hamminess in the director. An actor should have a general idea of the character he is going to play, and there is no reason to bar him from the rushes. While we look at them together, I tell him what must be improved, even in something so basic as makeup. I take my entire crew to see the day's rushes so that I can make observations to them about the next day's work. The director is not a magician; he doesn't make things happen by himself.

S: Some directors prefer to use actors as if they were inanimate objects that are moved through space.

C: To a certain extent that is correct, but it is the director's job to animate them.

S: Did you encounter new conditions when you moved to England?

C: Nothing much, except that the pace was slower. Alexander Korda had wanted me to make a film for him when I was still in France, but since I had a free hand here, I refused. Then he showed me a story called "Sir Tristram Goes West" that I liked so much that I wanted to buy it. He wouldn't sell it to me because he wanted me to shoot it for him. Then I went to London, where all my films were successful, even *The Last Millionaire*. It was shown at a royal charity ball, and I was very worried because the film pokes fun at royalty, but, as a friend told me, the English never care unless it is their royalty you are mocking. Later I had dinner with Alex, and since I had just flopped in France, I told him I was a little tired of making films here. He then offered me a treatment of that little story, and then my troubles began. With a ghost as the central character how can you make a film? He can't make love, can't eat, can't even travel; he can only be a ghost. So Alex called me and said I was to drop the whole idea and make *Cyrano de Bergerac* with Charles Laughton. Since I loved the play too much to reorder it, as I always do to the material I shoot, I wired Alex that I had a brilliant idea for the ghost picture. So he said, "Come back to England, and we'll start next week." I had no idea, but in a week I wrote the synopsis. Then Bob Sherwood was called in to write the dialogue. Most of it is his. I wrote only the love scenes.

S: How do you feel about the film?

C: I don't know. It was a tremendous success in England, and when a film is a success, you begin to believe it's not as bad as you thought.

S: It seems to me that *I Married a Witch* is greatly harmed by Fredric March's performance. He's a good actor, but he has little comic talent.

C: He has some, but I don't think he was right for the part. I don't know why he was assigned to the picture, but of course, you don't turn down an actor of his importance. Veronica Lake was so childlike that maybe the age difference was a hindrance.

S: One of the scenes—the fire in the hotel—doesn't come off well. Did you have trouble shooting it?

C: Censorship trouble; the censors protested because when the witch comes through the smoke, she is nude. I told them that the audience would see no more of Veronica Lake than if she were wearing an evening gown. We see only her shoulder; the rest of her is in smoke. They replied that the audience might not see her, but March would!

S: You mean to tell me that they were protecting the morals of movie stars?

C: Isn't that preposterous? If you start protecting the virtue of Fredric March, you'll find yourself very busy!

S: What do you think of *It Happened Tomorrow*?

C: The last twenty minutes are the best thing I did in Hollywood. The real story only starts at the end, when the hero learns he is going to die.

S: I wondered why you were interested in a story that defeats you for so much of its length.

C: Two young writers had produced a synopsis that interested everyone but was eventually turned down because no one in Hollywood felt comfortable with fantasy. When Jed Harris offered it to me, I refused because I thought the story could not work in a contemporary setting. However, I thought it would go if we pushed the action back. I offered it to Paramount, but they didn't want it. Arnold Pressburger then bought it, and when I separated from Paramount, he asked me if I would do it for him. I agreed on the condition that I had Dudley Nichols to collaborate on the script. What interested us was the technical problem of happily ending a film in which a man's death is accurately predicted. We found the answer in a little story by Lord Dunsany that another producer had under option.

S: What do you think of the casting of Linda Darnell?

C: She was even more beautiful than she looks in the film. Shuftan, my cameraman, and I were in despair because we could never show her true beauty on the screen.

S: Do you think she was charming enough?

C: She was beautiful!

S: What about Jack Oakie? His style is so different from yours.

C: No, he is exactly the type I would always like to have worked with. His timing is perfect.

S: Why did you make *And Then There Were None*?

C: I had a very bad time in Hollywood during that period. The war had broken out, and I felt terrible being separated from my country. Second, most films made at that time were about war, but I could never shoot actors "dying" when a real war was going on. Nobody wanted to make my sort of film, and I needed to make a living. *Ten Little Indians* was then a very successful play, so I went to Dudley Nichols and said, "Let's do that one." But I have never considered it one of my films.

S: How did you return to Paris?

C: As soon as I was able to get my passport from the temporary government of De Gaulle, I left as an unofficial ambassador between Hollywood and the French motion-picture industry. My wife remained in California, and my son served in the American Army, so I returned to the States with a vague project of making an American-French coproduction. After months of delay, that turned into a contract between RKO and Pathé, and I went back to France to make the film.

A silent film being made.

S: It seems so appropriate that your return to France should take the form of a retrospective look at French movies. Did you intend that?

C: No, but probably the nostalgia that had developed while I lived in America caused me to remember the days of my youth so that I wanted to evoke that period. It was originally written for Raimu; when he couldn't do it, I took Maurice Chevalier.

S: Did you try in this film to say anything about film?

C: No. The early film era serves in *Silence Is Golden* only as a background to the main story. I have always avoided making a movie about movies.

S: Why?

C: Because an artist must invent and should not become autobiographical.

S: When you made *The Beauty of the Devil*, you said that what drew you to the Faust legend was a problem in construction.

C: Yes. I had always felt dissatisfied by every version of the story that I knew. Since artists as great as Goethe and Marlowe had failed, I thought I too could make an imperfect try. Moreover, like everyone at that time, I became interested in the possibility that the earth would be destroyed, a possibility that comes directly from the devil. Here is where the problem of construction comes in: Marlowe's *Faust* is marvelous in the beginning and at the end, but the middle is silly. Faust throws things at the Pope, and you don't need the devil for that. About Goethe, Stendhal was right when he accused the play of invoking heaven and hell only to explain how a German student had knocked up his girlfriend. Goethe himself realized that, which is why he wrote Part II. That has some poetic beauties, but it is not a good play. I sat down to discover how all these geniuses went wrong and learned that if your character is in league with the devil, then everything is possible, and if everything is possible, then there is no drama. Furthermore, the existence of the devil proves the existence of God. Since Faust is the most intelligent of men, it is implausible to think he'd risk eternal damnation for only a few years of pleasure. My Faust thinks he can trick the devil because my devil doesn't ask Faust to sign a contract when he offers him happiness. My devil asks for nothing, expecting to get Faust to sign the

contract later. That was my great invention in retelling the story.

S: Michel Simon, who is one of France's best actors, gives a brilliant performance in the film. How was he to work with?

C: Very difficult. I admire him. He is an intelligent man. But he has an impossible character. I thought I had a gift with actors, since I never have any trouble with them; with Simon, my gift vanished. He was totally unreliable. One day he was charming; the next day—if he had not slept enough or had spent too much time in a brothel—he would not even speak to anyone.

S: Gérard Philipe's metallic laugh, when he plays the devil, is amazing. Was it amplified in any way?

C: No. Gérard had the projective power of an opera singer. Whenever you thought he had reached his limit, there was still more.

S: Isn't this the most expensive film you ever made?

C: It's difficult to say because the costs were computed in Italian money. Curiously, the French producer made a lot from the film, but not the Italian.

S: In your commentary on the film you said that you made a mistake to include Marguerite.

C: Not me; it's the fault of that son of a bitch Goethe who invented her.

S: But you enhance the mistake by keeping the passion away from us because it is the only reason for having her in the film. When they kiss, you put them behind a tree. Why?

C: Because it isn't a love story. Marguerite is just a sort of symbol of goodness.

S: It's appropriate that you made a film called *The Beauty of the Devil* because there is no evil in your work; even the devil turns out to be a delightful character. Do you really believe this?

C: No. I believe in evil, but I don't like it. I am always surprised and even a little frightened by those of my colleagues who can work for months on a subject that is so disheartening. I always suspect that such people are a little queer. How can one enjoy working through a world filled with nasty people?

S: What of the triumph to be had in comprehending and accurately representing a reality that is awful?

C: It is certainly an achievement, but I always wonder about the person who achieves it.

S: Are you saying that you can't stand the discomfort of living with such a subject?

C: How can one get up and go to his desk every morning to write about suffering? No, I couldn't.

Ermanno Olmi

Rome, April 23 and May 3, 1971

Feature Films: 1959 *Il tempo si è fermato* (*Time Stood Still*); 1961 *Il posto* (*The Sound of Trumpets*); 1962 *I fidanzati* (*The Fiancés*); 1965 *E venne un uomo* (*A Man Named John*); 1968 *Un certo giorno* (*One Fine Day*); 1969 *I recuperanti* (*The Scavengers*); 1971 *Durante l'estate* (*In the Summertime*).

Since Ermanno Olmi is surely the least known director in this collection, some brief words of background seem necessary. In my experience, Olmi is the best exemplar of the neorealist style, with its disdain for dramatic contrivance and fictive invention. His films offer slices of life, with indefinite or inconclusive endings: they simulate documentary methods in staging and photography; they aspire not to proposition or evocation but only toward accurate representation. The later works depart from the neorealist style of *The Sound of Trumpets* and *The Fiancés*, but even they are characterized by non-discursiveness. It is therefore surprising to discover that this most circumstantial of directors is personally given to abstractions and ideology.

Commitment to his avowed ethic of responsibility was evident from the events of our interviews. Session one took place during the latest hours of a week during which he had come to Rome for some television shooting and for the press screening of *In the Summertime*. Since he speaks no English and since I was not sure that my Italian would get me through the interview, I invited him to the apartment of my cousins, Dr. and Mrs. Enzo Martinelli, where the latter served as interpreter. Forced to return to his home in Milan, Olmi could not finish our talk. A week later, although urgent business required that he be in Florence, he drove all day so as to reach Rome and conclude the interview.

Olmi is about six feet tall, with close-cropped red hair, and a monochromatic appearance. In his early forties, he seems like an average workman, deviating from the type only because his manner is apparently the result of cultivation. But his softly regular voice becomes sonorous and his diction becomes heavily emphatic when he expresses his convictions.

SAMUELS: What interested you in becoming a director?

OLMI: I wanted to communicate my love of the ordinary things in life. I began by taking pictures of objects and people sheerly for the love of them. Shooting these pictures also was a way of coming closer to the world of work that I shared with my colleagues. I then started making documentaries, but soon I felt the need of doing something with greater significance.

S: In your films don't you try to portray not what separates your characters from the viewers but what unites them?

O: The public contains my characters.

S: You seem to say that you discover your subjects in the streets.

O: No, I discovered my first subjects in myself. For example, the boy in *The Sound of Trumpets* is me; the worker who goes to Sicily in *The Fiancés* is also me. The young boy in my first film, *Time Stood Still*, is certainly me. Each film, except,

obviously, *A Man Named John*, was about me—until *One Fine Day.* When I started writing that script and realized that once more I was being autobiographical, I put it away. Instead, I decided to explore the world of advertising, a world in which I am very interested. What I did was use my original idea to provoke in the agency personnel stories that I could use to construct a script. I wanted to work in the mode of *commedia dell' arte,* which is the greatest style of theater. In that style, a master of ceremonies appears and announces a show that the viewer feels represents his own private drama. Leaving aside the Greeks, who were incomparable, every great dramatist has merely modified the essential formulas of the *commedia.* By arranging its basic types, Molière could write a play in one night. In *One Fine Day,* I tried to find my own variation of this style. I moved into the advertising agency and lived among the workers so that when I interviewed them they would accept me as a co-worker and thus present themselves frankly. The screenplay I wrote is nothing but an arrangement of the stories they told. All I held back from them was my theme (individual responsibility), and they provided me what I needed to flesh it out. As if I were talking to actors, I told them that they shouldn't tell me about themselves but rather about people they knew. Therefore, they were more candid than they would have been had they thought I was gathering personal secrets. When I finally came to shoot the film with people from the agency actually taking the roles, the man who played the hero said that although the events in the film didn't correspond to his own life, he almost felt that they did. Anything that occurred to my nonprofessional actors during the course of filming and that also seemed interesting I incorporated into the script. For example, there wasn't any subplot originally, but during the shooting I arranged to have the girl who plays the interviewer and the boy who plays the artist meet. Then I shot a scene of their meeting in the very studio where he lives. Afterward I told him that I would see him again a month later to shoot another scene, because I was certain that he and the girl would see each other in the interim. I knew that the backgrounds and characters of these two people would dispose them to fall in love, and I arranged things so that this could happen.

S: Then you shot the two scenes between these characters exactly in their order in the film?

O: Yes. I went on shooting the film and didn't call the boy back until a month had gone by and the two had fallen in love.

S: The girl who plays the interviewer is extraordinary. In the scene when she first talks to the artist in his studio, she suddenly looks at him and says, "You want me, don't you?" Her delivery of that line is one of the best I've ever encountered. How did you get that inflection from her?

O: Look, when young people meet, the subject of desire is bound to come up, and besides, this particular girl has exactly the personality in real life that she portrays on the screen. I didn't get this inflection; it is an expression of her deepest self. This girl works as a market researcher; she isn't the sort of person who waits for things to happen; she got her job because she is able to impose herself on others. If I had written that scene before our improvisations, I certainly wouldn't have put that line in her mouth. This is the way I operate: If, for example, I wanted to shoot a scene with you and this young lady in it, I would simply place you and her beside each other and wait to see what comes into your speech.

S: That sounds like *cinéma vérité*.

O: But there is a difference. In *cinéma vérité*, the person plays himself and therefore is his own creator. Instead, my people are impersonating characters in a script I have written by assembling from all the things they say during rehearsal those that I want in the final film.

S: You are very similar to Bresson, who spends months talking to his amateur actors before he begins shooting the film. Like him, you seem to be searching for what the people don't realize is in them. But Bresson has criticized all you Italian directors for dubbing in the voice because he says that the voice is the most profound indication of personality. What do you think of his point?

O: Bresson is absolutely right. In *Time Stood Still* I did not dub. *The Sound of Trumpets* was dubbed by the very people who had played the roles.

S: But even when you use the voice of the original actor, the fact that he is saying the line after he performed the original moment must change its feeling.

O: I'm not so doctrinaire as Bresson. Since the visual element is the most important thing in a film, dubbing isn't too harmful. Furthermore, one touches up the visuals; why shouldn't one also touch up the sound track? However, I *do* try to take sound directly whenever that is possible. But when I shoot in 35 mm, I can only take the sound directly when I am not using a hand-held camera, because obviously I couldn't find a machine small enough that would also record sound. When I need to be free of trolleys and so on, I dub. I never tell my actors how to speak a line, for then they would try to imitate my inflection, though I suppose they are influenced by my inflection in explaining motives or the significance of a scene. I also never say, "Stop, everybody, we are ready to shoot," because that creates tension, whereas, above all, I want things to be natural. I never shoot a scene more than three or four times. If it isn't right by then, I completely change it so as to keep my actors from performing mechanically and speaking in the inflections of theater rather than those of life. The terrible thing is that even an amateur begins to sound like a professional after two or three days of shooting.

S: Bresson also says he wants to preclude theatrical inflection. That's why he uses non-professionals, as you do. Why did you break with that practice in *A Man Named John,* and how did you find directing professionals?

O: I used a professional for the role of mediator in that film because the role was that of an actor who impersonates other people. I also wanted a professional actor, like Rod Steiger, who normally plays people like Napoleon or Al Capone but who

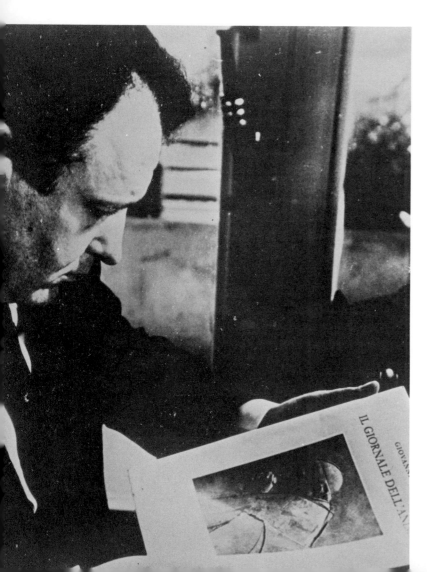

here says, "I am not going to play a character but rather myself as a human being." I wanted to present Pope John not through his physical dimension but rather in his soul. However, after a week I knew that I was defeated because Rod Steiger could not simply play a human being but insisted on projecting his personality as an actor.

S: I think this is your least successful film, and I want to explore some of its shortcomings. Why, for example, do you sometimes show Steiger observing the action and sometimes appearing in it as Pope John? Moreover, why don't you make it clearer that he is moving from one role to the other?

O: If I were to tell you a story, you would initially see me only in the role of storyteller, but as you became caught up, I would seem to assume the role of the character about whom I am speaking.

S: I understand that. Let me see if I can get at the problem in a different way. When Rod Steiger becomes Pope John, he presents the man at different stages in his life, yet Steiger himself is always the same age.

O: In John's *Diary of a Soul* he said that his relations to people never changed regardless of his age; that is what I am trying to represent by not showing Steiger aging physically. I am trying to show that age is not a physical sign but a deepening rapport with life.

S: All right, but at the beginning of the film you do have a child enact the role of John as a child. That seems to me, especially in the light of what you've just said, to disorient the spectator thoroughly.

O: In those early scenes I wasn't interested so much in John as in the environment.

S: Let me try another example. During the sequence of John's mission to Bulgaria, the man who is his attendant suddenly steps out of that role and speaks a commentary directly at the viewer.

O: I don't think that's a mistake because this character also acts, like the mediator, sometimes as a character and other times as a commentator. In fact, all the characters in the film are just mediators between us and Pope John.

S: Yet you said that in the early scenes you wanted to show the environment, and in fact, the people seem thoroughly realistic. They do seem to be playing characters rather than mediators.

O: Of course, these people are real peasants, but they are not the actual peasants in John's life. They are people called by Steiger to impersonate roles. John came from a world that still exists, but that world is not only stones, walls, and trees, but also the people who represent the human material of the countryside. So these people mediate between that and us.

S: When I saw the film in America, a title said it was supported by Gulf Oil. Why is that so?

O: I know nothing about that. So far as I know, the film was financed by Harry Saltzman. But maybe Pope John had given Gulf his special benediction.

S: Your producer Labella collaborated on the script. Did that cause any special problems?

O: Actually Labella didn't produce the film. He merely proposed the project to me in the name of Saltzman and put me in contact with a man who had been the Pope's secretary and who gave me a copy of his diary. He worked on the script only because he knew a great deal about the Vatican. When he first came to me, I refused because I thought it would be irreverent to make a film about Pope John. But he replied that this wasn't necessarily so. Therefore, I decided that maybe I could make a film showing not the well-known affection and sweet nature of John, but rather the reasons for these characteristics. I wanted to understand why people flocked to this man's smile and talk—why, at his death, they came from all over to give their love and pay their final respects. Many politicians smile, but their smiles do not move people the way John's did.

S: Do you think you succeeded in getting behind that smile?

O: It is an error to think you can show spiritual comportment in a film. If the spiritual is not incarnated, it remains too abstract for cinema. The most serious contradiction in the film is not the one you mention (between mediator and character) but that incarnating a spiritual essence in flesh distorts it. The message of this film is that you shouldn't make a film about this kind of story.

S: Don't you think that Bresson succeeds in showing the soul?

O: Yes, because he shows the soul in travail.

S: Then you're saying that your portrayal of the soul doesn't work because it lacks drama.

O: Let's not remain abstract. I can make my point with an example. If I wanted to make a film about problems in love, I would show people living these problems, not discussing them. If someone tells you his troubles, you become annoyed. But if he acts them out, you become fascinated.

S: Mr. Olmi, I understand why you selected a professional, but why did you select an American actor who couldn't even speak Italian?

O: Because I wanted an actor who had prestige, as if I had chosen a great violinist to impersonate a great composer.

S: Did Steiger have such prestige in Italy? He didn't in the United States.

O: He had just finished making Rosi's *Hands on the City,* and in Italy he did have prestige. But, in any case, I didn't choose him. This is the one film that I made within the industry. I don't mean that

Saltzman or the others were at fault; I was interfered with by the system. In fact, Saltzman did everything he thought would help me. He gave me a troupe of thirty people, but that only disgusted me. I would walk into the hotel lobby in the morning to find them all waiting for me. Often I didn't want to do anything on a certain day, but I had to give them something to occupy their time. After a week I understood that nothing was working properly. I felt like a man who has fallen out of love with a woman and doesn't know how to get rid of her.

S: Let's return to a happier subject: How did you get your chance to direct your first feature film?

O: Through a betrayal. The electric company which I worked for didn't want to produce features but only documentaries because they feared that if they went into feature production, the stockholders would worry that too much money was being spent. Therefore, I told my boss that I would make a documentary though I intended to make a feature. When they discovered my lie, they were extremely angry. But luckily, the critics liked the film, so peace was restored.

S: How are your films received in Italy?

O: Let me first speak of the critics. With the exception of a number that you could count on one hand, people who write about film are journalists who went into this field because they didn't know what else to do. Instead of helping get an audience for the director, they damage him. A man works more or less seriously on a film for a year only to find his work reduced to some circles on a page. Unlike writers in other fields—like politics—these people aren't even respectable; they are hangers-on at festivals. As for the public—people are always wondering why my films don't play at their neighborhood theaters. Because they don't go to see them!

S: Isn't that because the films are so difficult? Not intellectually, but because you are so inexplicit. All your meaning is contained in the action.

O: You are absolutely right. In commercial films the characters constantly explain themselves, so there is nothing to understand. But do you know why most people choose a film? To interrupt their normal lives. They enter the theater suffering indigestion (nothing counts more in the reception of a film than the state of the audience's stomachs), and the whole world of film is organized so as to make them forget the way they actually feel. It is like a county fair. If people went to the theater before dinner, when their heads weren't full of pasta, you'd see very different films on the screen.

S: I wish you were right. I think, however, that your films will always seem difficult because people are not trained to "read" images.

O: No, the problem is not one of comprehension. The public wants to evade reality because any reality portrayed on the screen demands that the spectator take responsibility for it. The average spectator is so reluctant to do so that if he actually saw himself there, he would deny that the character corresponded to him. I remember a scene in a film played by Charles Laughton, where he is a worker razzing his boss. The spectator identifies with that sort of person precisely because he would never have the nerve to razz his boss in real life. Most films subvert culture because they encourage evasion of responsibility. In my view, society must be made up of responsible men, for those who do not take responsibility for their own lives are ripe to be led by a dictator.

S: This suggests what I regard as the central theme in your films. From Natale's speech about the good old days in *Time Stood Still*, through the depiction of an office in *The Sound of Trumpets* and a factory in *The Fiancés* one can trace the notion that modern technological society militates against the existence of free and responsible men.

O: I'm not saying that technological society is bad; I'm saying that the men who formed it were irresponsible.

S: In what sense?

O: Men have always understood that they must resolve certain problems: work, shelter, etc. So they produced a society rich in consumer goods. But men don't act the role of responsible protagonists of their own lives; rather they become passive—this is the problem. It's not that we have cars, refrigerators, and television sets; it's the way we use these things. People who make television programs aren't responsible men; they don't, as being men of cultivation they ought to, lead their audiences. They follow what the society dictates; they sell their cultivation for money.

S: But don't your films contain nostalgia for the past? Your first film, *Time Stood Still*, has a great speech about the days when the young respected the old, and your latest film, *In the Summertime*, takes as its hero a man who lives by old chivalric values.

O: I don't want to go back and lose what industrial society has given us. At the same time, I don't want to lose a certain kind of man. In a former era, when farmers seeded the earth, they didn't understand the chemical process that made their crops grow, but they worked from a faith that gave them responsibility for their lives. I have three children. When I come home, they run to me, kiss me, and call me Daddy. When they grow up, they won't do these things anymore; they will express themselves in the gestures of maturity. So with our farmers. They cannot farm, as farmers used to: by an act of faith. They now understand the earth's chemical processes. But in this progress of knowledge they must not lose the sense that the earth is human. I, who believe in God, can no longer accept Him unquestioningly. It is by questioning and taking responsibility for our questions that we who live in an industrial society can be responsible.

S: Don't you agree with the speech against modern life that Old Du makes at the end of *The Scavengers*?

Old Du haranguing Gianni about the latter's acceptance of work.

O: Du, who belongs to the mountains, can achieve freedom only in that world. The young man, on the other hand, becomes responsible and free by saying he won't go into the mountains. He will find freedom in an entirely different ambience, with construction, roads, light bulbs, missiles that go to the moon. . . .

S: What then is the relationship in *The Scavengers* between the fact of work and the reality of World War II?

O: The war presents the hero with his problem. He must find work so as to be able to marry, but in his village, at that moment, there is no work. He could go to Australia, but he won't leave home. Then he meets Du, who proposes that they scavenge; the work is dangerous, but it pays very well. Then construction begins in his village. Now he must decide whether to continue his dangerous, profitable work or to build houses.

S: What your films show is that men are tied to dangerous or enervating jobs because they have been taught to think only in terms of economic necessity.

O: *The Scavengers* is about our postwar period, when all we thought of—with reason—was economic recovery. Unfortunately, the motive that was so justified then is still primary. We all need to eat, but we have become obsessed with eating. Instead, as a person matures, hunger shouldn't play so great a part in his life as it does for an infant. As hunger decreases, he can show the effects of conscience. But we do not act from conscience. We are like students who refuse to graduate. Our society wants to remain infantile.

S: That is why I think *The Fiancés* is the most successful of your films in expressing your ideas. I think it criticizes all previous films in the neorealist style, because the others show that everything a man did he was forced to do because of economic necessity. Instead, you show that poverty doesn't excuse this couple, that their estrangement is a result of the man's deficiency in love.

O: The situation of the film is two people who ought to get married after a long engagement but who think they can't because they lack an ideal economic condition. Instead, they are kept apart by moral and spiritual factors. So when the hero goes to Sicily, thinking he is going for money, only then does he fall in love with his fiancée. In fact, the film ends as if the two had met for the first

In The Fiancés, *the lovers come closer, ironically, through letters than they ever could in person.*

time. Now he no longer hides from her behind the excuse of money. He makes his most beautiful declaration of love; he says, "Today I won't go to work."

S: I want now to go back to something you said about The Scavengers. You said that the path of Old Du and that of the young man are simply two different ways of being responsible. But I don't think the audience can see this because Old Du is so much the more interesting character that we believe him.

O: Yes, that danger exists. It is like the fascination exercised by the old agrarian world, which is not ours anymore. How often do we see an old abandoned building in the countryside and say, "Ah, how I'd like to live there!" But if we lived that way and improved our lives a bit, we would be evading our responsibilities. Our responsibility is to keep faith with the values we believe in and to search for some way to live out those values in whichever society we find ourselves.

S: I don't think the film itself—the events, characterization, even the camera setups—is neutrally respectful of both characters.

O: I myself sympathize more with Du, but I also recognize the validity of what the young man says. He must aspire to the same liberty enjoyed by Du, but in his own way, in a world very different from Du's world—a world of houses, modern hospitals, electricity. . . .

S: Aren't we supposed to agree with Du when he tells the young man that the latter's way of life makes him society's slave?

O: Recall The Sound of Trumpets. When the boy reaches the position at the desk before the end of the film, we realize that he has become a cog in a wheel, but if he wants to, he can still remain a free man. Freedom is not the ability to wander in the mountains or to live outside

Moving up a desk constitutes a precious victory in the meager office world of The Sound of Trumpets.

society; it is internal. In that office there is a character who everyone thinks has no personality, but when he dies, they discover that he had always been a writer.

S: Why did you make *The Scavengers* in color? I think that keeps one from remembering that we are in the immediate postwar period.

O: Perhaps you're right, but I wasn't very interested in giving the film a historic character. Otherwise, I would have made it in black and white.

S: Why didn't you?

O: Because by now we are so used to color that we simply accept it as another cinematic technique. I could, however, have made the tones grayer.

S: As in *One Fine Day*, where the color is good, not because I prefer gray but because beautiful colors don't suit a tale of privation and difficulty.

O: But *The Scavengers* isn't completely realistic. It is an attempt at parable. Indeed, the personality of the old man was taken from a character who was dead when the novel was written, a character who, by now, belongs to the world of legend.

S: He is also a character in your personal world of fable because this film obviously reworks *Time Stood Still*.

O: Except that the earlier film is thoroughly realistic.

S: Not thoroughly; think of the nonrealistic background music.

O: But there is music only at the beginning and end.

S: And in the skiing scenes.

The hero plays a childish game in the snow, accompanied by light-hearted background music.

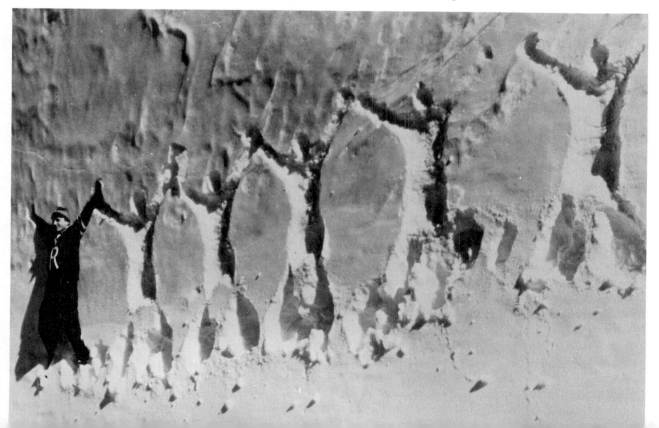

An earlier idyllic walk sans music.

O: Ah, yes. Well, it was my first film, so you must realize that I wasn't yet completely clear on all such questions.

S: I'm puzzled by this, however. I think your films are the most realistic ever made, outside the field of documentary. Why then do you use evocative background music? I think, for example, of the scene in which the couple walks through the street in *The Sound of Trumpets.*

O: You hear only a distant piano.

S: But that's not real.

O: Tennessee Williams has said that when we remember a happy moment, it is accompanied by the sound of violins. You can have a pleasant encounter with someone, in the midst of traffic, but your interior happiness blots out the traffic noises and all you hear is a sort of music brought by your feelings. Very often when we are talking or even thinking to ourselves, the talk or thinking has a musical accompaniment—psychologically speaking.

S: To get back to *The Scavengers:* Why do you include so much suspense about whether the protagonists will be blown up when the film isn't meant to be a thriller?

O: Obviously, scavenging is very dangerous work. Although some bombs are handled very easily, others must be picked up with the delicacy of a surgeon. With these, the old man exaggerates the danger in order to dramatize himself. You recall the scene in which he tells that story while dismantling a bomb—

S: May I interrupt for a moment? Where did you find that wonderful tall tale?

O: We made it up, but it is a variation on a well-known tradition. In those mountain villages where it snows six months of the year and the villagers huddle in stables, they tell such stories, full of fabulous hunts and enormous foxes. But you were right to ask a question about the suspense. I included that scene where two workers are found dead of an explosion in order to provoke the young man into saying to Du, "What kind of work is this we're doing! It's worse than war." Then Du answers, "Shepherds get killed in tornadoes. All work is worse than war."

S: That's an instance of the greater number of explanatory speeches in this than in your other films.

O: That's true, because the encounter of these two characters represents the collision of old and new worlds. Furthermore, this is the only one of my films based on a novel. I made it—I won't say on commission, but on request.

S: Yet it is, as you seem to agree, so similar to *Time Stood Still* that it seems a revival of your own ideas.

O: You're right. It's not only that both films take place in the same mountainous region but that they both concern the meeting of generations. In each case, I felt very tenderly toward the subject, perhaps because, owing to the force of circumstances, I spent many years living with my grandmother, a peasant woman of great wisdom (not scholastic wisdom, but the fruit of a life lived with utter clear-sightedness). As a result, I feel a great deal of tenderness toward such old sages. The most regrettable flaw in modern society is its separation between old and young. We adults spend our lives entirely among the efficient, whereas the old and very young have time for reflection and contemplation. Our society has destroyed the human family; that is why we build nurseries and nursing homes.

S: Why, as a beginner, did you choose to make a film in CinemaScope?

O: Because it had just been discovered, and the story I was getting ready to shoot seemed to me to be right for it: two people at opposite sides of a great distance.

S: Why haven't you used it again?

O: Because it is cumbersome. I prefer hand-held cameras.

S: The last scene of the film shows the characters taking shelter in a church. Did you intend to suggest that the old man's strength came from religion?

O: That church was built from 1915 to 1918 by people native to the Alps. It was the only cement and rock building in the area, so naturally my characters, who lived in a wooden shack, went there during the storm. I'm a Catholic, so I might have subconsciously felt what you suggest, but that wasn't my intention.

S: The storm is very authentic. How could you shoot anything during that turbulence?

O: It was fake. We made it with an airplane motor. I started my career with that whole bag of cinematic tricks—CinemaScope, special effects—but gradually I have tossed them away. In *The Fiancés* I used a real storm, though it was hard to find. That's a story!

S: Tell me about it.

O: You must remember that in Sicily it never rains during August and September. You shouldn't tell anyone this story, because he will laugh at me! It exemplifies the mentality of a Catholic and a peasant. Here I was, needing a storm when there couldn't be any, so I started up an internal dialogue with my grandmother, who was no longer alive then. I kept praying for her to help me, and I went slowly on the retakes in the hope that she would. One day that oppressive Sicilian heat was so dreadful that no one could sleep, so we worked through the night. When I finally got to sleep, I had this crazy dream: I was shooting my last scene in a downpour so terrific that it was actually painful; even the trees were bending under it. I went on filming, while my grandmother looked on, happy and satisfied. Imagine how I felt when I awoke from that vivid dream to see an utterly clear sky. Nevertheless, I told everyone to get ready for work because it would rain that day. They looked at me as if I were crazy. We went to the salt flats [where the scene takes place] and worked all day, without one drop. But by afternoon a storm came. Suddenly I found myself exactly as I had been in the dream, shooting in a downpour, with trees swaying all around me. In a half hour it was all over, and we all were standing in our underwear, drying our clothes on the hoods of our cars. But another cameraman whom I had sent to do some shooting three kilometers away came back dry. It rained only within a radius of three kilometers. With machinery you can make rain, but not a storm like that.

S: Why did you want a storm to end the film?

O: Because storms are special moments; since peasant times, they signify a pause. In life we all need pauses now and then, which is what the storm brings my hero.

S: Lamberto Caimi worked as an assistant on *Time Stood Still* and as the cameraman on your next films, but then you began to do your own shooting. Why?

O: In *Time Stood Still* my cameraman was a conventional technician who never agreed with me on the lighting. Toward the end of the film we quarreled, and I took over. Caimi was my co-worker at Edison, from which I invited him to become my assistant. Practically speaking, I photograph my films, but I've always thought it just to give my assistants credit. By now Caimi has established himself. My early collaborators were fellow workers whom I brought to the cinema. Because I thereby changed their lives and made them leave their regular jobs, I was anxious always to make sure that they stabilized themselves in their new profession.

S: *The Sound of Trumpets* is different from your other films because it is so funny. Did you intend this humor?

O: When *Time Stood Still* appeared, the press called it a documentary; since I began by making industrial films, it was assumed that anything I made would be a documentary. I wanted to rebel, to wink at the front rows and, above all, the critics. So I decided to put gags here and there in this film.

S: I'm glad you did because—

O: Let me tell you something: Apart from *A Man Named John*, which was a mistake, this is the film of mine I like least.

S: Why?

O: Just because it has all those gags.

S: I disagree. I think the comic scenes are brilliant. For example, the personnel exam. How did you decide exactly how far you could depart from realism in the direction of humorous exaggeration?

O: One shouldn't do such things coldly; one should do it instinctively. However, I did see a comic aspect in exams like this one that I had witnessed at Edison.

S: You should know that René Clair thinks this film one of the few comic masterpieces since Chaplin.

O: The comedy was intentional. Perhaps that's why I love it less.

S: How did you find the principal actors for the film?

O: I began the film with another boy, but after seeing a week's rushes, I gave up shooting for a month. The girl never worried me; all I needed was an innocent face, a blank page. But for the boy I needed someone who had reached the precise stage in life of my hero, someone who would not need to be taught the things that worried my character. In fact, I found such a boy in Treviglio, who was trying to fulfill his family's aspirations by placing himself in the big city. That's why I set the film on the outskirts of Milan, in the agriculture district where twenty years ago his parents were probably farmers. Having arrived at the position of workers, they regard the city as a place where one achieves a tranquil

station in life. But this station they look toward is also the renunciation of responsibility. That's what the mother tells the boy in the film, "Once you get there you're set for life. You'll have no more worries or responsibilities."

S: That's a kind of death.

O: Precisely. When a person renounces responsibility, he dies. It's as I show in my film, where the workers war with one another just to get a desk that's slightly closer to the front of the room.

S: But to get back to your search for the protagonist.

O: One of the ways I tested people for the role was to ask them to answer the telephone, moving toward it with hesitancy. I saw immediately that the boy I found had the right rhythm for the character, and once you have a performer like that, it is easy to make a film. For the girl, I had assistants photograph girls as they came out of school, and to some of them I gave screen tests. As I told you, I wasn't worried about finding her, but I still hadn't when we already reached the stage in the shooting where she enters the story. Then I remembered a face that hadn't been

among those tested, but it was getting so late I feared I would have to interrupt the film. I searched without success until one day I put on a suit I hadn't worn for a long time. In the pocket I found her picture; I had taken it out because even then I realized she had the right face. On the back of the photograph, her address was written.

When we finally reached her, I asked her to do a test that required only that she take a seat and ask someone a question. I set my camera up and said, "Go," but nothing appeared in the viewfinder. I kept saying, "Go," but there was still no movement; the girl was too terrified even to walk. She had to be brought to the chair so we could photograph her.

S: The presentation of the office building suggests Kafka. Do you agree?

O: I learned this after the film came out, from the French critics. I had no such intention.

S: The film also makes the factory into a continuation of school.

O: Yes. In fact, in the factory where I worked there was a supervisor who handed the work out as if he were giving assignments to students. Like a teacher, he would sometimes pretend he was reading a newspaper so as to be able to spy on the workers.

S: The montage in *The Fiancés* is much more complicated than that in *The Sound of Trumpets*. Were you influenced by the similar technique of Alain Resnais?

O: Remember that in *The Sound of Trumpets* I used intercuts to show the families of each person who worked in the office. That had nothing to do with Resnais, whose meaning is wholly metaphysical.

S: How did the audience respond to *The Fiancés*?

O: They were confused. So were the critics.

S: Sometimes you make the terrible factory in this film also beautiful.

O: Yes, because it has its own kind of fascination, though behind it there is tragedy.

S: What do you think of *Red Desert*?

O: I haven't seen it.

S: Of Antonioni?

O: He is our most lucid director, the first one to see the weakness and emptiness of our world. I esteem even his mistaken films because he ignores spectacle and even poetry in giving way

to the fear that overcomes him when he contemplates modern society.

S: He told me that he loves the modern world.

O: Sometimes when one loves a woman, one says he hates her or vice versa. Even more than private individuals, artists fall into such contradictions, but they tell the truth in their art.

S: Why are you so fond of sound bridges from one scene to another?

O: To show that the psychological state remains even though outward reality changes.

S: How did you film the festival at Acireale that occurs midway in *The Fiancés*?

O: As it actually occurred.

S: Do you mean us to find a similarity between the float that shoots fireworks and the rivets that scatter when the hero works at the factory?

O: Yes, but you're the only one who understood this.

S: Why did you include the scene where the hero enters church?

O: The same thing happened to me when I worked in Sicily. I entered this church in an isolated village where I saw a priest thundering from the pulpit at an audience of little children. Then the gravity of the scene was destroyed when a little dog that wandered in barked back at the preacher's sermon. I wanted this scene to capture that culture with its heavy Spanish solemnity that can be ruined by the smallest intrusion.

S: How did you get the remarkable color in *One Fine Day?*

O: Through slight underexposure.

S: During the early scenes you habitually cut during the action. Was this a deliberate attempt to render the fast pace of the hero's life?

O: Yes. This frenetic pace makes it impossible to do one thing at a time. Each gesture is superimposed on another, and nothing is free from distractions.

S: Why did you so completely eliminate humor in this film?

O: It's almost gloomy, you're right. I had just finished *A Man Named John* and had spent three years without making any films. Then I found myself in a world of men who were acting without meaning or significance. People seemed dead, alive only through small gestures.

S: How could you portray the world of advertising in which the film takes place without criticizing it?

O: I did not want to criticize because it too has its purpose. I simply wanted to study a man who fully understands the mechanism of psychological manipulation and all the means of contemporary society, but who neither knows nor wants to know himself. He knows why customers choose one product over another, but he does not know why he himself chooses anything.

S: You externalize interior states of mind in this film. Would you like to work further in this vein?

O: Look, I'm taking a three-month vacation now because I must make a difficult choice: whether to become, how can I say, a true professional who makes films from likely projects or to remain one who makes films to express himself, as a way of life. Up until now I had many roads open to me. But by now choices I've already made foreclose the future. My last film, though only a small parable, allowed me to treat fundamental questions concerning human relationships and the nature of nobility. Where do I go from there?

S: In the scene where the hero meets his mistress in the hotel, why did you choose to have

her watch a violent TV program as she waits for him?

O: Because violence is an important element in contemporary society, one that, as it were, violates us. We watch scenes of violence on television while we drink our after-dinner coffee, and we think we are detached; but I am convinced that it changes our lives.

S: Why is such an ordinary man as your protagonist so pleasing to women, particularly to one so unusual as the interviewer?

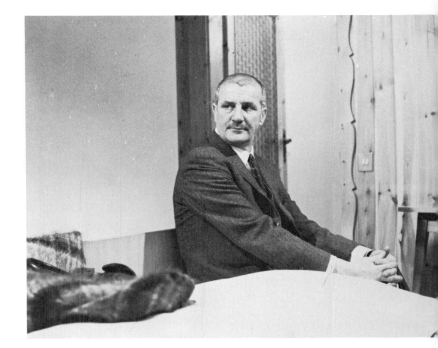

O: Because he's a big shot. Why do today's girls go for motorcyclists? They seek power; success is one sign of it. But although the interviewer accepts his offer, when they are in the bedroom, she dominates him. When she says, "I came here because I wanted to," he is struck dumb. This isn't a sentimental, not even a sexual encounter; it's a power struggle. It was inconceivable before that a woman shouldn't be merely a conquest. For men like him, the woman must always be something of a victim in love.

S: When the hero and his boss walk through the latter's farm, you maintain the sound level of their dialogue even when you switch from close-up to very long shots. Why do you permit this violation of realism?

O: I wanted these two men to seem very small in the surrounding countryside, but at the same time, their conversation had to be heard. I'm interested in reality, but I want it to serve me. Throughout life we select from the reality around us certain details. We listen to a group of men discussing profound matters but hear only the girl among them who is saying stupid things.

S: Now we come to your most recent film. I want to ask some questions about details. For example, why do you show the professor always having trouble making phone calls?

helped to bring it into being. I love this man who is, for me, one of the greatest living philosophers. He has also written two marvelous books about the United States.

S: Why were you interested in a character like the professor?

O: Because I believe that crazy people will save mankind. I am not talking about pathological cases, of course, but those who see more profoundly than the sane—like that man in Dreyer's *Ordet* who lives on a level of wisdom above the earth.

O: He is listened to only by the humble, the abandoned, the excluded. He tries to call those more highly placed, but they won't hear him.

S: Why did you use a collaborator on this script, and what did he write?

O: Fortunato is almost as important in my life as my grandmother was. He has been the person who most helped me clarify my ideas. He didn't write the script, but he merits credit for having

S: Do you think that we have reached the point where we require such a savior?

O: I now believe in men of feeling more than in scientists, and it comforts me to know that the greatest scientists in the past were those who expressed themselves in formulas as one expresses himself in verse. We have arrived at a moment of desperation when we need such men.

S: But aren't they dangerous? Can't it be said,

for example, that the professor ruins the young girl's life? By convincing her that she is a princess, doesn't he doom her to the same problems that he has always faced?

O: According to the logic of current society, what you say is true, but he gives her a sense of dignity such as she never had. He makes her a princess just as he makes the porter a nobleman.

S: But the porter hides when he should come to the professor's aid.

O: Like Peter renouncing Christ. My whole film is based on the Gospels. In life, we daily renounce not Christ but ourselves. At the end of the film the girl has stopped renouncing.

S: Why do you now make films for Italian television?

O: Because the circus world of movies rejects me, and since I must make films, I go to RAI, which gives me the wherewithal. Perhaps they will appear only on television and never circulate, but at least I can make them. I want to tell you something: I believe only in what a man does. Declarations, protestations, ideas mean nothing. Christ allowed Himself to be crucified to manifest His belief. What does it matter if a man speaks of such beautiful words as "honesty," "justice," "liberty" if he doesn't live them? Only actions have meaning.

S: Do you like Camus?

O: As a matter of fact, I was asked to film one of his novels, and I want to do it. I must decide during my future vacation.

S: You should film *The Plague*.

O: Isn't that funny! An English producer has already proposed it to me!

S: Why haven't you done it?

O: I don't know. I have another idea, too, but it hasn't caught fire yet. It's a story that derives not from a single text, but from a narrative tradition, a story about a young man who asks questions.

The professor is denied help at the crisis.

As children we all ask "why" continuously, but after a certain age we stop. Instead of asking questions, we start giving answers. Intellectuals offer definitions before they have even learned what it is they are going to define, and I consider that enormously presumptuous. The life of the farmer was one great question posed to nature, whereas industrial society thinks it can provide all the answers. The great mystery of life is that it is never so mysterious as when you think it has been solved. We should always ask ourselves new questions, touching on all matters from the most mundane to the most metaphysical. Job was the last great questioner because he questioned God. I would like my next film to be nothing but questions.

Federico Fellini

Rome, April 29, May 2 and 4, 1971

Feature Films: 1950 *Luci del varietà* (*Variety Lights*); 1952 *Lo sceicco bianco* (*The White Sheik*); 1953 *I vitelloni*; 1954 *La strada* (*The Road*); 1955 *Il bidone* (*The Swindle*); 1956 *Le notti di Cabiria* (*The Nights of Cabiria*); 1959 *La dolce vita* (*The Sweet Life*); 1962 *8 1/2*; 1965 *Giulietta degli spiriti* (*Juliet of the Spirits*); 1969 *Fellini Satyricon*; 1970 *The Clowns*; 1972, *Roma*. Episodes: 1953 "A Matrimonial Agency," *Love in the City*; 1961 "The Temptation of Dr. Antonio," *Boccaccio '70*; 1967 "Toby Dammit," *Spirits of the Dead*.

This interview is in three parts. Session one took place at Rome's Grand Hotel, to which Mario Longardi, Fellini's publicity manager for *Roma*, invited me to lunch. Eager to meet the director, I arrived at the hotel ten minutes before my appointment, but suspecting that Fellini would like to arrange the scene before my entrance, I decided to stroll about so as to come in a bit late. Outside, I enjoyed the spectacle of Fellini barreling up to the Grand parking lot in a long green Mercedes; inside, there was his ample figure towering over the corwd and hovering above some rum concoction that looked like a Felliniesque version of what millionaires drink in the tropics. "Ah," he said, "you're the journalist I'm supposed to meet." Next, he waved aside my assertion that I was a professor by handing me his drink. Finding that I liked it, he ordered replicas for his assembled colleagues, who were introduced as someone who would correct his English, someone who would correct his errors, and someone who would correct his lies. "If that isn't enough," he assured me, "we can bring others from the studio."

Fellini would clearly prefer not to be interviewed. While he looks about the lounge, rises to acknowledge the presence of various friends, and generally disports himself like the King of Rome I have later occasion to call him, I try to ingratiate myself with his troupe, hoping that they will encourage the enterprise when once we start. This, Fellini suddenly signals, but when I unwrap my gear, lunch is announced.

The first course comes; Fellini tells me to set up the tape recorder. I do, but the interview must contend with full mouths, greetings across the room, and a couple of phone calls. During one of them, Signor Longardi informs me that eight calls are par at lunch and that today I am in luck. Fellini, he says, would like to live with phones in his pocket; also, though the director is fascinated with talk about diets, "look at how much he eats!" Part one (which was spoken in Italian and later translated) is, by force of circumstances, brief:

Fellini directing The Clowns.

SAMUELS: You co-directed *Variety Lights* with Alberto Lattuada. What was the distribution of responsibilities?

FELLINI: It's very hard for me to remember things because I am so totally and passionately absorbed when I make a film that afterward my memory of it doesn't correspond to the truth. For *Variety Lights* I wrote the original story, wrote the screenplay and chose the actors. Moreover, the film recalls some worn-out routines I saw presented by a vaudeville troupe with Aldo Fabrizi. Lattuada and I formed a company with our wives, and everything was a cooperative venture. I can't remember exactly what I directed or what he directed, but I regard the film as one of mine.

S: The film is characteristic because of its emphasis on the life of the theater. I'm interested that you, a man of the cinema, should be so fascinated with the theater.

F: I'm not fascinated by theater; I'm fascinated by all forms of spectacle: theater, circus, cinema itself. These all contain congenial elements; when I show the atmosphere of show business, I speak of myself, because my life is a show. I am a man wholly devoted to spectacles; I am one of those who tells stories to others.

S: Both as a writer and director. Could you have been only a writer?

F: Since I became a cinematographic author, you can tell that exclusively literary expression isn't congenial to me.

S: Why?

F: You might as well ask my why I didn't become a surgeon. In a certain sense, however, I am a literary man. The exigencies of production require me to write down what I intend to do, not only for myself, but to instruct my co-workers. I must tell the set designer about the world which the actors will inhabit, must send notes to the wardrobe mistress, must even keep records of what the film costs. I started my career writing story ideas for other directors, but now that is only the necessary first step in clarifying my own conception and thus of bringing me closer to making a film. A story idea merely fires the furnace, and a screenplay merely instructs the various sectors that must work to produce a film.

S: Did you become a director rather than a writer because you enjoy that audience response which the writer never sees?

F: But directors don't see it either.

S: You can go into the theater, as you must certainly have done—

F: No.

S: Never?

F: Occasionally, I've accompanied a film to a festival or a premiere, but I've always felt distracted and detached. A film's success with the public doesn't concern me. I made the film I had to. Then it becomes a prostitute, lives a commercial life; what it does for the public is the public's business. Working for the public doesn't interest me. I think that my films are produced by a wholehearted sense of vocation.

S: In *Variety Lights*—

F: We're still on *Variety Lights*?

S: I'm afraid we've only begun. In *Variety Lights*, you show the theater with obvious love, but you also ridicule it. This is common in your films. It's as if while photographing a beautiful woman you showed her dirty feet.

F: But the dirty feet are also beautiful. I try to love everything in life, not only what we usually consider proper, honest, charming. I always like to show both sides of a thing.

S: So you show both sides of the theater because they both exist?

F: They exist together. The ideal and disillusioning sides of theater are two faces of a single truth. Both represent man.

S: In the process though, you deglamorize theater. For example, if we think of *Children of Paradise*—

F: That film by Truffaut?

S: No, Carné. Films like that glamorize theater; you want to present show business.

F: I don't want to do anything. I never ask myself about my goals, and if I asked and answered, what good would it do? That's the critics' and public's business. For me, the important thing is not to know why I do something but simply to do it.

S: *Variety Lights* also gives us our first example of something more obvious in your later films: the

The ludicrous, tawdry aspects of theatrical performance:
early in Variety Lights
middle in Vitelloni
and even as late as La strada

Fellini's quintessential parade. Guido as ringmaster to all the characters in his life at the end of 8 1/2.

Fellini parade. Why are you so fond of showing actors walking in parade formation?

F: There is no answer that would satisfy you. I could invent ten answers, but if you want something sincere—

S: Perhaps the answer is—

F: If you know, why do you ask me?

S: I want to hear whether you agree. At the beginning of *The Clowns* you present yourself as a little boy watching the circus. Couldn't this love of parades have that origin?

F: I don't know. An artistic creation has its own needs which present themselves to the author as indispensable. You're playing a game. If you are drawn to this type of cocktail party analysis, and if you have goodwill and some intuition, you can discover the reasons, but what good does it do? If I wanted to, I could explain that when I show a parade, I am showing the façade of life, people displaying themselves, etc.

S: That's interesting.

F: But it's not true.

S: It's interesting even if it isn't true—to someone who wants to understand how you see your own work.

F: More likely, the truth of the matter is this: The sequence in question forces you to accept it nonrationally because you sense that artistic fatality that is independent of any explanation.

S: There's a wonderful scene in *Variety Lights*—

F: More *Variety Lights!*

S: I'm sorry, but—

F: We're making this a long lunch.

S: —there's a scene between a cowboy and a Negro jazz musician that is not, strictly speaking, necessary to your story. Why did you include it?

F: I really don't remember the film.

S: It's a good film.

F: That's nice, because I made it. Certainly, I agree with you, but—

S: In this scene, and others, each character speaks his native language. This isn't usual in films.

F: He was an American Negro; therefore, he spoke English.

S: Usually a director, aiming his film at an audience of compatriots, has everything spoken in the native language.

F: Often I mix languages to express the truth of a situation.

S: You've said that all your films have the same theme and seem so alike to you that you can't even say which you prefer. But I've noticed more specific similarities: in situation and images. For example, in *Variety Lights*, there is a scene in a piazza where a gypsy—

F: Plays a guitar.

S: Right. Slightly altered, that scene reappears in *The White Sheik* when the fire-eater performs in the piazza. The finale of the orgy in *La dolce*

awakened conscious state, and it's clear that consciousness involves intellectual presumption which detracts from creativity. Thus, an artist who realizes a dream always senses a diminishment. I don't remember the specific question you asked me, but in any case, whenever you ask me why I did this, that, or the other thing, I can only answer that this particular moment brought me that perspective, light, words, characters, face. If the question interested me and I remembered, I might be able to answer when it concerns my sense of craftsmanship, but that is all. This answer takes care of all my work, eh?

S: I'd like to continue discussing your assertion that realizing the idea diminishes it.

F: Yes. I think, for example, that Nervi's idea of a bridge must have been more beautiful than the bridge he finally designed; he thought of Bridge and only built a bridge. That "a" sets limits on an idea that was originally unlimited. An image in the unconscious is not framed; it has the fascination of the vague and indefinite, of the inexpressible. This obscurity makes it more exciting. But when you realize the idea, you take away the mystery, the imprecision that makes things more than just themselves. The authentic, happy artist is one who maintains some sense of the arcane.

S: By your definition, which of your films diminished its original conception least?

F: The one I am making—but I really don't know. I never see my films again and therefore can't give a judgment.

S: Why don't you see them?

LONGARDI: He doesn't keep photos, clippings, scripts.

S: Then the repetitions I mentioned can occur because you don't monitor your films; they are recurring images, symbols of your deepest interests.

F: Are you happy now? OK, eat your lunch.

vita takes the form of Marcello riding on a woman as if she were an animal. This also takes place in the nightclub scene of *Variety Lights*. There is the famous sea beast in *La dolce vita* and another in *Satyricon*. I could go on. Why do you repeat these things?

F: There is no answer. A film takes form outside your will as a constructor; all genuine details come through inspiration. And what do we mean by inspiration? The capacity for making direct contact between your unconscious and your rational mind. When an artist is happy and spontaneous, he is successful because he reaches the unconscious and translates it with a minimum of interference. Unfortunately, we all make mistakes because education, culture, personal tics, and personal taste deform things that otherwise would be pure and instead mark them with the taints of our conditioning. The transformation from dream to film takes place in the

II

I close the tape recorder, not wholly in regret, for by this time I am beginning to feel stomach pangs. But to my horror, I realize that Fellini considers the interview finished. Before he can rise to bid me farewell, I tell him about the length of my other interviews and protest that we haven't got very far. Since this appears not to impress him, I recount long discussions I had with my students during the period when I taught some of his films. This piques some interest, but he quickly closes the opening by asserting his surprise that we had found so much to say. By now, probably because they feel he is not being polite enough to the "press," his associates have tendered sufficient compliments to make me feel I can risk some grandstanding. "Today you have perhaps discovered that I am not a cretin," I declaim. "Tomorrow we can have the interview."

Luckily, Fellini takes this with good humor and begins reviewing his schedule to see whether the day is free. Sunday would be better, he decides. I can come to his beach house at Fregene, spend the day, and get everything I need. I thank him for the invitation and, now that I have my appointment, feel that remorse which always overcomes me when I am relaxed enough to put myself in a director's place and think how I too would dislike constant harassment by interviewers. I express regret at having joined the disagreeable throng, but he allows that they too are part of a director's work. "We only got as far as my first film," he says. "Sunday we'll do the last one." "If we do," I return, "I'll make up all your answers for the middle."

My satisfaction at having got a second appointment is soon dashed, however, because Fellini calls me the following day to say that business forces him to grant me only an hour Sunday morning at his office on Via Margutta. I try to extort a promise that this meeting won't be our last, but he refuses to commit himself.

When I arrive at the typically Roman building in this fashionable area of art galleries and antique shops, Fellini is waiting at the door; he explains that the porter is off. He also tells me that he didn't want to appear "precious" at the Grand but that he has given so many interviews he feels like a fool, always saying the same things. I insist that I will get him to say new ones, but he tells me I can't. Then, as if to make sure my spirits are dampened, he informs me that "another journalist" will attend the meeting, adding to the annoyance of his constant and—as the transcript shows—deliberate mistake about my profession, the uneasiness I feel about the presence of an eavesdropper. I remind Fellini that this is *my* interview, and he assures me that "the other journalist" has come along to record what he says about *Roma*, the film in progress. As things turn out, we never get that far.

S: What did Antonioni contribute to *The White Sheik?*

F: If I remember correctly, Antonioni made a short about the sentimental side of the *fumetti.* I forgot its name.

S: *L'amorosa menzogna.*

F: Then he wrote a story for Ponti, which he was going to direct, and Ponti called me and Pinelli to turn it into a screenplay. There really was no contribution by Antonioni to *The White Sheik* except for that original contract with Ponti. We gave Antonioni screen credit, but actually we never even saw him.

S: Do you see any point of similarity between his films and yours?

F: I have seen very few of his films. We share the same passion, the same lack of reserve, the same sense of authentic vocation.

S: I think most viewers would agree that your films are more Italian than his.

Wanda's first meeting with the fabulous "White Sheik."

F: According to you! I never give judgments about colleagues. An artist can no more judge another artist than one child can judge other children. Each artist has his particular vision. You can't wear someone else's glasses; they would fit badly, and you wouldn't see. The artist's glasses only work when they are put on nonartists, whom they move, exalt, surprise. Of course, sometimes private and esoteric material becomes part of a more general discourse. It's clear that Joyce is appreciated by other artists because his vision of the world is marked by that neurosis, conflict, and unhappiness which all artists share.

S: When *The White Sheik* was first presented, it failed. Why?

F: It's ingenuous to ask an author to justify his failures. He can always find many reasons.

S: Let me suggest one. The film is too satiric about Italian life.

F: That's a sensible justification because it doesn't require me either to mortify myself or to offer inflated excuses. Perhaps the film was ahead of its time. It's an ironic story and Italians don't like irony—sarcasm and buffoonery, but not irony. [Aside.] Listen how he makes me talk!

S: Do you think that you made your subsequent films more tender in part because of your experience with *The White Sheik?*

F: I had no experience; experience never teaches me anything. I have always been reproached for my caricatures, deformity, grotesqueness.

S: In *The White Sheik* one first sees a marked characteristic of your work: fast cutting. For example, at the beginning—

F: [On phone.] Hello. Oh, hello, Valentina. How are you? . . . Good. Listen, come to Fregene today. Listen, Valentina, are you awake? Are you absolutely sure you're awake? . . . If you like to come. . . . Okay, at four thirty I'll pick you up at the Hotel de la Ville. . . . Good-bye, baby. Good-bye. [To journalist.] She's half-drugged, dreaming.

JOURNALIST: La Valentina?

F: Yes. One has such blurred conversations that you have to cut them short.

J: She's an actress!

F: Sure, but ours is a truly bestial cinema world, so confused that you can never meet its like anywhere.

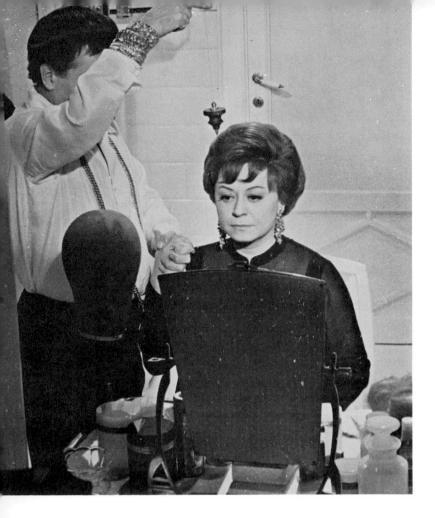

S: Back to *Juliet of the Spirits*. When Juliet puts on her makeup—

F: You can't ask an author why he put an adjective in a sentence.

S: Some authors do answer.

F: I'm one who doesn't.

S: If you don't want to, you obviously don't have to.

F: You have to realize, my dear friend, that all artists aren't alike.

S: I'm perfectly aware of that, and—

F: Poe wrote an essay telling—conceitedly—exactly how he wrote "The Raven." If you ask me how I shot a particular scene, I can answer for three days with a pack of nonsense. There is only one answer; I had to shoot it that way.

S: I don't think so. [Fellini curses.] It's interesting for other people to learn what you thought you were doing.

F: What use is all that? Of course, let's continue talking. I answer because I agree that you are right in the sense that my answers are also me. But practically speaking, everything you do to translate an irrational fact into an image diminishes . . . tends to deform . . . [Knock at the door.] Who's there? [The maid enters.] *Madonna mia.* What do you want? I don't need you. Didn't I tell you to leave me in peace today: . . . Look, everything that seeks to clear up an obscure process is totally academic. You only invent categories. I do things, and then I forget them. I seem to recall there is a hurried effect in the scene you speak of, but that is because Juliet realizes that her husband is coming home and is in a hurry to make herself up for him. So the cuts mirror her agitation.

S: But even in the *Satyricon*, when there isn't such an explanation. . . .

F: Where?

S: At the beginning, for example, we see Ascyltus crawling on the floor of the baths and the camera moves.

F: The shots in the *Satyricon* are fixed.

S: But the effect is of flying. . . .

F: That's because you saw it on a moviola.

S: I saw it in a theater.

F: The shots are fixed to suggest a lost world contemplated through a series of frescoes.

S: All right. Why then do you impose movement by having Ascyltus crawl back and forth while delivering his lines?

F: I wanted to give immediately a sense that he was an animal that could not be restrained. So he was naked, perspiring, moving on the floor—with muscles like something alive. What a question anyway; really crazy! [To journalist.] Look at all this heap of questions he has prepared!

S: At the end of *The White Sheik*, the Catholic Church becomes the ultimate spectacle. The characters run off to St. Peter's as if they were going to a movie.

F: Of course. Seen from the perspective of Ivan

Cavalli and his relatives, the church is a spectacle, like the Colosseum or the Quirinal, something to tell others about back in the provinces.

S: And the church always fails to do anything worthwhile in your films. For example, in *8 1/2*, when Guido's producer asks him to visit the cardinal for technical advice, all the man does is recite some ridiculous words of Diomedes.

F: Well?

S: Is this what you think of the church: that it always fails?

F: My feeling about the church is so clear: a reaction against my education that nevertheless bears fruit. Even going to prison can be a precious, necessary conditioning for a creative nature. Tyranny, slavery, superstition—all those things that tend to restrain the vital instinct—provoke in a creative nature an opposite response. While reacting, he may become a bit deformed because his stimulus is oppression, but he is always liberated in another direction. When an artist—I use this word too often, but what should I say. . . . A plumber? . . . Okay, when a plumber. . . . No. The animosities of a creative nature are only pretexts to stimulate his creativity. An authentic or serious artist—and when I say "artist," I mean only a certain kind of individual of a certain psychological type—when an artist exhibits antipathies, he is not to be wholly identified with them. One artist needs antipathies; another, ideology; another, love; another, memory. Depending on the season and his temperament, every artist needs one or another of these things simply as a pretext that will fire his creative furnace. You understand, I am speaking only of real artists, men of personal vision. For such men, after it has been used to create a work of art, an idea is used up. They can then use a totally opposed idea so long as it will inspire another fantasy.

S: When Ivan goes searching for Wanda, he crosses a square and is almost run down by a parade of *bersaglieri*. Why?

F: As the professor has noticed, *The White Sheik* is a satiric film. Thus while Wanda follows the White Sheik as her dream romantic hero, the husband follows his own mythology, consisting of the Pope, decorum, respectability, *bersaglieri*, the nation, the king.

S: You know perfectly well what your films

mean. Let's go further. I think of the great moment in *The White Sheik* when Ivan comes out of the *questura* and a clerk asks him to help carry some papers. When they move the papers about, great clouds of dust emerge. This is your comment on Italian bureaucracy, isn't it?

F: I only said that I can't explain my means of expression: why something merges with those distances, those vistas, that rhythm. But when you speak of those papers and clouds of dust, it is clear that the thing didn't happen by accident.

S: I think I know why you did it, but—

F: If we both know, why talk about it?

S: For my readers. They want to know how a given director sees himself.

F: It is all useless. I hope you're not insulted by what I say. [On phone.] Dovagnoli, I am being submitted to the kind of work that drives me mad. Listen, Dovagnoli, go to the Hotel de la Ville at four thirty. You'll meet Valentina there, and you can both come to Fregene. We'll photograph the artichokes, the mushrooms, the cats—everything. Okay? Good-bye. [To journalist.] Three years. Three years *Life* says it wants to do a "Fellini story"! I must have spoken already to thirty journalists and four or five serious writers. [Turning.] That one who wrote about the *Satyricon* was serious.

S: Eileen Hughes.

F: What was her book like? I never read it.

S: Not very good.

F: Why?

S: Like most writers about you, she treats you as if you were a legend rather than a real person. I don't think that's right, and that's why I'm fighting. After all, you can also make a work of art of yourself.

F: And now you are helping me to make another one.

S: Presumptuously, I am searching for the truth.

F: The truth. You know what that is? The films are the truth. You confuse the truth because you make me say silly things just to please you. Something comes into my head; I say nonsense.

S: I haven't made myself clear. I will try to—

F: Don't. I am full of respect and admiration for your work, done in spite of me.

S: Let me ask a question that will take us past *The White Sheik*. Your first three films are neorealist—

F: *You* say that.

S: All right, I say it. By the time you get to the *Satyricon*, however, you're saying things like this: "I read all these books about Rome so as to forget what Rome was like."

F: I can't be accused of what I say in interviews.

S: Haven't you become less realistic as your career progressed?

F: What does "realistic" mean?

S: I want you to tell me.

F: The professor astonishes me! You need me to explain it! For me, the only real realist is the visionary because he bears witness to his own reality. A visionary—Van Gogh, for instance—is a profound realist. That wheat field with the black sun is his; only he saw it. There can't be greater realism.

S: There is a difference between that detail in *The White Sheik*—

F: I don't see big differences among my films. Words like "neorealist" are just comfortable tags. Too much has been made of it. De Santis wasn't a neorealist; he was a follower of D'Annunzio, who took calendar art shots of the sea. If we define neorealism properly—and definitions mean nothing to me—Rossellini is the only true neorealist. De Sica is not a realist. He merely adapts sentimental romantic rhythms to stories that Zavattini tells out of ideological necessity. If by "neorealism" you mean the opposite of manufactured effects, of the laws of dramaturgy, spectacle, and even of cinematography, then Rossellini has made the only neorealist films. Neorealism was mistaken for social realism. When people saw a badly made shack, they mistook it for neorealism. When

they saw two tramps, they said, "Neorealism!"

S: Still, there is a distinction. When Ivan goes to the *questura*, the official, who thinks Ivan is mad, offers him a cigarette to pacify him, and Ivan politely reaches for one that has been cut, but the official says, "No, take one of the whole ones." That detail refers to a specific set of social circumstances, and there are fewer and fewer such details in your films. Or am I wrong?

F: That story was recounted like an anecdote, so it had to be told in a certain way, with its own vision and laws. An artist evolves; he goes through changes like any other man. When I was ten, I loved lollipops, but now I love other things. The seasons of a creative nature are conditioned by the seasons of the man himself. Impoverishment, enrichment, falling in love with certain styles and ideas—these changes occur, but I don't find them important. To myself, I seem always to be making *The White Sheik*.

S: Alberto Sordi's tango is wonderful: that splendid gesture of raising his fingers. . . .

F: [Aside.] My God, he noticed everything!

S: Was the scene improvised?

F: Alberto Sordi, a great comic talent, used to try to outdo himself all the time and was very inventive, though by now he has become a bit fossilized. He has established such rapport with his audience that he no longer tries for variety. In that scene I gave him general directions, but the gestures were his.

S: The film seems to me your greatest, but there are a few small imperfections. When Sordi takes the girl into the boat in order to seduce her, some of the background shots are sets, aren't they?

F: Yes. That was the first scene I directed myself, because earlier Lattuada had given me technical advice. I had done little landscape shots, but nothing more. This was my actual debut as a director—I mean with forty people looking on, that terrible Roman troupe, looking at their watches, and with faces that would happily end your career. When we started shooting, we and the camera were on the high seas in an enormous boat, and the little boat with Sordi and Bova was in front of us. It was a very complicated scene because the ocean obviously makes unpredictable movements. You look through the viewfinder, but by the time you are ready to shoot everything has changed. It was terribly difficult for a beginner. In fact, I shot nothing that first

day. I couldn't tell the sea to stop; it was a disaster. My legendary reputation for audacity began at this moment, because this is what I did: The next day I had a big hole dug on the beach and placed the camera in it. I placed the boat with Bova and Sordi on the beach and shot up at them. For a while it worked well, but after two hours the tide receded and you saw the waves hitting the sand, so later I had to include some shots to cover this up. However, I could give you an esthetic justification: Cinema is an art of illusion, and sometime the illusion must show its tail. A great magician pretends to make a mistake sometimes. In that scene, I pretended. And that's where the professor finds an imperfection! I made that imperfection because I was sure that someday someone would arrive who had found it out. [I begin to put a new tape on the recorder.] Tell me, how did Antonioni behave with you? Did you ask him such questions?

S: Yes, and though he hates to talk, he tried his best to answer them. Moreover, though he was in the midst of editing *Zabriskie Point*, about which he was deeply worried, he gave me four hours of his time.

F: But one must ask Antonioni many questions. On the other hand, my films are entirely clear. Anyway, I'll give you four hours, too.

S: In the scene toward the end of the film, when Ivan finds Wanda in the hospital, we track down the corridor and see a catatonic wheeled by in a crib.

F: It's a hospital!

S: Behind the police there's a nun with a mustache. Why?

F: Certain forced vocations make the organism grow irregularities. Obligatory chastity, like that of a nun, can well bring such hair to the face. Satisfied?

S: All these touches provoke a charge against you. People point to them and say that you are reveling in the grotesque merely to amuse us.

F: I think it is significant if I amuse you. And the nun belongs there. After all, Ivan and Wanda want to see reality in an idealized way, so it is clear that the author, at such a moment, puts a nun with a mustache, instead of one with a Fra Angelico face, in order to provide some contrast.

S: But to the general point: People said that *Juliet of the Spirits* was almost a freak show—

F: Who said that?

S: People.

F: People! I say it isn't true. Furthermore, I'd ask to see the faces of these people. I would put a mirror before them and ask them to say, "Fellini puts monsters in his films." Perhaps they don't see or recognize themselves.

S: What do you mean to suggest as the future of the Cavallis?

F: [Aside.] Here's one I didn't expect. To begin with, I must tell you that Trieste and Bova [the actors] were not married. It was all make-believe. You know I think they are still unmarried. To anyone anxious to know what will happen to that marriage you can safely say, "They're not married."

S: All right, I'll switch to *Vitelloni.* Why does the Sordi character dress like a woman at the carnival?

F: Because at a carnival one wears a mask.

S: But the whole film seems unified by examples of deficient virility.

F: There is also a legend that I am impotent. "Starting with neorealism, by the time of the *Satyricon* Fellini has reached the buttock stage."

S: I'm not identifying the characters with you. I'm merely saying that all the men in the film are missing—

F: Their mothers. They all come from the provinces.

S: Then the theme is deficient masculinity?

F: It's a story of men who haven't grown up, and the infantile state is ambiguous. There can be no heroic posturings, no virile poses.

S: Why didn't you go on to make "Moraldo in città"?

F: Because I had written *La strada* before *Vitelloni* and wanted to make it but couldn't. The producers didn't like the story and didn't want Giulietta. I was party to a contract for three films, so when the producer didn't like *La strada,* I quickly made *Vitelloni.* But after I was finished, it became clear that *Vitelloni* had revived a whole series of recollections, which I took up in "Moraldo in città." Meanwhile, De Laurentiis decided to produce *La* strada, so I thought to make "Moraldo" afterward. But every film leaves certain shadows, unresolved fantasies. It isn't easy to free yourself, and when I'm finished with a film, I want to make others of the same type. That's another reason I don't like to see my old films; they are like diseases, the germs of my fantasy. One wants to make the film quickly in order to free oneself. The sign that I have to make a film is given by my hatred for it. It's like having a guest who sleeps in my bed, eats my food, puts on my clothes, and follows me when I make love. It's always there, and if I didn't throw it off my shoulders, I couldn't do what I wanted to. I truly hate the film and make it in a mood of hatred. What was the question? Oh, yes. After *La strada* an atmosphere of travel followed me, so I made *Il bidone.* "Moraldo" became grayer, paler; but it fermented, and I used it as the basis for *La dolce vita.*

S: How did you get involved with Zavattini's project of a narrative newsreel, *Love in the City?*

F: Because of this circus world of cinema—and because of timidity. Someone like me, without strong ideology, always feels a sense of guilt when confronting all the Communists. Then I become uncontrolled, tell them to go to hell, and call for the emperor and Pope. It's a very childish reaction. But so is my fear at being excluded from social feelings. After the war and the mythology of the resistance, I felt left out of all that soldierly heroism, so probably to prove that I could also be a good little soldier, I made this episode in a film which intended to inquire into Roman life after the war. But the demonic, Romagnolo side of me caused me to tell Zavattini that everything in the episode really happened: that there really was a matrimonial agency in my building and that a girl came to it and was willing to marry a werewolf. Zavattini kept saying, "How true," "How one can feel the truth." But I made it all up. Finally, I admitted that, but he wouldn't believe me.

S: You told Pierre Kast that all your films concern characters who want to free themselves from moralist inhibitions. But the girl in "A Matrimonial Agency" isn't trying to free herself from inhibitions; she's trying to realize her dream of a better life. Her life is so awful that she'd even marry a werewolf to improve it. It seems to me that all your films are about people fantasizing a more marvelous life than the one they live, until you yourself in *Satyricon* have such a dream.

F: If you say so.

S: This seems crazy to you?

F: No.

III

As Fellini ushers me out, I receive his promise for one more meeting. He asks me to call at Cinecittà, where he is shooting; after several attempts, I get the appointment. He agrees to meet me at the Villa Hassler, whose grand-manner lobby he enters ten minutes late, confused about where we can sit down. Since I had depended on his making the arrangements, I can offer no help. We wander through the hotel's public rooms: Fellini, the giant, and I trotting behind with my tape recorder (we must look like a big shot pursued by a shoeshine boy). Fellini eventually threatens to perch in what seems a ballroom, where a pianist tries hard to inspire the advertised thé dansant. "Look," I tell my quarry, "I had crockery for part one, a journalist for part two; I'm not having genteel piano accompaniment for part three." Agreeing that I, at least, deserve a quiet background on the tape, he suggests we go back to his office.

Although I can't get the tape recorder out, I seize a few additional minutes by interviewing him in the taxi. We talk about La strada, whose heroine, Gelsomina, Fellini says he wholly imagined. "I liked that childlike quality, that hopefulness," he confesses. When I compare her with Cabiria, he rightly notes that Cabiria is Gelsomina grown-up and living in town.

We then discuss his casting of Richard Basehart as the Fool. I wonder why he used a foreign actor who had to be dubbed into Italian and ask if he would have done this had he not been an Italian director (in Italy, all films are dubbed). Characteristically, he fires back, "If I weren't Italian, I wouldn't be Fellini." But he doesn't seem determined to make the quip climactic this time. Instead, he volunteers a story about Stanley Kramer. While shooting The Secret of Santa Vittoria, that director had been infuriated when he heard a slight unplanned noise in the streets. According to Fellini, Kramer then dispatched "a troupe of SS men," but their efforts uncovered only a woman frying an egg. Fastidiousness that stops a whole company because of a slight sizzle, Fellini finds absurd. "Film is only images," he says, "You can put in whatever sound you want later and change and improve it."

In his office we are, as before, interrupted by phone calls (though none as suggestive as those I transcribed), and I am beginning to feel not only exasperated but as tired as Fellini, who continually yawns. After a while, however, he shuts off the phone—to my relief—and becomes, I believe, more yielding.

S: *Il Bidone* was intended for Humphrey Bogart. Were you satisfied with Broderick Crawford?

F: I thought of Bogart because the confidence man who told me the story looked like him: the same dry wolfish face, a face desperate with the knowledge he would end badly. I always have models in my mind. So at the beginning, I say I will use Mae West and the Marx Brothers for the *Satyricon* as part of my quest for the ideal faces that will realize my characters. But by the time I started shooting *Il bidone* Bogart was sick, so I used Crawford.

S: Why do you always use the same music in your films?

F: Because all have the same author, story, atmosphere. Moreover, Nino [Rota] writes the music in my company. It is a harmonious collaboration that I haven't felt like changing. His music is a kind of frame that is very true for my story and images.

S: In *Il bidone* you give the first of many pictures of corrupt middle-class life. But I'm struck, for example, at the party that Basehart and Massina attend, that you can't think of anything more squalid than those men who ask the girl to strip so that they can see if she's wearing falsies.

F: You want something more corrupt; that's your problem. I don't want to shock. I only want to be true to the story I'm telling.

S: What about the orgy that ends *La dolce vita?*

F: *La dolce vita* was considered scandalous— all over the world! The police wanted to take my passport away; they wanted to kill me, to put me in prison!

S: What is corrupt one year seems tame the next.

F: Of course. But anyway, I didn't want to show corruption. There are never polemical intentions in my films.

S: Not even in *La dolce vita?*

F: The title of that film came to have a meaning exactly the opposite of what I'd intended. I told

that story about Rome because I know Rome, but it could have taken place in Bangkok, Paris, Babylon, anywhere. The city is an internal city. I wanted the title to signify not "Easy Life" but "The Sweetness of Life."

S: That's not the way it comes out. Marcello looks like someone wallowing in trouble. Think of that scene in which he sees an angelic girl, played very much like the one in *8 1/2* by Claudia Cardinale.

F: That is a result of the myth produced by a Catholic upbringing: a wish for some purity, something morally complete and angelic—stamped at the bottom of our minds and leaving us with a nostalgia for something rarefied.

S: If he could attain that, wouldn't he be better off?

F: No, he likes *la dolce vita*. His infantile fancy has its form of integrity, but *la dolce vita* is very fascinating.

S: At the end, he makes a gesture of resignation.

F: No, he says, "I don't hear. I don't understand." It could also be considered a bantering gesture: "I don't hear you because I don't want to hear you."

S: What about the scene with his father? Doesn't that show that something good and stable can't exist in the sweet life? The father has a heart attack in Rome.

F: Because he tried to fuck.

S: Why did you revive the character of Cabiria after *The White Sheik*?

Cabiria, the good-hearted whore, making her first appearance in The White Sheik.

F: Because I liked her nocturnal vagabond spirit that is so typical of Rome.

S: But she is different in the two films, don't you think?

F: A little. In *The White Sheik* she was a minor character: a night spirit in love with flame. In *Nights of Cabiria* she became something larger: a woman in love with love.

S: I am disturbed about the film's ending. François Perrier seems so sincere, so true, until the last scene when he dons dark glasses. Why didn't you give earlier signs of his villainy?

F: There are signs: that toothpick he keeps in his mouth, and his face and neck—those of a Robespierre. You are an American, innocent like all Americans. A European sees immediately that he is no good: the way he talks, the saccharine insistence, the exaggerated timidity behind which he hides, that mustache, those moles on his skin that give him the look of a rat.

S: Why do you show the family that buys Cabiria's house just before she goes to get married?

F: They are other wretches who will fill the house with their own misery and desperation.

S: Her reaction to them is important.

F: She feels that they are invaders, mice and weasels to whom the house has been sold. She is like children who say yes and then change their minds.

S: One of the great touches in the film is the mascara that runs down her face in the final close-up. Was that planned?

F: Everything is planned. Making a film is like putting an astronaut in space.

S: Don't you ever improvise?

F: No. "Improvisation" is an offensive term to an artist. I don't improvise; I try to keep myself open to all suggestions, to all changes that occur

while the film is growing day by day. When I start a film, I know where I want to end up because I have already gone through all those evocations and that magic which cause a fantasy to take shape. But after the first two or three weeks a film assumes its own will, face, and voice; it becomes a different person whom I do not know until I begin to make it. Therefore, if I tried to be strictly faithful to all my original plans, I would confine the film. I prepare everything, more than is necessary, but then I want the film to grow and tell me itself what I must do. This is not improvising; this is humble service to a creature of one's own who is growing and has its own needs. When you start the film, you don't yet know what the faces will look like or how much the props will weigh. I can write a three-page scene which is very beautiful and then suddenly discover that a certain light accomplishes all that those three pages did. I don't improvise; my films grow as part of a vital process. There are other methods: I think that Hitchcock couldn't do as I do since his films are manufactured with the precision of a Swiss watch. Mine are different.

S: When you edit a film, do you do much revising?

F: No, because I film with a pretty clear idea of what I need. It's rare for a shot of mine to be cut from the final print.

S: In *La dolce vita* when Sylvia and Marcello are in the Trevi fountain, the water is shut off. Why?

F: It is a trick of dramaturgy.

S: Are you upset by those who argue that this action symbolizes an aborted moment of sexual contact?

F: Everything in life is symbolic. At this moment, I also wanted that silence, that moment of suspension between them.

S: Do you think that Steiner is a convincing intellectual?

F: In Rome there are many such theatrical intellectuals. And not only Italians are this way. Look at Norman Mailer.

S: He'd like to be thought an intellectual, but he isn't one.

F: So much the better for him.

S: Why do you end the film with the sea beast?

F: It's a childhood memory of a sea monster that a storm had thrown up on the beach at Rimini. The beach was very crowded, full of

journalists. I recall that Beltrame, who used to paint covers for *La Domenica del Corriere*, used this monster one Sunday. It remained vivid in my memory, and I always wanted to make use of it. I wanted to place it in the scene when the *vitelloni* take a walk by the sea, but it seemed too powerful an image for that. I even thought of ending *I Vitelloni* with the monster, but that would have been excessive. But in *La dolce vita* it seemed to fit.

S: Why?

F: As an expression of absurdity, irrationality.

S: Because of its subject, as well as its many brilliant inventions, *8 1/2* is probably your most important film, but the film has been attacked as a grab bag, an empty sack into which you could put—arbitrarily—whatever entered your mind.

F: Who said that? *8 1/2* got fabulous reviews all over the world! And anything can be called an empty sack, even *The Divine Comedy*—to give an example.

S: You said that the film was your attempt to make friends with yourself, fearlessly and without hope.

F: I say so many things. But even though I said that, it is true.

S: But doesn't the film ask that Guido be forgiven for all his wrongs?

F: What wrongs? Who is guilty? No one is guilty. We become guilty only when we try to live up to schemes that don't conform to reality. I, who am fifty, would be guilty if I tried to live like an eighteen-year-old.

S: If one is honest, he isn't guilty?

F: One is guilty only for having regrets. Perhaps Guido is guilty in that sense.

S: Don't you think he is also guilty for making the juvenile request of his wife that she accept anything he does? Isn't that what any man wants, when he is not thinking of responsibility, to have every other woman in the world without angering his wife?

F: *8 1/2* is also a comic film. Next to the camera I placed a card on which I had written, "Remember, this is a comic film."

S: The fantasies in the film are either memories (like the scene in which he is put to bed) or wish fulfillment (as in the Turkish bath), but in the latter he fantasizes something that I find difficult to accept as his wish: the revolt of his harem.

F: That comes from his sense of the practical. I show what would happen if his dream were fulfilled. Since he is not an Oriental caliph but rather an Italian Catholic, his dream isn't spontaneous but only a response to frustrations built up in him by his Jesuit upbringing. Therefore, his dream carries its own punishment. For that reason, the sequence quickly changes from joy to sorrow.

S: Are you using the critic in the film to raise all the objections that the audience might raise?

F: Not the audience; other critics.

S: So you're trying to prevent the critics from having power over our response?

F: No. That critic represents an intellectual who is rarefied, unvital, stifling. Also, for a creative nature like Guido's, criticism is profoundly foreign. He cannot accept that mentality and so has to kill it. Otherwise, he would not be able to give full vent to his fantasies, his world of games and marvels.

S: But there is a critic inside you, too, isn't there?

F: Yes, and once in a while I stab him. I am a builder, and building involves both intuitive and rational operations; but I have to reach an equilibrium. I know all the categories, and I must choose; but choosing means judgment, which delimits things. I need that critical sense that selects, eliminates, and chooses by taking account of my experience.

S: Doesn't a critic do the same thing—even though he doesn't create films or plays but merely writes about them?

F: I don't know. The critic merely by saying, "I am a critic," inflates himself and causes himself to see not what exists but what he thinks ought to exist. But things are only what they are. Therefore, the critic is usually mistaken. A truly humble critic would look at things from the inside, not from the outside. If the thing is vital and you look at it from your external point of view, you

will never understand but will only project onto it what you think it should be.

S: Not necessarily. And even when the critic is trying to posit corrections, he doesn't refer to himself as such but rather to his experience of what other artists have done in a similar situation.

F: Just as bad. When a critic tells how the work should be according to his taste, which has been formed by a certain culture and certain artists, he is still judging by what is congenial to him. That is totally alien to me.

S: Not totally. You are very concerned about critics. You are hostile to them, but they crop up in your films, even in *The Clowns*. There is a scene in which you and a critic sit discussing the film, only to be covered by overturned pails.

F: He's not a critic; he's just a newspaperman.

S: But he is raising a critical question: "What does this mean?"

F: It's a stupid question.

S: *You* consider it stupid. Why don't you leave it alone then? Why do you keep creating characters who put this question to your alter ego so that you can debunk it? If it's so clearly stupid to you, why don't you just ignore it?

F: Because my pictures are also about stupidity.

S: Who is the girl in white in *8 1/2*?

F: She is the most disturbing sign of Guido's impotence, and he projects through this figure all his own confusions, his desire for an ideal woman who would tell him, both as man and artist, what to do; she is his nostalgia, his childish desire for protection, his romanticism. These all are embodied in a figure who mocks him because she is only an abstraction.

S: In another episode showing Guido's relations with women, are we to find La Saraghina sexy or funny or both?

F: She is sex seen by a child. Hence she is grotesque, but also seductive to one so innocent.

S: Later, when the priests berate him for watching La Saraghina, he is brought before his mother in the seminary. Why does she wipe one eye and keep the other open?

F: She is trying to see whether or not Guido is contrite.

S: She is hypocritical?

F: No. She is controlling. She wants to see that her exaggerated desperation has an effect on the child. But since the boy is intelligent, he remembers his mother as being a bit hypocritical here.

S: Later he goes to confession. When he departs, you hold on some decoration in the confessional booth. Why?

F: It is a horror, a big ghost, a black bird.

S: Let's pass on to *Juliet of the Spirits*. It seems to me similar to Bergman's *Hour of the Wolf*—

F: I made my film first.

S: I know, but I'd like to compare them. Have you seen Bergman's film?

F: Yes. He showed it to me when he came to Rome. Its fantasy is completely different from mine, more Nordic. I would call *Hour of the Wolf* Bergman's *8 1/2*. Indeed, he confesses candidly that he has seen all my films and cites them in his own. Being a rich, an authentic artist, he can borrow from others without being guilty of plagiarism. I value Bergman. He is a real man of spectacle and images, one of the best.

S: Why was there so long an hiatus between *Juliet* and your next film?

F: I had written the scenario for a film that would have been my most beautiful ("The Voyage of Mastorna"), but through a mysterious series of circumstances, I never was able to make it. I got sick, for a long time. You know, it's good sometimes to fall sick because illness ruptures the daily routine and forces you to think about things in a new way. One imagines he will always be vital and active. Suddenly, there comes a pause. As a result, new fantasies emerge.

S: Why did the new fantasy become "Toby Dammit"?

F: Why, why, why! I was still under contract with De Laurentiis to make "Mastorna" and so was in total confusion. Then along come these French producers who beg me to participate in a

multi-episode film, although I have never agreed to work with anyone else. But they assured me that of the three stories, I would make one, Bergman another, and Welles the last. So I said yes. Then it turned out that they had lied about Bergman, and Welles, who didn't trust them, refused to sign. I continued anyway, simply because this was a way of freeing myself from De Laurentiis. When they told me my partners were to be Malle and Vadim, I could have legally refused. With me, Welles, and Bergman—three visionary artists whose images have richness of meaning—there would have been some common quality in this homage to Poe. That's why I signed; not for monetary considerations. But you see, I was emerging from a period of crisis; I was overwhelmed with troubles, had not worked for two years. I could have broken the contract, but that didn't seem right. So I proceeded. And now I am glad I did because, although I'm not able to judge my own work, because I never see it when it is finished, I think this film is perhaps my most representative.

Terence Stamp as Toby Dammit.

S: I agree, and that's why I'd like to ask several questions about it. First, where did you get the idea of characterizing the devil as a young girl?

F: In Poe's story, which, as you know, was only my jumping-off point, the devil is a man with a black cape and a beard. I didn't like that; it seemed too eighteenth century to me. Moreover, I thought this was the wrong kind of devil for a drugged, hippie actor. His devil must be his own immaturity—hence, a child.

S: She is infantile but also terribly knowing. Did you feel that you put into the film some of your own ideas about success?

F: No.

S: Not even in the interview sequence?

F: In the interview I reflected my sense of the uselessness of this procedure. Excuse me, have you found that I'm the only director with such a negative attitude about it?

S: Many have your feeling, but none so strongly. When Toby enters the airport, we see many fantastic things going on. There is an ugly man pawing a cowboy, a girl standing at a bar next to a sort of Fu Manchu, etc. Why do you fill the background with such grotesque figures?

F: The airport in Rome is like that. Furthermore, this is all seen from a drugged perspective.

S: Why don't you tell us why Toby sold his soul?

F: You're asking too much from a short episode.

S: During the drive through Rome, there are sometimes sets and sometimes real objects. For example, the bus going under the aqueduct is a painted flat.

F: I do this sort of thing very often.

S: Why?

F: Because I like to joke. It makes the image disquieting. And the whole tale is meant to have that effect: a drive toward death. Even that cowboy you mentioned has a mask on his face. These are all small tricks.

S: One of the tricks I'd like to ask you about concerns the head of Terence Stamp at the end of the film. It seems so phony. . . .

F: The film is make-believe.

S: I feel the need of something stronger there.

F: Why, isn't that head frightening?

S: No. Nor is it frightening in the *Satyricon* when Alain Cuny's head is cut off and falls into the sea. That image is marvelous, but it seems to me to be adulterated when the body hits the deck and the top of the torso is obviously wax.

F: That's because you saw it a hundred times on a moviola.

S: No, I saw it once in a theater.

F: Actually, we really cut the head off but since we had two takes and Cuny had only one head. . . .

S: You told Eileen Hughes that "Toby Dammit" was a deliberate attempt to parody your style so that you could never return to it.

F: That's not true. I said that since the film was made after a long period of crisis and inactivity, it reflects a certain anger. . . . There are many things I say just to say them. Yes, I did tell that to Eileen; I don't know why.

S: In an article you wrote for *Show* in 1964, you said you would never adapt a literary work. What made you change your mind?

F: *Satyricon* is a work in fragments. I didn't illustrate a book; the book was simply a pretext.

S: Why did you cast Tanya Lopert as the emperor?

F: Because she was the producer's daughter.

But she also gave a feeling a neurotic asexuality, so that one can't tell what sex she is—and that was fitting.

S: Why do you so emphasize sickness and deformity in this film?

F: I don't think I do. I wanted to present an unknown world about which we know only impressions, mostly gleaned from an idealized neoclassicism. I wanted to forget all that and make a science-fiction film, as I've often said. It is the discovery of an unknown planet in which the forms are disquieting. Moreover, as you know, there was no penicillin at that time, no antibiotics, so terrifying illnesses must have been common. A long life then lasted twenty-seven years. Most people must have been sick.

S: Why don't you show the homosexuality more directly?

F: I do.

S: All we see is one man kissing another's wrist.

F: What, did you want to see the prick going in? I wasn't making a film about homosexuality as seen by a prurient Catholic. I wanted everything to appear as if on a fresco.

S: In the picture gallery scene—

F: What did you want, men kissing on the mouth?

S: In the scene at the picture gallery, a platform loaded with people passes before the window. Why?

F: I will never tell you.

S: Is it a secret?

F: It was pretty. . . . I liked to see those people go by. . . . I did it so that Samuels could ask me why.

S: Why do the guests jump up and down in Trimalchio's bath?

F: Because I liked that human wave.

S: There is no other reason?

F: Look, in the *Satyricon* the actors are always doing bizarre things because they have to evoke a world that we don't know. They look like Italians whose gestures seem incomprehensible to an American tourist.

S: Why did you include the episode of the widow of Ephesus?

F: I thought of cutting it out, but since it is one of the more significant of Petronius' fragments, I was sure that eliminating it would have sent the whole cultural world of universities, Latinists, and professors of Roman history into an uproar. So I let it stand.

S: But there has been an uproar anyway, a claim that you've violated the spirit of Petronius.

F: Who knows what that really is? So little of Petronius survives. How can we tell his point of view? To understand that, we should need to have the whole of the novel, to learn how the characters end up. I was faithful to the fragmentary state of Petronius, that ruined temple which is more fascinating because we project onto its broken pillars all the past that has vanished. I am not an illustrator of other men's work. I was faithful to the darkness that surrounded the *Satyricon*, to all that which is incomplete, interrupted, mutilated, and therefore more seductive.

S: Let's move on to your latest film. Why did you include Anita Ekberg in *The Clowns*?

F: I met her one day, and I like Anita. Besides, she has a circus personality

S: Why the scene with Victoria Chaplin?

F: I met her in Paris where I needed to shoot a small scene of two clowns auditioning for Buglione (which I had witnessed in real life). I asked her and her boyfriend to play the scene because they live in the circus world. Also, it was a way of paying homage to her father.

S: At the beginning of the film why do you show men in jail also watching the circus tent as it goes up?

F: For no particular reason. It's just that in Rimini, where I was born and this scene is taking place, there was a jail near the piazza that the circus used.

S: It seems very effective to me, though, because men in prison would find the circus particularly grand. Tell me, how did you come to select "Ebbtide" as the final song?

F: Because I like it and it is a typical circus number.

S: In America it is regarded as very corny. When I saw the film, the audience laughed at it.

F: That is very dangerous because it is the end. Well, it's too late to change.

S: We've finally arrived at *Roma*. What can you tell me about it?

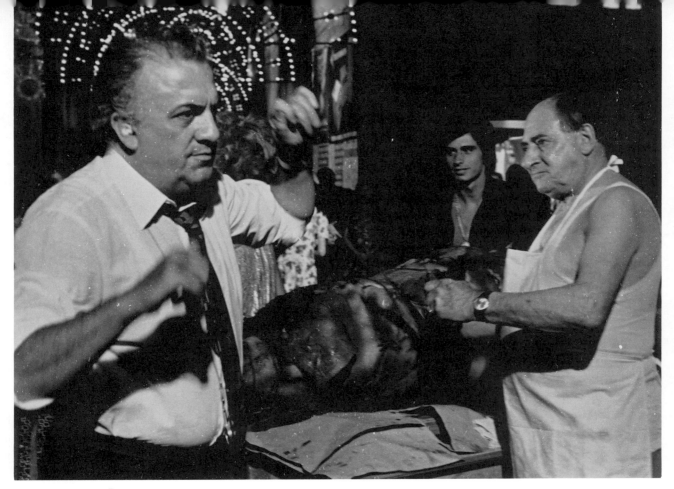

Fellini directing Roma.

F: Nothing much. It is a film I am making in stages because the production is so difficult to organize that I've insisted we stop from time to time. It's a film unlike any other—but, as always, it seems to be turning out like all my previous films. It's a conversation about the city. I can't say more now.

S: What about the sequence concerning the foreign literary colony—Gore Vidal, Muriel Spark, etc.—are you making that?

F: I don't know. Many ideas that I've had turn out to be suicidal and collapse.

S: In the few times I've seen you, you give me the impression of being a kind of King of Rome. The whole city seems like your own living room. And you are so well recognized. How does that make you feel?

F: Sometimes very comfortable, sometimes embarrassed, sometimes threatened.

S: I want to suggest one threat. It's said that you are surrounded by friends and admirers. Isn't that dangerous for an artist?

F: Surrounded by friends? I am always alone. I have only about two good friends, and them I see

rarely. I am surrounded by people who want to work in my films, by journalists.

S: Are there no friends who appreciate you so that you have confidence in their criticism?

F: Maybe not enough of them. I don't know. But anyway, I don't like to talk about my work. It is impolite.

S: Impolite?

F: My work is so representative of my personality that talking about one is like talking about the other. It isn't polite to talk about yourself all the time.

S: People are interested in your work, and, as you've said, your work is you. The one interest leads to the other. We can't make a separation.

F: But I must.

S: And you are not only a good, but a unique director; there is even an adjective: Felliniesque. You've made yourself public property.

F: I don't want to repeat myself. I don't want to become presumptuous or ridiculous. I don't want to become an external being whom I must look at in a detached way. I want to be free. It is dangerous to identify with the public image one has made. Success is a construction that it is so easy to become accustomed to. But one has to forget, to think one has done nothing. I am speaking not of humility, but of freedom. If I am obliged to talk and talk about Steiner, Gelsomina, and the others, I am forced to remain tied to what I have done, whereas I want to forget it all.

S: I don't want to tie you, so let me ask a new question. What do you regard as the distinction between a simple entertainment and a work of art?

F: I don't want to talk about entertainment vs. art. I want to distinguish between a film with an author and one that is made for consumption. A film made by an author reflects a human creature and his ideas. The other, which may contain pleasant images, shows you nothing, and you like it precisely because it is unreal. Why does a commercial film succeed? Because it doesn't disturb the spectator. He leaves the theater in the same darkness with which he entered it. People who go to these films don't want to be disturbed; they don't want responsibility; they want to stay asleep.

S: As you say, your films represent an individual consciousness; that's what makes them art. It also makes people interested in your consciousness and causes you to be interviewed etc. It's your excellence that has trapped you.

F: I accept this conclusion since you want to leave the impression that our interview is useful. And it is. I only want you to understand why I have been so reluctant; not because I am uncouth or ungrateful to someone who has studied my work with such care and enthusiasm. My reaction springs more from timidity. This long and searching talk about past work ties me to exactly what I want to forget.

S: In 8 1/2 Guido is constantly asking to be freed.

F: I am Guido.

Vittorio De Sica

Rome, May 9, 1971

Feature Films: 1940 *Rose scarlatte* (*Red Roses*), *Maddalena, zero in condotta* (*Maddalena, Zero in Conduct*); 1941 *Teresa Venerdi* (*Mademoiselle Friday*), *Un garibaldino al convento* (*A Policewoman in the Convent*); 1942 *I bambini ci guardano* (*The Children Are Watching Us*); 1946 *La porta del cielo* (*The Gate of Paradise*), *Sciuscia* (*Shoeshine*); 1948 *Ladri di biciclette* (*The Bicycle Thief*); 1950 *Miracolo a Milano* (*Miracle in Milan*); 1951 *Umberto D.*; 1952 *Stazione Termini* (*Indiscretion of an American Wife*); 1954 *L'oro di Napoli* (*The Gold of Naples*); 1956 *Il tetto* (*The Roof*); 1961 *La Ciociara* (*Two Women*), *Il Giudizio Universale* (*The Last Judgment*); 1962 *The Condemned of Altona*; 1963 *Il Boom* (*The Boom*); *Ieri, oggi, domani* (*Yesterday, Today, Tomorrow*); 1964 *Matrimonio all'italiana* (*Marriage, Italian Style*); 1965 *Un Monde nouveau* (*A Young World*), *After the Fox*; 1967 *Woman Times Seven*; 1968 *A Place for Lovers*; 1970 *I girasoli* (*Sunflower*); 1971 *Il giardino dei Finzi-Contini* (*The Garden of the Finzi-Continis*).

Vittorio De Sica is a familiar presence from his many screen roles. Meeting him, I was surprised only that his matinee-idol looks have survived into his seventies and that his speech and manner are so mild, for as an actor he is characterized by *brio*. Perhaps the mildness was the result of fatigue. Although he had just returned from a month-long business trip, he graciously agreed to see me that evening. The interview was conducted in Italian, my proficiency in which provided another test of his grace.

De Sica lives in a well-furnished but by no means opulent apartment near the Colosseum. The measured luxury of his surroundings lent a peculiar poignance to what quickly became the leitmotiv of our conversation.

Vittorio De Sica as he appears in "The Gambler" segment of Gold of Naples (1957).

SAMUELS: Signor De Sica, how did you meet Zavattini and what made you decide to collaborate with him?

DE SICA: I met him when I had decided to film a novel by Cesare Giulio Viola, called *Prico*. A short time before that, I had met Zavattini in Milan and had thought, "Here is a writer I would like to work with." I admired his style, which had just then been revealed in his novel *They're Talking So Much About Me*. The film we made together, *The Children Are Watching Us*, had a great success because of the poetry and melancholy of a marriage failing before the witness of a child, who learns that adults make mistakes, who is forced to suffer his mother's adultery and his father's suicide. But when it came out, we were in the middle of our Fascist period—that absurd little Italian republic of ours—and I was askkd to go to Venice to lead the Fascist film school. I refused, so my unfortunate little film came out without the name of its author.

S: Your collaboration with Zavattini seems to me the most fruitful partnership between director and writer in film history. Has it been completely untroubled?

DS: Sometimes producers, after discussing a project with Zavattini and me, have turned to other writers, thus disturbing our rapport. But in these so-called betrayals, I was never at fault. Unfortunately, our producers often make films with American backing, so sometimes they say they want an Anglo-Saxon flavor and hire an English-speaking writer. But I stoutly maintain that a good film must reflect the country of its origin. A French film must be truly French; a Yugoslav film, truly Slavic; etc. When one starts making these Italo-English, Italo-American films, he is bound to fail.

S: Would you go so far as to disown those films you made outside of Italy, such as *A Young World*?

DS: Not *A Young World*, because that film deals with an international problem which is still being talked about. When we decided to make it, a million women a year were dying in France because of abortions. The film was a defense of the birth control pill, and it argued that abortion should be a recognized fact, dealt with efficiently and not hidden. At this very moment, there is a scandal in France because of all those prominent women who declared they had had abortions in order to oppose the law against it. Look at all the trouble their sincerity has brought them!

S: Signor De Sica, you are one of the most famous of neorealists. What does neorealism mean to you?

DS: I recently discussed this question with a British journalist. You know, people think that neorealism means exterior shooting, but they are wrong. Most films today are made in a realistic style, but they are actually opposed to neorealism, to that revolution in cinematic language which we started and which they think to follow. Because neorealism is not shooting films in authentic locales; it is not reality. It is reality filtered through poetry, reality transfigured. It is not Zola, not naturalism, verism, things which are ugly.

S: By poetry, don't you mean scenes like the one in *The Bicycle Thief*, where the father takes his son to the *trattoria* in order to cheer the boy up only to be overcome with the weight of his problems?

DS: Ah, that is one of the few light scenes in the film.

S: But sad at the same time.

DS: Yes, that is what I mean by poetry.

S: Was that scene improvised?

DS: It was written in advance, but of course, during the moment of filming, gestures are produced by the actors that reflect their dreams and taste. I knew there must be some shift in the scene to show the change in the father's heart, and I directed toward that end.

S: You say that neorealism is realism filtered through poetry; nonetheless, it is harsh because you forced your compatriots right after the war to confront experiences they had just suffered through. Didn't they resist?

DS: Neorealism was born after a total loss of liberty, not only personal, but artistic and political. It was a means of rebelling against the stifling dictatorship that had humiliated Italy. When we lost the war, we discovered our ruined morality. The first film that placed a very tiny stone in the reconstruction of our former dignity was *Shoeshine*.

S: Usually, audiences resist such reconstruction.

DS: In fact, *Shoeshine* failed. It is easy to see why. After the war, Italians were hungry for foreign films. They flocked first to American, then to Russian movies, but both proved a great disillusionment. Slowly, bit by bit, the public came back to their own. Rossellini, Zavattini, and I came out too early. Many films that were shown then would have a greater success if they were new today.

S: Do you know the films of Olmi?

DS: Of course.

S: What do you think of them?

DS: I like them very much. He is a very delicate director. He doesn't try to *épater le bourgeois*; he says what he thinks in his own way: simple, modest, humble.

S: Without popular success.

DS: Because he is too good, too delicate.

S: I'd like to know what you think of his contemporaries. Bellocchio?

DS: I don't like him. He is too propagandistic and presumptuous.

S: Pasolini?

DS: He is good, particularly in his Roman films, like *Accatone*, but I also admire his *Oedipus Rex*.

S: Don't you find his theme banal?

DS: Perhaps Pasolini is a bit too literary, too educated. It's been said that Shakespeare is better played by ignorant than by overly cultivated actors. Pasolini imposes his immense cultivation on his work; he could probably use more freedom, greater simplicity.

S: I find that Godard has badly influenced most of these directors.

DS: Godard is a master, a totally personal artist, but the inventor of the New Wave. He created followers, imitators, and imitation is always deplorable.

S: What about his most important Italian imitator, Bertolucci?

DS: No, Bertolucci is our best young director. I liked him from the first, when he showed *La commare secca* to me. He is a young man with a new vision of cinema.

S: How do you compare his *Conformist* with your *Garden of the Finzi-Continis*?

DS: They are totally different.

S: They have similar subjects and the same leading lady.

DS: Okay, but Sanda is not very good in his film. Still, the picture is very beautiful, except for a certain willful and eccentric estheticism. For example, when the father's madhouse is made to look like the Roman Senate, I find the effect too *recherché*, too painterly. Bertolucci admits that he follows Magritte. Another young director I like is Carmelo Bene; unlike all the others, he has a sense of humor. And he doesn't make propaganda, which for me isn't art.

S: How do you feel the younger critics treat you? For example, the *Cahiers du Cinéma* group.

DS: They have never liked my films, and they are welcome to their opinion. I am never affected by critics I don't esteem. I go my own way, mistaken or not. I trust my conscience and my sensibility. On the other hand, I have listened to those critics who said that De Sica made no important films since *Umberto D.* and who, fortunately, feel there has been a revival with *The Garden of the Finzi-Continis*. They are right, because I made too many films that depended on the will of American financiers. For example, I made a film with Sophia Loren, which earned her an Oscar. I made films that are . . . too industrial, not as deeply felt as *Umberto D.* When I offered that film to Rizzoli, he said, "Why do you want to make *Umberto D.*? Why don't you make *Don Camillo*? I will give you a hundred million lire, half of the grosses." But I was full of noble intentions then; I didn't make *Don Camillo*; I made *Umberto D.* But soon my money ran out—because I financed *Umberto D.*, *The Bicycle Thief*, and *Shoeshine* myself—and I became dependent on producers, who wanted me to make films I won't say that I didn't believe in but that I would rather not have made.

S: Are you nostalgic for the earlier days?

DS: Very. *Umberto D.* was made absolutely without compromise, without concessions to spectacle, the public, the box office.

S: Even fewer than *Bicycle Thief*?

DS: Look, for me, *Umberto D.* is unique. Even though it has been the greater critical success, *The Bicycle Thief* does contain sentimental concessions.

S: Nevertheless, it is wonderful. How, having made such films, could you produce a thing like *A Place for Lovers*?

DS: That was the result of a misunderstanding. I had read in the papers that a friend of mine, Rondi, had an enormous theatrical success with a play of his called *The Lovers*. I told my manager about it, and without even giving me time to see the play, he purchased the rights. I kept saying, "Wait. I only read about it in the paper." But he didn't wait. Still, the play was not a bad one; it simply wasn't good material for a movie.

S: Why?

DS: *Love Story* is a great success, but in my film the lovers are adults of forty and thirty-six. A love affair between adults isn't as touching as one between young people.

S: What about *Brief Encounter*? Your rule doesn't hold up.

DS: Yes, *Brief Encounter* is beautiful.

S: Even allowing for the ill-suited subject, why did you smother it in such beautiful scenery and chic costuming? It seems to me a film about Faye Dunaway's wardrobe.

DS: Faye Dunaway brought her personal dressmaker with her. That's the way with all actresses!

S: Such a film gives ammunition to those who use your later works to dismiss your entire career.

DS: It was a mistake. Like all artists, I make mistakes.

S: Why do you use professional actors now, whereas you made your best films without them?

DS: In Italy there are about a hundred actors; fewer, if you are critical. In life there are millions. If I find a person with the particular appearance, virtues, and defects that fit my character, I take him from the streets when I cannot find what I need in a professional. For example, in *The Garden of the Finzi-Continis* Dominique Sanda and Lino Capolicchio are perfect for their parts,

but Sanda's father I found in the street. Her mother is a Turinese countess, her grandmother a Russian extra. For *The Bicycle Thief* only one producer would give me money. David O. Selznick was the only one who saw value in the project, but he wondered whom I would cast as the father. I replied that I wanted a real Italian worker because I found no one suitable among the available professionals (Mastroianni would have done, but he was too young then, only eighteen). You know who Selznick wanted? Cary Grant. Grant is pleasant, cordial, but he is too worldly, bourgeois; his hands have no blisters on them. He carries himself like a gentleman. I needed a man who eats like a worker, is moved like a worker, who can bring himself to cry, who bats his wife around and expresses his love for her by slamming her on the shoulders, the buttocks, the head. Cary Grant isn't used to doing such things, and he can't do them. Therefore, Selznick refused to give me money, and I had to beg to finance the film, as I always have had to beg. For my commercial movies, money was always available. I want to make Flaubert's *A Simple Heart* now, but the producers want me to amplify the love affair in it. You can't betray Flaubert. If they will let me make *A Simple Heart*, I will; if not, not.

S: How do you direct nonprofessionals?

DS: I explain and explain, and I am very convincing. I seem to have a special gift for making myself understood by actors. Either I play the part or I explain it, slowly, patiently, with a smile on my face and never any anger.

S: Do you have many takes?

DS: No.

S: If it isn't right?

DS: If it isn't right, I sometimes repeat, but usually I keep what I have shot. But I rehearse and rehearse and rehearse.

S: Is it difficult for you to act for others, as, for example, in *General della Rovere*?

DS: That was my best role because the film was made by a director I esteem.

S: You are also very good for yourself, especially in *The Gold of Naples*.

DS: That was painful. I couldn't see myself and kept asking the cameramen and mechanics, "Do you believe me? How am I doing?" A line of dialogue can be said a thousand ways; you need someone behind the camera to tell you which is the right one.

S: You have the rushes.

DS: Yes, but in Italy there is never enough money. Producers always tell you that once a thing is shot it must remain that way.

S: You've explained why you made your commercial films, but I still can't fathom how you and Zavattini, not only neorealists but leftists, could have made a film like *Woman Times Seven*, a wish fulfillment for the middle class.

DS: *Woman Times Seven* was a compilation of sketches that Zavattini had lying about. We were among the first to make films of sketches, and when Joseph Levine asked us to make another of them, Zavattini pulled some out of his drawer. It was a bit dishonest. The film is too long, but there are some cute things in it.

Shirley MacLaine in Women Times Seven.

S: Bresson complained to me that you neorealists were violating reality by dubbing, since the voice is the truest expression of personality.

DS: It's not the voice; it's what one says.

S: Still, why do you dub?

DS: Because I didn't have the money. *The Bicycle Thief* cost a hundred thousand dollars,

Shoeshine twenty thousand. With such budgets, I couldn't afford sound cameras.

S: You've worked in color and black and white. Which do you prefer?

DS: Black and white, because reality is black and white.

S: That's not true.

DS: Color is distracting. When you see a beautiful landscape in a color film, you forget the story. Americans use color for musicals. All my best films were made in black and white.

S: What do you think of the color experiments of Antonioni?

DS: He is an esthete. He takes red apples and paints them white.

S: Most critics today maintain that the true film artist writes what he directs.

DS: That's not true. Directing is completely different from writing; it is the creation of life. If *Bicycle Thief* had been directed by someone else, it would have been good, but different from the film I made.

S: Does this mean that you think dialogue less important than images?

DS: Images are the only important things. Let me give you another example of what I mean. Five films have been made of *The Brothers Karamazov*, all bad. Only one came close to Dostoyevsky: the version by Fedor Ozep. That's how the director is an author. In all these films the same story was used, but only one of them was any good.

S: You have often said that you greatly value Rene Clair and Charlie Chaplin. How have they influenced you?

DS: In no way.

S: Not even in *Miracle in Milan*?

DS: No, that is a wholly personal film. I detest imitations. In fact, I sometimes don't go to see a certain film for fear I'll want to imitate it.

S: How does your success affect you?

DS: Success has never made me drunk. I have never told myself one of my films is wonderful; I have always thought I could have done better. I want always to improve. When I have done something badly, I recognize it; when I do something well, I want to do better.

S: Do you see your old films?

DS: Yes, and sometimes I am pleased by them. Recently I saw that unfortunate film *Good*

Morning Elephant, which was signed by Gianni Franciolini but which I directed and in which I and my wife, Maria, played. It is delightful. Another film of mine, that had no success, *The Roof*, seems to me one of my best.

S: That film seems unusually polemical, am I right? Under the credits, for example, we see the Italian flag. The film seems your judgment on Italy.

DS: To a certain extent, because, you know, the housing problem is still an issue for us. But I was primarily interested in recording a way of life. You see, it is customary to place a flag of Italy atop a house when it is completed. To me, this film is sincere and interesting, as well as humble. The actors are delightful.

S: But too pretty.

The lovers in The Roof.

DS: No. I'll tell you a story about that. Sophia Loren wanted to play the feminine lead. In fact, she has always reproached me for not letting her. But, as I told her, if she were in that situation, people wouldn't give her a little shack but a palace. She is too beautiful, whereas Pallotta was a dumpy girl with a fat ass.

S: Could the film have succeeded if the lovers were ugly?

DS: The cinema has certain terrible requirements. One is that love stories be told

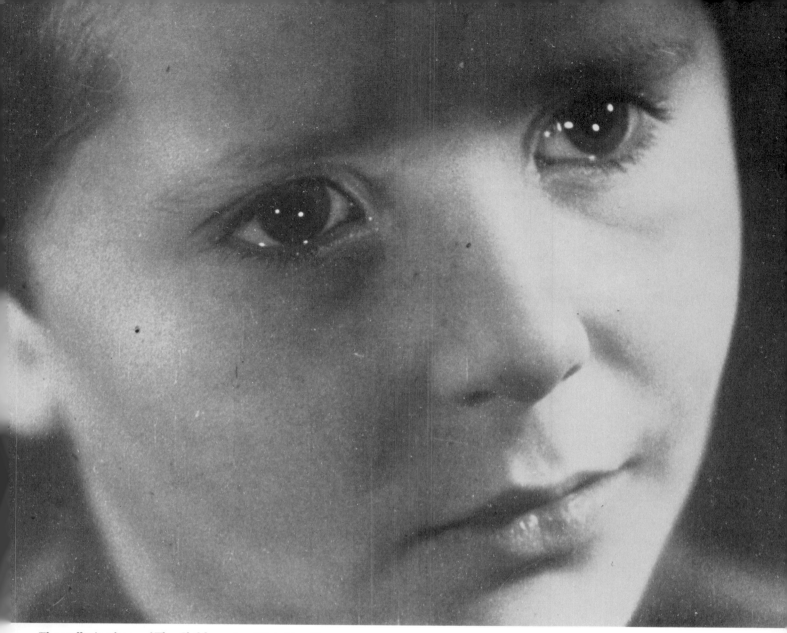

The suffering hero of The Children Are Watching Us.

about beautiful people. I know of only one film where this rule was ignored: *Marty*. Unfortunately, the public is not convinced when lovers are not handsome.

S: Why are there so many sounds of jets in the film?

DS: I'm glad you noticed them; they were an important auditory element to me. That sound evokes faraway worlds, power, the joy of escape.

S: Why are you so drawn to the destruction of young children as a theme for your films?

DS: Because children are the first to suffer in life. Innocents always pay.

S: This is what you show in *The Children Are Watching Us*. But something even more remarkable in that film is the general decency of the characters. Even that nosy neighbor turns out to be all right, in the moment when she brings the maid a glass of water. Does this represent your belief about mankind?

DS: All my films are about the search for human solidarity. In *Bicycle Thief* this solidarity

The solidarity of father and son in The Bicycle Thief.

at the train, we also watch the leave-taking of that vulgar young couple.

DS: A prostitute changing bordellos and her young man. I put that in as an ironic comment on the similarity between this good and well-intentioned husband who will be betrayed by his bourgeoise wife as if she were a prostitute.

S: Did you believe in your next film, *The Gate of Heaven?*

DS: No. I made it only to save myself from the Germans. As a matter of fact, the Vatican didn't find it orthodox enough and destroyed the negative. We were in the middle of the war then. I

occurs, but how long does it last? Twenty-four hours. One experiences moments, only moments of solidarity. That glass of water is one of them. Two hours later there will be no more union; the people won't be able to bear one another.

S: But it is important that the moment occurred.

DS: One needs something that lasts longer.

S: Is that possible?

DS: No. Human incommunicability is eternal.

S: Incommunicability or egoism?

DS: Let me tell you something. I wanted to call my films from *Shoeshine* on, not by their present titles, but "Egoism #1, #2, #3." *Umberto D.* is "Egoism #4."

S: One of the greatest performances on film is given by the man who plays the father in *The Children Are Watching Us.* Who was he?

DS: A dubber named Cigori.

S: The film is splendid. With so many traps for sentimentality, I marveled at how you avoided them. And the characters are so rich, except the aunt.

DS: Ah, she was a bourgeoise truly of the second rank, a coquette. But you are talking of a film that I made over thirty years ago and scarcely remember.

S: There is a strange shot in the film: The grandmother's mill seems to be made up of two photos joined at the middle.

DS: I spliced the shot because there was no mill on the set.

S: A particularly fine moment occurs when the father is leaving the resort. As Nina sees him off

was invited by a messenger of Goebbels to go and direct a German film school at Prague, because, you see, I was then at the top of my fame as a director. I told the envoy to give me time to think, but in truth, I was shaking because I knew they could put me on a train any time they wanted to. Then the Italian Fascists began insisting that I go to direct their school in Venice. I was saved by a marvelous man, D'Angelo, who was truly an angel and who asked me to make a film for the Vatican. I said yes immediately, knowing that the Vatican tie would keep me alive. All the time the Fascists kept asking me when I would finish that Vatican film and come to Venice, and I kept telling them I was at work on it. It took me two years; I completed it the day the Americans entered Rome. It was made to order. There are some good things in it, but the final scene of the miracle is horrible. It was a film made only to save me from the Fascists.

S: *Shoeshine* is more polemical than *The Roof*, isn't it?

DS: Of course. That is the result of the war, whose first victims were those poor youngsters, ruined by Americans, money, the black market in cigarettes. And then we put them in prison!

S: How did you get the details of prison life?

DS: I frequented the jails and spoke to the inmates. But, you know, the idea for this film was born years earlier. As soon as the war was over, three men and I formed a film journal, which was forbidden to publish after four numbers because it reflected Communist ideas. In the journal we ran a series of interviews with directors, including myself. In my interview I said that I wanted to make a film about shoeshine boys, and I even photographed some of these youngsters and published the results. One year later a producer asked me to make this very film, but he gave me a plot line that was terrible. I said that I would make the film but not with that story. Instead, I went to Zavattini, and we came up with this tale about the boys and their love for that horse.

S: One theme in the film is not developed: homoerotic love among the adolescents. Why?

DS: Because it revolted me.

S: It comes out very strongly in the shower scene where one of the boys beats Interlinghi [the hero].

DS: Yes, the element is present. The boys are nude, and the motive for the fight is jealousy. You're right, but it isn't developed.

S: Is it possible that you instinctively felt that development of this theme would harm the polemic?

DS: Yes. The other is a peripheral tragedy, a secondary unhappiness.

S: Don't you find the ending of the film melodramatic?

DS: I had intended to shoot the last sequence outdoors, but the producer didn't have the money to wait for good weather, as one must in exterior shooting. I wanted to photograph several sunrises and sunsets, and this would have required a week. He gave me two days, so the scene had to be shot indoors on a set. The original ending was beautiful, but I didn't have the money to shoot it properly. The film cost only twenty thousand dollars.

S: The ending isn't convincing.

DS: Twenty thousand dollars!

The boy's real love for their horse photographed on a painted set.

S: Why do you use music in *The Bicycle Thief* so often to provoke an emotional response?

DS: I am against music, except at a moment like the end of *The Garden of the Finzi-Continis* when we hear the Hebrew lament, but the producers always insist on it.

S: You said that this film contains a compromise. . . .

DS: Not a compromise; a concession. A small, romantic sentimentality in that rapport between father and son.

S: But that is the most moving thing in the film.

DS: Look, I agree that *Bicycle Thief* and *Umberto D.* are my best films, but I stoutly maintain that the latter is superior.

S: So do I, but you've no need to denigrate the earlier film. The son's forgiveness of the father isn't at all sentimental. It is the dawning of his maturity. It is absolutely essential to the meaning of the film.

DS: I am pleased to hear you say that. So many have criticized me for it.

S: Don't listen to them. I've also heard criticism of the end of *Umberto D.* by people who don't realize the dreadful irony that Umberto is saved only because of the dumb brute instinct for self-preservation that makes his dog refuse to be run down by the train.

DS: Yes, that ending is ironic.

S: In *The Bicycle Thief* why do you have Ricci put up a poster of Rita Hayworth as Gilda?

DS: Because she is so far away from his world, and he clumsily ruins this image of that woman.

S: Why did you include the scene of the workers rehearsing a show?

DS: In that Fascist period, it was dangerous to show a Communist cell. I included a polemical discussion of salaries and unemployment, but I made it take place as the workers are trying to divert themselves with a badly made spectacle that also contrasts with the melancholy of the hero in search of his stolen bicycle.

S: Why did you turn to fantasy after these neorealist films?

DS: After the success of *Bicycle Thief* Zavattini and I were afraid that neorealism would become a formula, so we decided to try the style in all genres of film, even fantasy and musical comedy. I liked and bought a book called *Let's Give Everyone a Horse as a Rocking Horse*, but, as a present to Zavattini, I decided instead to make a film out of his old novel *Toto, the Good.* That made him very happy.

S: Why did you present the angels as you do?

DS: I turned to an American makeup man, whom Alexander Korda had recommended to me. This man, who came from Hollywood, was a drunkard. The makeup for the film cost more than everything else, because the man got a thousand dollars a week and took so long. Besides he wasn't any good; that's why the angels look that way.

S: Too balletic.

DS: Exactly. The makeup is the worst thing in the film, and it cost the most. The film cost five hundred thousand dollars, half of that for makeup.

S: Why in *Umberto D.* did you choose a professor for the title role: a man whose life is so different from the character's?

DS: Battisti was a dignified bourgeois. All the neorealist films were made in favor of the proletariat, always forgetting the poor middle class. Furthermore, at that time, one kept reading in the newspapers stories of suicide. When a young man with his whole life ahead of him kills himself, he is crazy. But when an old man hasn't the strength to face his few remaining years, he represents the maximum grade of human despair. That's what I wanted to show.

S: How did such a man learn to act a character like Umberto when he himself was, in real life, famous and powerful?

Battisti as the bourgeois Umberto D . . .   *and the ruined old man . . .*

directed by De Sica.

DS: He was the character physically. Rizzoli, the producer, always complained that Battisti was so unpleasant. "Why don't you make him up?" he would say. "Why don't you take Ruggero Ruggeri instead?" I kept saying that I could not imagine changing Umberto D.'s face and that Ruggero Ruggeri was too aristocratic, with a magnificent voice—a great actor, but not Umberto. I looked for Umberto D. everywhere. I went to every old folks' home. I went to see retired people, old workers in pensions. I searched every institution but never found him. One day I saw Battisti on the street and knew immediately that he was the man. I followed him to the university where he was giving lectures, and I stayed put so that he wouldn't disappear. I took him to my office and gave him a test right there.

S: Was he reluctant?

DS: He was totally bewildered. A man like that, a man of letters and high culture, he didn't know me or the cinema. . . .

S: In the film, he seems crotchety, a bit of a pedant.

DS: He had to be like that. I needed an old man who was totally antipathetic because the old are unpleasant. He fights, but he cannot make it any longer. Reality is stronger than him, so he wants to kill himself.

S: Now we come to your awful *Indiscretion of an American Wife.* What kind of trouble did Selznick give you on that film?

DS: Every day he sent me forty- or fifty-page letters, detailing everything. They were in English; when I translated them, I arrived at work no earlier than noon. So I stopped reading them and began throwing them away as soon as they arrived. I would agree with everything he said and do things my own way.

S: Do you agree with me that this film is a failure?

DS: It's funny: You don't like it, but many people did.

S: Don't you think that Montgomery Clift and Jennifer Jones are terrible?

DS: The film was made for Jones. I found myself in Hollywood, where I was to make a film taken from a television comedy. Thornton Wilder and I prepared a script that was wonderful. Then the imbecile producer canceled everything. He started saying that we couldn't film the picture on the streets of Chicago but must make it in

Hollywood with back projection because that cost less. I broke the contract, paid my penalty, and left, thanks to Selznick who had purchased the script for *Stazione Termini* from Zavattini. I accepted this assignment in order to return to Italy.

S: Jones' neurosis is so great that I can't believe the love affair.

DS: She was hypersensitive in real life, too. I had terrible problems with that production. I produced the film myself and spent my own money to rent Terminal Station at night and to fill it with trains and people. At least twice, she arrived distraught, having quarreled with her husband, Selznick, and she threw her hat in the toilet, so that we had to fish it out because we had only one which she used in every scene in the film.

Clift, Jones, and the hat.

Then she took her shoes off and ran back barefoot to the hotel, leaving me and all the other people in the railroad station. Twice she pulled that trick on me, and it cost me four million lire each time.

S: Another problem with the film is that Clift doesn't seem too masculine and some of the dialogue, by Capote, doesn't give the right impression either.

DS: Yes, they were both pederasts.

S: Why didn't you make any film for the five years between *The Roof* and *Two Women?*

DS: Because I was in America.

S: What did you do there?

DS: Nothing. I lost a year on that script with Thornton Wilder. I lost time working with poor Dudley Nichols. I lost a year being under contract to that madman Howard Hughes.

S: Madman?

DS: He kept me a whole month in Hollywood without showing up. My contract forced me to stay in Los Angeles, and people kept saying, "Don't you like Los Angeles?" "Sure," I answered, "but I want to work. I'm not used to being kept, like a prostitute." I was well cared for. They gave me this marvelous hotel, this swimming pool, birds singing outside my window all day. But I wanted to work.

S: Why did you make *Two Women* in CinemaScope?

DS: Because it was the fashion in that period.

S: Do you think it a good method?

DS: No.

S: What do you think of the Moravia novel?

DS: I like it. It tells about the countryside where I was born.

S: Don't you find it melodramatic? Can you believe that the young girl, after being raped, would so quickly turn to sexual license?

DS: That's the way it is in the novel. She does it for revenge.

S: It seems opposite to the kind of truth I find in *The Children Are Watching Us* and *Umberto D.*

DS: Yes, it is forced drama.

S: Are you satisfied with that moment in the film when they find the girl nursing a dead baby?

DS: No, but that too is in the novel. Perhaps it is too contrived, but, then, women did lose children in the war.

Sophia Loren confronting her daughter (Eleanora Brown) with the evidence of prostitution.

De Sica in one episode of The Last Judgment.

S: Do you like *The Last Judgment?*

DS: Very much. You know, it was never exported.

S: That's regrettable. I think it a first-rate film. I was very surprised to discover it and *Il Boom* here. Only the scenes with Mercouri and Manfredi seem wrong to me.

DS: That was a mistake.

S: But I thought, while watching the film, that it must have been made in a mood of great gaiety.

DS: Yes, I was very enthusiastic about it. De Laurentiis lost money on it, however, and it has never been widely shown. That is too bad, because it's one of my best films.

S: I agree. Perhaps it doesn't appeal because of its cynicism, which is exceeded by *Il Boom*. In the latter film, when Sordi goes to the rich woman he thinks will settle his financial problems by taking him as her lover only to find that she merely wants to buy his eye for her husband, why do you end the discovery scene by holding on that wooden angel?

DS: He has false hopes of a profitable adventure with a rich old woman, and she, out of her egoism, entertains equally false hopes. Amid all this asking of favors and false hope I show a false angel.

S: Isn't this type of symbolic detail new to you?

DS: Yes. Robbe-Grillet has made popular this

use of objects surrounding the character. It is a new mode.

S: Has this influenced you much?

DS: No, but Robbe-Grillet has been a great influence on Antonioni.

S: Why did you make another American film, *The Condemned of Altona*?

DS: Ponti wanted it; I didn't.

S: It is wholly uncinematic.

DS: You know, Antonioni called it an essay in direction, an anticinematic text that De Sica made with a skill one wouldn't expect him to show.

S: The play is good, but Abby Mann's script diminishes Sartre.

DS: I agree. This film was one of the causes of a breach between me and Zavattini. Zavattini had written a screenplay, but Ponti insisted on having Abby Mann.

S: Why did you use that pompous music of Shostakovich?

DS: Shostakovich wrote me a letter saying that I used this music for a Fascist film, but where is that film Fascist?

S: How do you feel when you direct actors like Robert Wagner and Fredric March?

DS: Melancholy. Someone who made *Umberto D.* cannot be making *The Condemned of Altona*. The producer asked for it.

S: I am deeply disturbed by such films; they give ammunition to those who want to forget your great achievements, and they cause works like *The Last Judgment* and *Il Boom* to be ignored.

DS: I have made many mistakes.

S: For money?

DS: For money. The lack of sufficient money to make the films I want makes me dependent on others. I want to make Flaubert's *A Simple Heart* now, but I must reply on American capitalists who want Flaubert turned into Erich Segal.

S: Did you participate in *Boccaccio '70* also for money?

DS: That sketch was merely a *divertissement*.

S: It's so sentimental. I can't believe that someone who sells her body for money could also be so fastidious as Loren.

DS: It was an entertainment, nothing serious.

S: In *Yesterday, Today, Tomorrow*, who had the idea of teaming Loren and Mastroianni?

DS: Ponti. But you know, this is the first film with sketches enacted by the same people.

S: I like the first and last parts, but the middle

is wholly unconvincing. I don't believe for a minute that Loren as the rich industrialist's wife really wants to change her life; hence the switch is no surprise.

DS: We needed a sketch in the middle to make three.

S: Your next film, on the other hand, is an entertainment that is highly skillful. Part of the excellence is due to a faster cutting tempo.

DS: That was inspired by the French New Wave directors, who gave us a push in that direction.

S: One of the best scenes in *Marriage, Italian Style* is Loren's signing the contract for her apartment. Did she contribute any of the gestures?

DS: I directed it all.

S: Do you believe the ending? Why should this woman, who knew the man so well, be happy at her marriage?

DS: She doesn't love him; she marries to give her sons a name.

S: Why did you use freeze frames in the wedding scene?

DS: To speed up a subject that is so banal.

S: How much of *After the Fox* is due to Neil Simon?

DS: Everything.

S: How did you find working with Peter Sellers?

DS: Sellers is a good friend, for whom I feel great affection. He had made films that I admired, and I wanted to make one with him myself; but I wasn't able to because of Neil Simon.

S: How do you feel about *A Young World*?

DS: It was very difficult for me. I was in a new, completely unknown atmosphere and so had to make myself over. Moreover, I had terrible fights with the French censors. In the original film there is a scene where a man sells himself to an older woman in order to get money for his girlfriend's abortion. The French wanted to send me to jail for it because I was exposing the existence of male prostitution.

S: And then we come to *Sunflower*. How could you have made this film?

DS: When I accepted that film, it was called "Giovanna," and Zavattini had written the script. It was a very simple story of a Calabrese woman whose husband had gone to Sweden to become a miner. When he doesn't come back, Giovanna leaves Calabria, makes the difficult trip to Sweden, and learns in Stockholm from some Italians there that the husband has gone to a town in the Arctic. Once there, she meets his wife and child, but she doesn't say who she is. She reports herself as her husband's sister, so the wife takes her in with great affection and tells her whole life story: how she met Giovanna's husband, about their baby, about their desire to go to Italy to meet his mother. Giovanna cries; in order not to show this, she washes her face in the sink. Immediately, her husband comes back from work, his face begrimed. They look at one another; she runs away screaming. The end. Now comes Mr. Ponti, who says, "Never can Sophia Loren be abandoned by any man. Mastroianni must have lost his memory in the war. He must go after her." Can you imagine that? What a nice story it was originally, so simple and so true. He comes in, she screams, and that is all.

So Mastroianni pursues Loren to Italy . . .

only to separate after a maudlin final embrace.

S: That's the moment I wished *Sunflower* would end.

DS: It doesn't, thanks to Mr. Carlo Ponti.

S: But how could you have agreed to it? Why didn't you abandon the film?

DS: So much time had already been spent preparing it. The shooting had started. It was weak of me not to have left.

S: And of course, you take all the blame.

DS: Yes; me and Zavattini, whereas the fault is wholly Ponti's.

S: And things are worse. In the film, when Loren returns from Moscow, she actually looks younger than before her ordeal.

DS: I didn't notice that. So much depends on the actress. I don't worry too much about makeup; I am interested in the performance. I didn't notice she had had this wig made to make her look younger. She has her personal makeup man, paid by her.

S: Is the battle scene in the film a stock shot or something you made?

DS: I think part was stock, but the rest was made.

S: Don't you think the superimposition of the red flag over the carnage is a bit artificial?

DS: That's a stupid effect which Ponti wanted. Anyway, I didn't direct it. It was shot by the second unit, headed by a Russian director.

S: That's the poignance of being a film director!

DS: My experience with this film was so terrible that I decided to rebel, and my rebellion is *The Garden of the Finzi-Continis.*

S: Why didn't Zavattini write the script this time?

DS: After *Sunflower*, Zavattini and I have been a bit estranged. Because even Zavattini sided with Ponti, so I was left alone, with Ponti, Zavattini, and Tonino Guerra against me. So I separated from Zavattini and made *The Garden of the Finzi-Continis* as vengeance. After the disaster of *Sunflower* I wanted to make a true De Sica film, made just as I wanted it. I accepted this subject because I intimately feel the Jewish problem. I myself feel shame because we all are guilty of the death of millions of Jews. Why were they killed? Because a criminal, a lunatic wanted that. But the Italian Fascists are also guilty. So am I. I wasn't a Fascist, but I belong to the country that collaborated with Hitler. I wanted, out of conscience, to make this film, and I am glad I made it.

S: I've heard that the author of the novel, Giorgio Bassani, renounces the film.

DS: Ah, because of the character of the father, which has been minimized in the film. But I think the character is well treated.

S: Why did you use foreign actors?

DS: I needed someone foreign for the heroine, Micol, because she is a difficult, ambiguous personality with an unstated incestuous love of her brother. I couldn't find among my Italians anyone with the face she needed. But Dominique Sanda is marvelous, with her hard, cold face.

S: Do you feel that the film shows the connection between Micol's private difficulties and the historic tragedy of the war?

DS: Micol's drama is far from the other. She only suffers the consequences of racial laws.

S: Don't you think the film should have been

The troubled love affair . . .

longer so as to give equal development to both subjects?

DS: Perhaps, but I wanted this effect: The

Germans come little by little. They are only the first symptoms. We are only at the door of the tragedy.

. . . and the family caught in a historical crisis.

S: That's true. But there are problems. For example, when Giorgio goes to the girl who runs the shooting gallery, she tells him that Malnate, who has been killed, used to be her lover, but we never saw that. Something crucial seems to have been left out. I have the impression of a film having to rush to include all the events of a *roman fleuve*.

DS: Yes, perhaps that was done too quickly.

DS: Because I made it very quickly, with very little money.

S: The garden is justly marvelous, but so is everything else.

DS: That's right. The second half shouldn't be so beautiful. I should have made it gray or reversed *The Last Judgment* and made the first part color and the second black and white. That's a good idea. I wanted to achieve effects like those

The in-color ending of The Last Judgment.

Four years go by too quickly. It's a defect of the screenplay.

S: Do you find the colors a bit in disharmony with the story. The color is so beautiful; the story so bleak.

DS: I should have done what Antonioni did, paint everything white, or what you say Olmi has done: use underexposure.

S: Why didn't you?

in Huston's *Reflections in a Golden Eye*, but my cameraman was incapable.

S: As far as you're concerned, why does Micol sleep with Malnate?

DS: Because she is jealous of her brother. Her brother loves Malnate, and she wants to take him away from her brother.

S: Doesn't she also do it to abase herself? She, who hates sex, goes to bed with a man who, as she herself says, she finds too hairy? But don't you find it coincidental that Giorgio arrives just in time to see this?

DS: That was in the novel. Like all true lovers, at a moment of crisis, he has a sixth sense.

S: If you could remake the film, would you want it to be grayer not only in literal color, but figuratively, in tone?

DS: Already it is very sober. It was a very difficult film to make. The novel was so difficult to turn into a motion picture. I had to read four horrible screenplays before I found the one we could use. I am being presumptuous at this moment, but I believe that it is a good film. I am happy that I made it because it brought me back to my old noble intentions. Because, you see, I have been ruined by lack of money. All my good films, which I financed by myself, made nothing. Only my bad films made money. Money has been my ruin.

Sir Carol Reed

London, October 23, 1971

Feature Films: 1953 *Midshipman Easy*; 1936 *Laburnum Grove, Talk of the Devil*; 1937 *Who's Your Lady Friend?*; 1938 *Bank Holiday, Climbing High, Penny Paradise*; 1939 *A Girl Must Live, The Stars Look Down*; 1940 *Night Train to Munich, The Girl in the News*; 1941 *Kipps*; 1942 *Young Mr. Pitt*; 1947 *Odd Man Out*; 1948 *The Fallen Idol*; 1949 *The Third Man*; 1951 *An Outcast of the Islands*; 1953 *The Man Between*; 1955 *A Kid for Two Farthings*; 1956 *Trapeze*; 1958 *The Key*; 1959 *Our Man in Havana*; 1963 *The Running Man*; 1965 *The Agony and the Ecstasy*; 1968 *Oliver!*; 1970 *Flap*; 1972 *The Public Eye*.

When I arrived at Sir Carol Reed's fashionable Chelsea townhouse, I was greeted by the maid and by the director's cordial wife. At the far corner of the living room (painted green walls, matching the carpet; couches and chairs in complementary floral prints; china; silver—enclave of traditional taste against the trendy but equally arranged bohemianism of the streets) sat Sir Carol, looking ill at ease. Rising to welcome me, he seemed discomforted, surprisingly so because he is not only a knight, but a tall and imposing figure; one would instantly take him for a presence, were it not for the rather tentative expression.

Sir Carol could not have been more cooperative, more anxious to provide any information I asked for. Since he suffers from a slight hearing loss, he invited me to sit close by—expressing also by this gesture a willingness to be candid.

One quality I could not reproduce, however much I might wish to, is Sir Carol's total subjugation of self to fact. Nothing so indicates his immersion in a story than the total absence of personal flourish when he tells it. A deadpan comedian, one might say, but that suggests guile. Instead, Sir Carol seems one of those entertainers who are too earnest about their work to display much pleasure in it. Or perhaps, whatever enjoyment he takes, he takes in private.

SAMUELS: You started working in the theater as an actor. Did that have any crucial effect on your career as a director?

REED: Yes. But, you know, I wasn't a good actor. I began as a spear carrier and then appeared through the countryside in repertory, but though I got decent parts and so on, I was never very good—except in playing a dope fiend. That's the easiest thing in the world: You just shiver and shake and people think, "Well, isn't that good!" Yet I'm very glld that I did it for seven years or so because it helped me subsequently in understanding the actor's problems. Actors don't like admitting that/they feel awkward, but having been an actor myself, I can tell those signs by which an actor shows he's been made awkward by the movement I've asked from him. The most important thing is that the actors enjoy themselves. Then they'll redo any take as often as you like.

S: Why did you decide to become a director?
R: Because I was disappointed as an actor. I became a stage manager because I always enjoyed the entertainment business. I joined Edgar

Wallace, the writer, who, in the late twenties, sometimes had two or three plays running in London at the same time. I would appear in one, supervise the others, and then direct the touring companies.

S: Was it by choice or chance that you moved into films?

R: Edgar Wallace, who had gone to America to do a screenplay for *King Kong,* told me—this was in 1930—that talking pictures (which had just come in) were the future of the business. He advised me to see as many films as I could during his absence. He had a studio (Beaconsfield, which later became British Lion) that had been formed to film his plays. I would go there during the daytime and return to the theater at night. After his death, I decided to go into films. Since silent directors had no experience with dialogue, whereas, of course, I had, I was engaged as a dialogue director—something that doesn't exist anymore. My job was giving the actors instruction in intonation and voice projection, but I had nothing to do with shooting films.

S: Tyrone Guthrie had this job on your first movie.

R: You're quite right. On *Midshipman Easy,* Basil Dean, the producer, thought it would be good for me to have a dialogue coach. Guthrie was wonderful. In our business, some people are always worrying where any particular job is going to lead, but Guthrie—who, even in those days, was well known as an exciting stage director—had no interest in films, so he cared only to help me.

S: Unlike most important directors, you don't write your own scripts. However, do you substantially influence your scenarists?

R: Yes. I work with the author from the original conception right through to the finished script. You've got to be willing to sit with him, to say, you know, "We could do this with a look rather than dialogue. . . ." You know, letting an inexperienced screenwriter—even when he is an experienced novelist or playwright—work alone won't do. I don't write, though I have written a few stories, some of which were filmed by other men. But I think I can be of help in interpreting the writer's ideas.

S: What, then, do you think of the *auteur* theory?

R: Of the?

S: The French critics' assertion that a director is analogous to a writer because of his stylistic impositions even on a script not of his own creation.

R: This is something I'm not familiar with. In any case, I don't think a director should stand out. The audience should be unconscious that the damned thing's been directed at all. There's a fashion now to give too much freedom to the director; people fought hard for that. But there was never any need to fight: If you made a couple of pictures that were commercially successful, as well as artistically good, you automatically got freedom. I mean, nobody would ever dare dictate to a man like William Wyler! They'd say, "My God, he's done well so far. Let's back a sure thing." Now directors want total control even on their first picture, which is destructive for the business. Your Thalbergs, Selznicks, your Darryl Zanucks and Hal Wallises—these were the people who built the business. They didn't think of their own country; they thought of what would entertain internationally, and they had a financial sense.

S: What of the argument that such men hampered film as an art form just because they wanted international appeal and hence had to search for the lowest common denominator?

R: A man like Thalberg—who probably made the best pictures that have ever been made—had more knowledge than any of the directors who worked for him. It's the distributor, who has now got the authority, who is most likely to interfere. But it's precisely because everyone fought to do away with the producer that power fell to distributors.

S: Speaking of interference, were you forced to end *The Fallen Idol* as you do? Would you and Graham Greene have preferred a less happy ending?

R: We had absolutely no supervision on that film. It was adapted from Greene's story "The Basement Room." As you know, the film is about a young boy who unnecessarily casts suspicion on his butler and causes the police to hunt him for a crime that was never committed. But all that wasn't in Greene's story. What do you think is wrong with the ending?

S: The film eventually becomes a thriller, inviting concern about the butler's fate, whereas its true distinction is quite another matter: the boy's

process of innocent romanticizing and subsequent disillusionment with the butler. What happens to the Ralph Richardson character is really irrelevant. The important thing is that the boy believed the butler's boasts of heroism and so thought him capable of a just murder, yet he finds that the boasts were empty lies. Why didn't you end with that discovery?

R: In "The Basement Room" the butler actually kills his wife, but I said to Graham, "Suppose the man hadn't done it, but that the boy thought he did." Consequently, neither of us felt that the boy's actions should actually make the butler hang.

S: We wouldn't need that! I'm simply asking why you spend so much time making the audience wonder what will happen to Richardson when he is only important as he affects the child?

R: As I recall, the happy ending is the return of the boy's parents. Now he won't be the lonely

child he was when he got mixed up with complications he was too young to understand.

S: You've handled such a wide variety of subjects, but are you conscious of any themes or ideas that constantly interest you?

R: That I myself want to put forward? No. It's always the project. I know that there are great directors, like Visconti and Bergman, who have a certain view of life, but I don't think that a director who knows how to put a film together need impose his ideas on the world. It's another matter, of course, if the ideas are in the subject. You must always take the author's side and believe it whilst you're making the picture.

S: What does tend to attract you in the stories you choose?

R: I tend to look for something exactly opposite from what I've just done. One can find a comfortable groove, your best way—but I find that boring.

S: How do you feel when you're characterized as a director of thrillers?

R: Nervous.

S: You should also be annoyed. Despite the brilliance of a thriller like *The Third Man*, I'd say your best film was your adaptation of the Conrad romance *An Outcast of the Islands*.

R: I'm glad you feel that way. When I'm done, I can never judge a picture. Whilst you're making it, you're desperately in love with the thing, but right after the first night one never wants to see it again. Then you see the faults. Sometimes when I happen to see my old films on television, I think, "Oh, why did I do this or that?" and yet I know that when I said, "Print that take," I was sure it was right.

S: Is *An Outcast* your favorite?

R: While I was making it, I was in love with it, but there were things that didn't come quite right. It was a tricky one to do: a large production with little money. I went to Borneo to search locations; but by the time the actors were ready to come the Korean War started, and the insurance companies refused to write the necessary policies. So I got some army cameramen to shoot backgrounds. Then I had to come back home, reorganize, go to Ceylon, and try to make Ceylon look like Borneo.

S: Are all the backgrounds location shots or were some made in the studio?

R: There was a bit of studio matching. You remember that throughout the story a little boy follows Trevor Howard in a canoe. I'd shot the boy in Borneo, without Howard. Then, when I went to Ceylon, where I had Howard, I hadn't the boy. As a result, through the film I had to show only the nose of the canoe whenever Howard was also in the scene.

S: Were the scenes where Ralph Richardson teaches Howard to guide the ship all done with models?

R: Yes. But the rocks were shot in the Scilly Islands.

S: Whose idea was it to film this book?

R: Whilst I was working on *The Fallen Idol*, Ralph Richardson asked me if I'd ever read *Outcast*. I thought I knew all of Conrad's books, but I'd never read that one. Immediately after I did, I fell in love with it and asked Ralph to play the captain.

S: This is your most passionate film. Everything in it is heightened.

R: I've not seen it for years. It must seem too melodramatic.

S: Not at all. There are so many extraordinary things in the film, like the driven quality of the hero's love for Aissa. It's so difficult to portray such pure sexual longing without making it seem contemptible or ludicrous, but you thoroughly succeed. And of course, Kerima is magnificent in the part. Where did you find her?

R: She'd never acted, which is why I never allowed her to speak until the end when she screams, but then we covered her scream with a thunderclap.

S: How did you direct her?

R: When you use an amateur with a good face or a child, you must always shoot very far or very close. When shooting close, you repeat everything, keeping only the few bits you want. I never let a child speak in a scene with professionals because when professionals have to play next to an amateur, they keep worrying that he'll forget his cue. What I do is shoot the scene until the child's line is due. Then I cut, do a separate take of the line reading, and then start again. This relaxes the professionals. And I never use a number board with a child because it breaks his thoughts: When he hears it, he looks at the clapper boy and wishes they could change places. Sometimes I speak the child's line myself, let the other actors go on with the scene, and later have the child dub his line in. Amateurs and children always remember their dialogue, but they always forget their cues.

S: This means that a director is more responsible for the performance of an amateur than that of a professional. Would you like the control that making a film entirely with non-professionals would give you? Would you like, for example, to work as De Sica does?

R: Every Italian is an actor. With English people, you can't use amateurs in speaking parts. The English are reserved; you'll never find a shy Italian.

S: Are there any directors you particularly admire or have felt as an influence?

R: I don't know how other directors work. Because I feel embarrassed about going on another man's floor, I've never seen anyone else work—unless it's a bit of location shooting I chance to come upon in the street. I don't want to know, anyway, because I don't want to copy. But as far as results go—I admire William Wyler enormously. People find geniuses so quickly today, but, you know, it's always easy to hit lucky with a picture: You've got a good story or someone gives an extraordinary performance. Among his thirty or forty films, Wyler has made some of the greatest, and his record is fantastic. Of the newer boys, I'd say Mike Nichols is the most exciting.

S: What do you think of Godard?

R: I'm very impressed.

S: Why?

R: He is so much himself, like Visconti. You can always see Visconti in every story; he's something unusual. I don't know enough about Godard, though. I've only seen two of his pictures.

S: The director with whom you're most often compared is Hitchcock.

R: Hitchcock is the greatest technician in the business. He knows more about making films than the rest of us put together. I remember him giving instructions to the propman for a wineglass that was to contain poison in *The Lady Vanishes*. "Make me up a glass six and a half inches high and four inches wide and shoot it with a fifty lens, the glass three feet from the camera and your actors five feet beyond that. Then with the glass in the foreground, it will seem menacing even though it's like the others." And, do you know, Hitch can do that sort of thing in his head. He knows his lenses, everything. But although his pictures are the greatest of thrillers, I sometimes wish he would try his hand at other subjects.

S: Your *Night Train to Munich* was a deliberate imitation of *The Lady Vanishes*, wasn't it? Launder and Gilliat wrote both scripts.

R: At the beginning it was called "Gestapo" and was rather serious. But when the war came on, we felt it was wrong to make something so heavy at such a time, so we made it more amusing, in the vein of *The Lady Vanishes*. Launder and Gilliat were so brilliant at this kind of story. They deserve more credit for the film than I do.

Viennese location shots help create The Third Man's *crucial mood.*

S: Did you feel under pressure of the comparison with Hitchcock?

R: Oh, no. In those days, one made four pictures a year, each shot in five weeks. I was under contract to Gainsborough and was handed scripts, with whose authors I was given opportunity to work for perhaps two weeks. There wasn't the importance put on films that there is now. You never even knew when the picture was finished—another department took care of that.

S: Are you satisfied with the final chase scene on the Alpine funicular? Do you think it was done well?

R: I think it was done appallingly. I remember at the time thinking that the mountains looked like ice cream. But the war was on then, Gainsborough had a small stage, and it was a very bad model.

S: The set destroys the terror.

R: That's right.

S: How did you feel while working on this scene?

R: I knew it wouldn't be good, but what could one do? You have a job, and you do the best you can. One feels miserable, but. . . .

S: I haven't been able to see four of your films. Can you tell me if you think they are important: *Laburnum Grove, Talk of the Devil, Who's Your Lady Friend?* and *Climbing High.*

R: Of the four, *Climbing High* was much the worst. *Talk of the Devil* I wrote myself. At the time, it was sort of all right. I'd worked for Basil Dean, who had rather a strange voice and was very impatient. He'd get on the phone and say, "Tomorrow I want this-and-this on stage four" and there it was—because Mr. Dean had asked for it. Without actually saying I was Dean, when I began directing for him, I got into the habit of phoning and, I suppose, imitating his intonation. Whenever I asked for anything, I got it immediately. I used that situation for the story. *Who's Your Lady Friend?*: not good at all. *Laburnum Grove* was very successful.

S: Why haven't you been able to see that each of these films was preserved?

R: There are an awful lot of films I've made that I'd rather weren't preserved.

S: You seem to take particular care in casting minor roles.

R: Yes. I go to the theater a great deal and watch television. Whenever I see a good actor, I jot his name down.

S: Do you encourage improvising in minor parts?

R: A bit. It's important to keep the minor roles from being minor, to give the actor a bit of business, you know.

S: You've said that much of the excellence of *The Third Man* is due to location shooting. If you had your choice, would you shoot everything on location?

R: Yes. I suffered a lot of opposition going to Vienna with *The Third Man.* One didn't, in those days, take actors on location. But here's an example of the way finance does dominate the business. If you've got five weeks' location, you know you've got to get all your shots in that period. We had a day and a night unit. The actors we used at night didn't work in the day and vice versa. We worked from eight P.M. to five A.M., then went to bed, got up at ten A.M., worked with the day unit until four, and then went back to bed until eight. That way we got double the work done in the same time. It's a bit of a rush, but it's better to rush than not get it all and have to match things in the studio.

S: Despite your expressed admiration for producers, you've often acted in that role yourself. Why?

R: Because on those particular pictures I didn't need a producer; the money was set. But a producer can be very valuable.

S: However, afil your best films, except for *The Stars Look Down,* are among those you produced yourself.

R: Well, I enjoyed them more. But I've never had problems with producers except when they've tried to rush me. Some producers are inclined to do that even when they know you're not behind because they hope to earn some time in case you fall back. When they do that to me, it has the reverse effect.

S: How much supervision do you give your editor?

R: I edit as I go along—during the lunch break. I never take lunch in the studio; I don't like to sit down or see anyone else sitting down. I feel more lively when I stand. I go into the cutting room at one every day to see the previous day's rushes. Then each Saturday I work with the editor (if we're not shooting) so that the final cut only takes two days after shooting's done.

S: Your editing is very brisk.

R: David Lean's told me I cut too much.

S: He cuts too little. Tell me, why did you use Robert Dearing to edit so many of your films?

R: I had no control. He was chief editor for all films made at Gainsborough. I didn't get on with him.

S: Could he change your work?

R: It was such a different business then. Bob Dearing was inclined to resent directors. Very often I wasn't even invited to see the editing. But a director *must* work with his editor. Directing is conveying to actors what you had in mind while working with the author. After that, the editor must understand not only what you did on the floor, but what the author had in mind—a man the editor's never even met.

S: Let's move from technique to content for a minute. Although several of your films are outstanding, they rarely move outside traditional practices—except in one particular. You like unhappy endings (that's why I find *The Fallen Idol* case puzzling). Is this a conscious rebellion against commercial formulas?

R: You must always do as you like, gambling on the possibility that what you like is also commercial. I used to be very much criticized for ending my films unhappily. At one time, it was thought that every picture must end with an embrace so that the audience could go out happy, but I don't think that's what it did. A picture should end as it has to. I don't think anything in life ends "right." The ending of *The Fallen Idol* is only partly happy. After all, the boy is now finished with the butler, although he used to adore him. In *The Third Man*, Graham Greene wanted Joseph Cotten to overtake Valli in that car; then the film would finish with the couple walking down the road. I insisted that she pass him by.

David Selznick had some money in the film (I think it took care of Cotten and Orson Welles' valet). I must say he was very nice and appreciative about the picture as soon as he saw it, but he said, "Jeezez, couldn't we make a shot

on about Noel. Alexander Korda, the producer, didn't care, however, so in the end I got Orson.

S: What was he like to work with?

R: Wonderful! Marvelous!

S: He didn't try to direct himself?

R: He was difficult only about the starting date, telling me how busy he was with this and that. So I said, "Look, we're going on location five weeks. Any week—give us two days' notice—we'll be ready for you. And give me one week out of seven in the studio." He kept to it. He came straight off the train in Vienna one morning, and we did his first shot by nine o'clock. "Jeez," he said, "this is the way to make pictures!" He walked across the Prater, said two lines to Cotten, and then I said, "Go back to the hotel, have breakfast; we're going into the sewers, and we'll send for you." "Great! Wonderful!" Comes down into the sewers then and says, "Carol, I can't play this part!" "What's the matter?" "I can't do it. I can't work in a sewer. I come from California! My throat! I'm so cold!" I said, "Look, Orson, in the time it's taking us to talk about this, you can do the shot. All you do is stand there, look off, see some police after you, turn, and run away." "Carol," he said, "look, get someone else to play this. I cannot work under such conditions!" "Orson, Orson, we're lit for you. Just stand there." "All right, but do it quick!" Then he looks off, turns away, and runs off into the sewers. All of a sudden I hear a voice shouting, "Don't cut the cameras! Don't cut the cameras! I'm coming back." He runs back, through the whole river, stands underneath a cascade over his head (all this out of camera range, mind you!), and does all sorts of things, so that he came away absolutely dripping. "How was that?" he asks. "Wonderful! Marvelous!" I said. "Okay. I'll be back at the hotel. Call me when you need me." With Orson, you know, everything has to be a drama. But there were no arguments of any sort at all.

where the girl gets together with the fella?" "It was in the original script," I said. "We chucked it out." "I'm not sure. It was a good idea." But I mean, the whole point with the Valli character in that film is that she'd experienced a fatal love—and then along comes this silly American!

S: Whose idea was it to cast Orson Welles as Harry Lime?

R: Mine. I was having dinner one night with Orson. I'd just gotten the synopsis from Graham Greene, which I thought was all right, so I told Orson that there was a wonderful part in it for him. He asked to read it, but I said, "Look, the script's not ready yet, but I'm sure you'll like it even though you don't come on until halfway through." "I'd much rather come in two-thirds of the way through," he replied. After a week, I got Greene's treatment, which I accepted. By this time David Selznick wanted me to do *Tess of the D'Urbervilles*, which I wasn't very keen on. He had a script, which we both thought pretty bad, so I asked him to have work done to it and meanwhile let me go ahead with *The Third Man*, since it was something we could knock off quick. I said I wanted Orson and Cotten, who I knew was under contract to Selznick, as was Valli. "Cotten and Valli you can have," he said, "but you can't have Orson." I asked why, knowing very well that Orson wasn't under contract to him and that he preferred me to use someone who was. Besides I think Orson one day had made a pass at Jennifer or something. Selznick was very strong on Noel Coward's playing Harry, but of course, that would have been disastrous. It went on and on. When I started the film, Selznick was still going

S: He improvised that scene! But surely not the famous hand coming through the grate!

R: That was my hand; I did it on location before he arrived because I knew that Harry must try to escape the sewers. The shot immediately preceding that was done with Orson in the studio, because in Vienna there isn't any staircase leading directly up to a drain.

S: Who was responsible for the marvelous business in the introduction of Harry: the great idea of his being exposed by the cat?

R: Oh, God, so many cats! That was all improvised.

S: How?

R: I do happen to remember this. I was worried about finding Harry in that doorway; I didn't want Cotten just to pass by and see him because then the audience wouldn't know who the man in the doorway was. When Cotten brings Valli flowers, I placed a cat on her bed whom Cotten tries to get to play with the string around the gift. But the cat just turns and jumps off.

S: Much as Valli won't respond.

R: Exactly. Then the cat jumps through the window. Whilst Cotten had been trying to get the cat to play, I had him say, "Bad-tempered cat." Then I worked in the line for Valli: "He only liked Harry." We next look out the window, see a man come down the street, and watch him enter a doorway. So far as we know, it might be anyone. But by going over to him and playing with his lace, the cat establishes that it's Harry.

S: Here's the director as author!

R: It was a little trick, you know. But we used so many cats: one in Vienna, running down the street; another in the studio on the bed; another to play with the lace. . . . What was difficult was to get the cat to walk up to it.

S: How did you do that?

R: Sardines! But how you bring it all back! The problem then was to get the cat to look up at Harry.

S: Let me search your instinct here. The devil is often shown accompanied by or in the shape of a cat. Is that what suggested this moment to you?

R: No. I just liked the idea of a cat loving a villain—the charm of the man! Furthermore, I wanted Cotten to shout at Harry, although not knowing what the audience knew: who was in the doorway.

S: Another brilliant decision in the film is the zither music. How did you decide on Karas?

R: When we were on location, I used to store props in a studio outside the city. Whilst the boys were unloading, I'd go to a store to get carafes of wine for them. Nearby there was a tiny beer and sausage restaurant, with a courtyard in which this fellow played a zither for coins. I'd never heard a zither before, thought it was attractive, and wondered whether we could use a single instrument throughout the film, especially since the zither is so typical of Vienna. I got Karas to come back to my hotel one night, where he played for about twenty minutes. I then brought a recording of that back to the studio to see if the music fought against the dialogue—as some did— but a good deal of it worked well. Karas then came to London to live in that little cottage adjoining this house, which we used also to own in those days. I had a moviola with a dupe of the film so's we could match his playing against portions of the action. One night he asked me to come back and listen to a new tune he'd done, what came to be called "The Third Man Theme." "Why haven't you played that before?" I said. "I haven't played it for fifteen years," he answered, "because when you play in a café, nobody stops to listen; music is just background for talk and drinking and shouting. This tune takes a lot out of your fingers. I prefer playing 'Wien, Wien,' the sort of thing one can play all night while eating sausages at the same time." It turned out he'd composed the tune himself but had nearly forgotten it. What's driven other zither players mad (they can never figure out how it's done) is that he played the tune, then with an earphone rerecorded it, adding thirds. In the ordinary way, no zither player could do it.

S: Apart from the pleasantness of the music, there is the precise matching of musical phrases or chords and dialogue or action throughout the film. Did you tell Karas where things should go?

R: Yes. For example, in the cat scene, I asked Karas to play a few sort of walking notes while the cat crossed the street and then, as it looked at Harry's shoe, ascending chords, which break into "The Third Man Theme" when it finally sees Harry and we hold on the cat's little face. That's the advantage of working with a single instrument. Usually, I talk to my composer, saying, "You know, we should have something amusing there, something romantic here." Then after

Typical off-angle shot from The Fallen Idol.

three or four weeks, he comes to me, plays the piano and says, "Here's what the drums are going to do," and then, "The strings are doing this." It doesn't mean a bloody thing to me. I just cross my fingers but don't know until we get to the first recording session, when it's too late to change.

S: Would you like to make a film without music?

R: I never have.

S: Would you like to?

R: I think music helps.

S: Why?

R: It helps. I don't know.

S: Don't you think it bullies the audience sometimes? Then there's also the problem of where the hell the orchestra's coming from.

R: Maybe. But in many cases, you don't realize that music is playing. When I was an actor, we often had violins playing in the pit. But music's probably going out of fashion. There isn't any rule. For example, my current picture calls for music. There's a lot of silent stuff in it while the detective follows the girl for days without ever coming closer than ten feet. You'd get fed up with the traffic noise! In such a case, music is very helpful. I think you're right about it, but I'm not going to fight the convention. But I mean, you can only compare music to canned laughter.

S: Another notable feature of *The Third Man*, although one is already conscious of it in *Odd Man Out*, is your penchant for off-angle shots. Was that a conscious effect?

R: I hope it's not noticed by someone who's less familiar with pictures than you are. I intend it to make the audience uncomfortable.

S: "I don't know why, but this view of things is off."

R: Exactly.

S: But you didn't use this shot before *Odd Man Out*, did you?

R: I don't think so. I used it so much in *The Third Man*, however, that I remember William Wyler, after seeing the film, made me the gift of a spirit level. "Carol," he said, "next time you make a picture, just put it on top of the camera, will you!"

S: But from all the possible devices for disorienting the spectator, why did you choose this one?

R: I shot most of the film with a wide-angle lens that distorted the building and emphasized the wet cobblestone streets (it cost a good deal to hose them down constantly). . . . But the angle of vision was just to suggest that something crooked was going on. I don't think it's a very good idea. I haven't used it much since—only when I need to shoot someone standing behind another person who's sitting and I don't want to cut off his head.

S: So you used it for effect in *The Third Man* and for efficiency later. Tell me, do you find critics of any use?

R: It's silly to say one doesn't read them. I care very much about certain critics: a couple in Berlin. In Germany critics work seriously; they're not trying to show off to the editor. The *Figaro* man is good, too. The French say a picture is bad and then give reasons. They don't say, "Oh, my God, how fat the girl's gotten," or quote a line that's embarrassing (every film has some). I remember a review in New York of Van Druten's *I Am a Camera*; the whole notice read "No Leica."

S: Do you think you've been treated fairly by critics?

R: Yes. Sure. But you see what the trouble with critics is: What they like here, they don't like in Germany; what they don't like in Germany, they like in Japan—which is a far bigger market. I make pictures because they reach an international audience; otherwise, I'd prefer to remain in the theater. I think there are good critics in America. I like Archer Winsten. I like Bosley Crowther. He was unfair to American films, though.

S: What about the *Cahiers du Cinéma* group?

R: I don't know them. But Crowther was a good critic. He would tell how a film could be improved. He loved films! I don't care what a critic says about a picture so long as he loves film, so long as he hates the particular example because he loves film in general. Some journalists write about it without caring.

S: Why have you been so reluctant to be interviewed?

R: I hate it. When I was quite young, my mother loved to read about me in the papers; and when something good was said, I was happy because she was so pleased. But really, you know, I hate publicity. If it's flattering, it's embarrassing; if it's bad, it depresses me.

S: Now to some more specific questions: What do you think of *Midshipman Easy*?

R: It was my first film. As I've said, after it's finished, you don't much care, except that it do well financially, because if there's no money, there's no business for any of us. Do what you want to do, but make sure that people are going to look at it.

S: How did you come to make *Bank Holiday*?

R: On loan to Ted Black.

S: Don't you think the romance in the film is markedly inferior to the comic depictions of mores?

R: You're absolutely right.

The romance and comedy come together when the lovers (Margaret Lockwood and Hugh Williams) find themselves on a crowded beach.

S: Was the opening montage of people leaving on holiday stock, or did you shoot it yourself?

R: We shot it all: Waterloo Station etc.

Leaving from Waterloo in Bank Holiday.

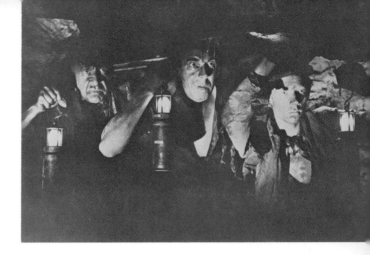

S: Why have you used Margaret Lockwood so often?

R: She was under contract to Ealing when I was a dialogue director there. When I moved to Gainsborough, she also went as a sort of resident ingenue. I thought she was very good.

S: But she's so proper. Even when playing a "bad woman," she never loosens up.

R: It was a matter of image. She was a big star because of the bow in her hair. You see, she made five or six pictures a year, and when the public likes a picture, they always give the actor credit. I remember when I wanted her for *The Stars Look Down*, she, Redgrave, and I all wanted to be released from our contracts in order to do the film. I remember telling Gainsborough how valuable this would be because, as there was nothing for us to do at the time, releasing us would save money. But when they received the script, they said she couldn't play the part; it would ruin her reputation to play a bad woman. There was a big fuss made. I remember, for example, the scene suggesting that she and Emlyn Williams had had an affair, which the production people particularly objected to. By this time Margaret, who had originally been reluctant, read the script and was crazy to do it. "All right," the producers said. "She can, but you must establish that she did *not* have an affair because she's married in the film." I had written a scene where Emlyn comes to her bedroom. It went like this:

"Are you happy?"
"Of course."
"Being married suits you?"
"Why not!"
"You don't care anything more for me?"
"Well, what do you think!!"

At the studio, they were delighted with this, but I directed it with reverse emphasis. [He demonstrates.] Do you see? It was obvious she was responding again. The producers objected when they actually saw the film, but I reminded them that the scene was word for word the one they'd passed.

S: Did you have any polemical intention in making this film?

R: No. I simply took the novel by Cronin; I didn't feel particularly about his subject [nationalization of mines]. One could just as easily make a picture on the opposite side.

S: Why did you include that final commentary about the forthcoming improvement in mining conditions?

R: What?

S: There's a shot of the sky with titles about the indomitable spirit of man.

R: That was never in the picture. It must have been added in America.

S: How were the explosions staged?

R: With models, though I'd been down to several mines for research and some location work was done at the pit head.

S: Why did you turn afterward to *A Girl Must Live*?

R: I liked the book.

S: Did you stage the musical numbers?

R: Yes. They were just tacky routines.

S: Did you want to make a real musical even that early?

R: Not particularly, but when I came upon *Oliver!* I liked the play and the music, though they are perhaps a bit saccharine.

S: You intended *Young Mr. Pitt* as an analogy for the English in World War II, didn't you?

R: Indeed.

S: So here is one instance of a film made polemically. Did you do much research for it?

R: Yes.

S: It's very authentic, but why did you permit such awful model shots?

R: I don't remember.

Setting up a model shot for Young Mr. Pitt.

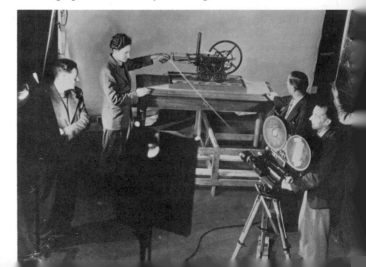

S: What drew you to *Odd Man Out?*

R: I liked the novel and went to Belfast to ask F. L. Green if he'd work on the script. It took only a month to write. We merely took the book and joined certain sections. Green had never worked on a script before. He had a gramophone; he couldn't write unless it was playing. I like the theme of someone who had done something wrong for the right reasons—and the incidental characters.

S: Do you think there's any justice in the charge of sentimentality? I think particularly of the ending, with the lovers dying in each other's arms.

James Mason and Kathleen Ryan in their final moments from Odd Man Out.

R: I had censorship trouble with that. Joe Breen was here on a goodwill tour, sort of instructing our own censorship people. He came to the studio one day and told me that the heroine couldn't shoot James Mason because that would be a murder in order to allow her lover to escape justice. He said, "Look, why not let the police shoot him while he's trying to escape." I agreed, but I got out of it: While the police are following them, she understands that Mason will never make it to the boat, so I had her turn around, fire at the police, and thus cause them to return fire and kill both. Everybody was satisfied. But I made her clearly fire toward the ground. Later, when I saw Breen, he allowed as how I'd done what was required to pass censorship, but he wondered about it. "The revolver didn't seem to be at the right level, don't you think?" "I don't know," I insisted. "I had her fire at the police, just as you suggested."

The censors also objected to Cotten shooting Lime in *The Third Man.* That's why Trevor Howard now shouts from off-camera range, "If you see him, shoot." Cotten isn't killing a friend, you see; he's only following orders.

S: Have you had no experience where yielding to censorship was ruinous?

R: I suppose just once: on *A Girl Must Live.* It was such a little thing! There was a song in which the girl sings "I've got lots of sex appeal." They insisted I cut "sex appeal" but the line had to rhyme with the next one and I had only one take. So I had to scratch the sound track. What you now hear is "I've got lots of———awk———" In 1938!

S: Why did you return to the thriller motif of *The Third Man* in making *The Man Between?*

R: It wasn't a particularly good story, but I liked the atmosphere of Berlin after the war, and I wanted to work again with James Mason. If you haven't got a story after finishing your last picture, a time comes when you say, "Let's take the next best thing that comes along." This was the best I saw at that time. Furthermore, Korda, who was financing films, had the wherewithal for the project. It didn't come out quite right because we were forced back from Berlin before the location work was finished, and we had to match a lot in the studio.

S: Was it a success?

R: It got its money back, but that's all.

S: Why did you suddenly turn to fantasy in *A Kid for Two Farthings*?

R: I loved that book! The film was all right in part and not in others. It cost very little money, but did well.

S: I think the most impressive aspect of *Trapeze* is its use of CinemaScope. Is this opportunity what attracted you to the film?

R: No. I wanted to work with Burt Lancaster, and Hecht-Hill-Lancaster owned this Catto novel, which, in fact, we used very little of in the end. Eventually, we decided the book was hopeless, but we got the idea of this crippled acrobat trying to help a novice learn the business. I'd committed myself before ever seeing the script. The story wasn't very good, but the photography was.

Trapeze made more money than any of my films. It was the simplest subject in the world, with scenes that were almost like musical numbers. It paid for itself in a single country: Japan! It did well everywhere! *Oliver!,* instead, didn't do well in France and very little in Germany. But *Trapeze* did well everywhere.

S: *The Key* was a flop, wasn't it?

R: No, it made profit.

S: Did Foreman, because he produced as well as wrote the film, meddle with you on it?

R: We didn't see eye to eye about certain things. My version was twenty minutes shorter; I didn't cut chunks out: I trimmed everything. But Carl was rather keen on putting things back.

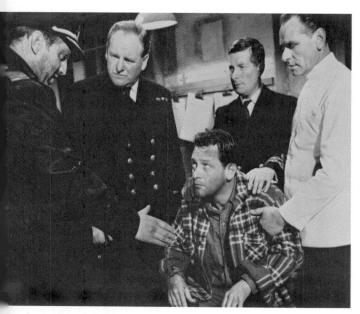

William Holden in The Key.

R: You liked that? It was improvised.

S: The film begins brilliantly, but its moral issues—raised by the deaths caused as a result of Guinness' self-protective plot—never get resolved. Instead, we get caught up in the banal romance between him and Maureen O'Hara.

R: I don't really remember the film.

S: He causes the death of several "spies." The

S: Your best film in this period is *Our Man in Havana.* Why did you and Graham Greene stay apart so long between *The Third Man* and this one?

R: Greene likes to work on his own books, and I liked that one. I would have done *The Comedians,* too, but I was busy at the time. We'll find something together again. Someday.

S: The film is full of good ideas. Whose, for example, is the running visual gag of the long seduction by the muscle man of the floozie?

Alec Guinness and Maureen O'Hara in Our Man in Havana.

film begins as a moral satire and turns into a silly love story.

R: It's really too long ago for me to remember the sequence of events in the story.

S: The period between *Our Man in Havana* and *Flap* is the most unfortunate of your career. It has done terrible damage to your reputation.

R: What?

S: It damaged your reputation.

R: What? *Our Man in Havana*?

S: No, things like *The Running Man*.

R: I don't think that did any damage.

S: You like it?

R: It did well. It didn't cost much.

S: But were you satisfied with it artistically?

R: It wasn't very good.

S: Nor *The Agony and the Ecstasy*.

R: That was supposed to have been much bigger. Darryl Zanuck had trouble with Twentieth Century-Fox then, so the budget was cut. We were prepared for big action sequences, and all we had in the end was the Sistine Chapel.

S: Can you tell me anything about your latest film, *The Public Eye?*

R: It's a light comedy; very very slight; I think it's amusing, and Mia Farrow's very good in it. And Topol. It's just a simple story. We shot the whole thing in eight weeks. Very few pictures are going longer now. I had nothing on my plate when Hal Wallis offered this. That's the value of producers. As an independent, from finding the story, to finding the money, to casting, you've spent two years before you can start shooting. If you like making pictures, you've got to go from one to the other—within reason. It's like being a boxer—there's no good just sitting down.

Michelangelo (Charlton Heston) and the Pope (Rex Harrison) peering up at the Sistine Fresco.

Ingmar Bergman

Stockholm, November 10, 1971

Feature Films: 1945 *Kris* (*Crisis*); 1946 *Det regnar på vår kärlek* (*It Rains on Our Love*); 1947 *Skepp till Indialand* (*Ship to India*), *Musik i mörker* (*Night Is My Future*); 1948 *Hamnstad* (*Port of Call*); 1949 *Fängelse* (*Prison*), *Törst* (*Three Strange Loves*), *Till glädje* (*To Joy*); 1950 *Sånt Händer inte Här* (*High Tension*), *Sommarlek* (*Summer Interlude*); 1952 *Kvinnors väntan* (*Secrets of Women*), *Sommaren med Monika* (*Monika*); 1953 *Gycklarnas afton* (*The Naked Night*); 1954 *En lektion i kärlek* (*A Lesson in Love*); 1955 *Kvinnodröm* (*Dreams*), ·*Sommarnattens leende* (*Smiles of a Summer Night*); 1956 *Det Sjunde Inseglet* (*The Seventh Seal*); 1957 *Smultronstället* (*Wild Strawberries*), *Nära livet* (*Brink of Life*); 1958 *Ansiktet* (*The Magician*); 1959 *Jungfrukällan* (*The Virgin Spring*); 1960 *Djävulens öga* (*The Devil's Eye*); 1961 *Såsom i en spegel* (*Through a Glass Darkly*); 1962 *Nattvardsgästerna* (*Winter Light*); 1963 *Tystnaden* (*The Silence*); 1964 *För att inte tala om alla dessa kvinnor* (*Now About All These Women*); 1966 *Persona*; 1968 *Vargtimmen* (*Hour of the Wolf*), *Skammen* (*Shame*); 1969 *En Passion* (*The Passion of Anna*), *The Rite*; 1971 *The Touch*; 1972 *Viskningar och rod* (*Whisperings and Cries*).

Aware that Ingmar Bergman is resolutely prompt and also that he would give me not a moment more than the three and one-half hours to which he had agreed, I arrived somewhat early at the Royal Dramatic Theater, where he had vacated his leadership but not a small office. Into this office, after a walk through seemingly endless corridors, I was ushered by a polite secretary who told me that Mr. Bergman would shortly arrive. While I waited, I examined the room, although one needed less time for that operation than I was granted.

Bergman's office is nearly as cold as the church in *Winter Light*, but here the austerity is secular and impersonal, rather than menacing. Moreover, the bare white walls are made radiant by light streaming in from the square and nearby seascape, which also bring in the noise of human bustle that served as background for our talk.

The room contains a pallet couch, fronted by a low coffee table (today offering two bottles of mineral water and a box of Droste chocolate), and a comfortable black leather chair, which Bergman first used but which he eventually gave up for the more rigid one that stands near the most important item of furniture: his desk. A color drawing of the theater hangs over the nearly empty bookcase (works by Strindberg, *Fellini Satyricon*, Lenny Bruce's *How to Talk Dirty and Influence People*, and a few others). The sole remaining ornament, also above the bookcase, is a child's toy: a stuffed red ant.

A few minutes after nine, Bergman strides in with hand extended. He seems uninterested in further introductions, but I am pleased that we can get down to business. During our talk, I am constantly amazed by the variety of expression that passes over his inherently bland face. This variety can no more be captured than the beautiful modulation of his voice, but both are so crucial to our encounter that I have departed from my usual methods in attempting to catch something of its manner, as well as our words.

From the beginning, I interrupted Bergman's sentences, sometimes completing them, sometimes anticipating a response that made me impatient to react. As the interview progressed, this became more frequent, and he also began to interrupt me. I have therefore reproduced nearly all the interruptions, whether of one man by the other or of one man by himself—I have also indicated (how I wish I could actually reproduce) some of the laughter with which Bergman increasingly punctuated the proceedings. For the man is passionate without being dour.

Although I have tried especially hard to capture much of the actuality of this interview, I have, as always, rewritten the text for readability. Bergman's heavily accented English, though very good, frequently falls into error when his mind outpaces his ease in the language. I saw no point in reproducing such errors, but one of them deserves remark. Whereas, midway in our talk, I put the word "tumultuous" in his mouth, what he actually said was "tumultarious," a portmanteau word, accidentally invented, that nonetheless perfectly describes a talk both "tumultuous" and "multifarious" in its concerns.

"Tumultariousness" is obviously meat and drink to Bergman. Even though our conversation absorbed him so that he inadvertently let it run an extra five minutes—thus, as frantic phone calls made clear, disarranging the meticulous schedule that is his daily regimen—when he escorted or rather trotted me to the elevator, he observed, with a broad and affectionate smile, "I think we had *such* a good talk, don't you?" Not only attending to film and theater business, he was in town that day, as I later learned, to make arrangements for his fifth wedding, which was to take place during the week.

SAMUELS: Mr. Bergman, I'd like to start with a rather general question: If I were asked to cite a single reason for your preeminence among film directors, I would point to your creation of a special world—the sort of thing we are accustomed to with great creative figures in the other arts, but rarely in film, and never to your degree. You are, in fact, very much like a writer. Why didn't you become one?

BERGMAN: When I was a child, I suffered from an almost complete lack of words. My education was very rigid; my father was a priest. As a result, I lived in a private world of my own dreams. I played with my puppet theater.

S: And—

B: Excuse me. I had very few contacts with reality or channels to it. I was afraid of my father, my mother, my elder brother—everything. Playing with this puppet theater and a projection device I had was my only form of self-expression. I had great difficulty with fiction and reality; as a small child I mixed them so much that my family always said I was a liar. Even when I grew up, I

felt blocked. I had enormous difficulty speaking to others and—

S: I want to interrupt you for just a moment. This description of your childhood resembles one classic description of the genesis of a writer. Was it only the accident of the puppet theater that sent you the way of theater rather than of books?

B: No. I remember that during my eighteenth summer, when I had just finished school, suddenly I wrote a novel. And in school, when we had to write compositions, I liked it very much. But I never felt that writing was my cup of tea. I put the novel in my desk and forgot it. But in 1940, suddenly—in the summer—I started writing and wrote twelve—

S: Plays.

B: Yes. It was a sudden eruption.

S: May I offer an hypothesis about this so that you can react to it? Your skill as a writer and your need to express yourself in words are fulfilled more in the theater and cinema because in these arts one also embodies his words and even sees the audience's response to them.

B: My beginning was otherwise, because when I began writing, I was suspicious of words. And I always lacked words; it has always been very difficult for me to find the word I want.

S: Is this suspicion of words one of the reasons why Alma makes Elisabeth say "nothing" in *Persona*?

B: No. Yes. In a way. But that wasn't conscious on my part.

S: Because "nothing" is the truest word, one that asserts least.

B: I don't know. I have always felt suspicious both of what I say and of what others say to me. Always I feel something has been left out. When I read a book, I read very slowly. It takes a lot of time for me to read a play.

S: Do you direct it in your head?

B: In a way. I have to translate the words into speeches, movements, flesh and blood. I have an enormous need for contact with an audience, with other people. For me, words are not satisfying.

S: With a book, the reader is elsewhere.

B: When you read, words have to pass through your conscious mind to reach your emotions and your soul. In film and theater, things go directly to the emotions. What I need is to come in contact with others.

S: I see that, but it raises a problem I'm sure

you've often discussed. Your films have emotional impact, but since they are also the most intellectually difficult of contemporary films, isn't there sometimes a contradiction between the two effects? Let me give you a specific example. How do you react when I say that while I watched *The Rite*, my feelings were interfered with by my baffled effort at comprehension?

B: Your approach is wrong. I never asked you to understand; I ask only that you feel.

S: You haven't asked me anything. I don't see you; I only see the film.

B: Yes, but—

S: And the film asks me to understand. Here are three performers under investigation for a spectacle that the authorities find obscene. The film continuously makes us wonder what the spectacle means, why the authorities want to suppress it, etc. These questions sit next to me. More and more, I feel them grab me by the throat—better, the head—so that I can't feel anything but puzzlement.

B: But that's you.

S: It's not the film?

B: No. *The Rite* merely expresses my resentment against the critics, audience, and government, with which I was in constant battle while I ran the [Royal Dramatic] theater. A year after my resignation from the post, I sat down and wrote this script in five days. I did it merely to free myself.

S: But then—

B: Excuse please. The picture is just a game, a way of kicking everyone's—not understanding—intellectual—

S: To puzzle the audience?

B: Exactly. I liked very much to write it and even more to make it. We had a lot of fun while we were shooting. My purpose was just to amuse myself and the audience which liked it. Do you understand what I mean?

S: I understand but—

B: You must realize—this is very important!—I never ask people to understand what I have made. Stravinsky once said, "I have never understood a piece of music in my life. I always only feel."

S: But Stravinsky was a composer. By its nature, music is nondiscursive; we don't have to understand it. Films, plays, poems, novels all make propositions or observations, embody ideas or beliefs, and we go to these forms—

B: But you must understand that you are perverted. You belong to a small minority that tries to understand. Ordinary people—and me, too. . . . Look, I have exactly the same feeling when I see a play. It is as if I were hearing a string quartet by Bartok. I never try to understand. I, too, am a little perverted, so I, too, on one level, control myself. Because I am a man of the theater, a professional, and this can—

S: Destroy spontaneous response?

B: Exactly. But it never does, because I feel that especially film. . . . You know, they always talk about Brecht's being so intellectual.

S: Whereas he's very emotional.

B: Yes. His own comments and those of his commentators come between us and the plays. Music, films, plays always work directly on the emotions.

S: I must disagree. My two favorites among your films—though there are about ten that I think excellent—are *Persona* and *Winter Light*. Each of these films works as you say a film should, but neither is like *The Rite*. I'd therefore like to compare them so as to explore the problem of a film that is too puzzling to be evocative. Let me start with *Winter Light*, which I think your purest film. By the way, do you like it?

B: Yes.

S: Although the film raises questions about what the hero thinks and about what he and his mistress represent as different ways of life, the drama is so compelling, the images so powerful that we don't sit there—I didn't sit there, perverted though I am—and say, "What does this mean?" I was caught. *Winter Light* typifies one of the ways you are at your best; in it, the audience's concern for the fate of the characters is more intense than any puzzlement about their significance. Do you see what I mean?

B: Yes. But I think you are wrong.

S: Why?

B: Because . . . because . . . when you say, "I like *Winter Light* and *Persona*, and I think these are two of the best you have made," then you say "we," and then you confuse "I" and "we," and you make generalizations, whereas for everyone, *Persona* and *Winter Light* are, I think, my most difficult pictures. So it is impossible for you to take this point of view.

S: I'll stop mixing "I" and "we"—

B: I must tell you, I must tell you before we go onto more complicated things: I make my pictures for use! They are not made *sub specie aeternitatis*; they are made for now and for use. They are like a table, or mineral water, or a flower, or a lamp, or anything that is made for someone who wants to use it. Also, they are made to put me in contact with other human beings, to whom I give them and say, "Please use them. Take what you want and throw the rest away. I will come back and make other new and beautiful things. If this was not successful, it doesn't matter." My impulse has nothing to do with intellect or symbolism; it has only to do with dreams and longing, with hope and desire, with passion. Do you understand what I mean? So when you say that a film of mine is intellectually complicated, I have the feeling that you don't talk about one of my pictures. Let us talk about the pictures, not as one of the best, or the most disgusting, or one of the stinking ones; let us talk about attempts to come in contact with other people.

S: I'm afraid I didn't make myself clear. We started with *The Rite*, and I said, "This is a film that I think. . . ."

B: I'm not interested in what you think! If you like, ask me questions! But I'm not interested in hearing what you think!

S: I'm not trying to tell you what I like or dislike for the purpose of giving you my opinion but for the purpose of raising questions. I won't say "I" anymore. Let's name a man X; I'll ask you about what X might want to know. Let's say that while watching *The Rite*, X isn't as emotionally—

B: No! It's clear! This is completely uninteresting! *The Rite* has been seen by millions of people who think. . . . It's completely uninteresting if one doesn't like. . . . You know, I live on a small island. The day after *The Rite* was shown on Swedish television, a man came to me on the ferryboat going to the island and said, "It was a nice play. Don't you think it was a nice play? My wife and I, we laughed and laughed, and we had a tremendous evening together." I was completely confused; as we would judge it, he had completely misunderstood the play. But he enjoyed himself! Perhaps he had been drunk; perhaps he had gone to bed with the old girl; perhaps he was being ironic. But he enjoyed coming to me and saying it was nice. Do you understand? So we must find some way of communicating. It's very important. If we continue this way, we will get nothing. We must find some sort of human communication, because if

we don't, you only make me irritated and I just want to finish. You know, I can sit down here and discuss everything in an intellectual way. I can say the most astonishing things because I am perfect at giving interviews. But I think we could find another way—do you understand—a sort of human—

S: Haven't you noticed that I've ignored all my prepared questions?

B: Yes.

S: I have been trying to respond to what you say as you say it. I have been trying to communicate. Please, by all means, tell me when I seem to be going astray. But, my God, Mr. Bergman, I've told you. . . . Look, I have a job: interviewing and writing about you. You've done the most important job already: You've made the films. But despite what you've said, I think there are people who would like help in understanding your films. I want, to the best of my abilities, with whatever aid you'll give me, to work for those people.

B: Of course. I understand very well that you're trying to reach contact, but this way you've started will only keep us sitting like two puppets discussing absolute nonsense—to me, it is completely uninteresting and, to everybody, completely uninteresting. Please let's try—

S: Let me suggest two alternatives, and you say which you'd prefer.

B: No! Go on!

S: No! I want to make human contact also. Here are the two ways: A few moments ago, you said you met this man who liked *The Rite*, yet you were surprised because—

B: He didn't say he liked it; he said he had a nice evening. Perhaps he was being ironic. But I liked his way of approaching, you know. . . . It was sort of. . . . He used my play. He used it.

S: Wouldn't you care to know why he found it useful?

B: That is irrelevant. He used it! Why and how people use are interesting to hear—as with *The Touch*, which got extreme responses: People either liked it or hated it. I like to hear about *The Touch* because it was not the picture I intended to make—for many reasons—especially the actors. You know that actors often change a film, for better or worse.

S: May I ask you how the film differs from the one you intended?

up, light, warm, gay. Suddenly, there is a jump cut to a long shot of her alone, drinking coffee, in an utterly quiet, utterly empty kitchen. This is a case in which the clarity of the surroundings immediately makes us understand her. Now we know why she goes to David.

B: I think this scene is mine, because the film was made about a woman I actually know. This transition from warmth to complete loneliness is typical of her whole life—and of every woman's life. That is why every woman laughs while watching that part of the film.

S: Do you ever do more than change a film for one of your actresses? Do you ever actually conceive of one to give her a chance to change? Let me give you an example. In *The Naked Night* Harriet Andersson plays a woman who epitomizes the power of sex. Then the next film

you made, *A Lesson in Love*, casts her in the role of a tomboy who is afraid of sex. Did you make the later film at all to reverse her performance in *The Naked Night?*

B: I intended to paint the portrait of an ordinary woman, in which everything around her would be a reflection. I wanted her in close-up and the surroundings clear only when near her. I wanted the portrait to be very detailed and very lovely and true. But when I joined the actors, they liked the plot more than I did, and I think they seduced me away from my original plan. I can't say if the result is better or worse, but it is different. Bibi Andersson is a close friend of mine—a lovely and extremely talented actress. She is totally oriented toward reality, always needing motives for what she does. She is a warm, fantastic woman. To her, everything is important, so she asked that what I wanted out of focus or shadowed be made utterly clear. I'm not criticizing her; I admire and love her. But she changed the film. When I give an actor a part, I always hope that he will join in the creating by adding something I didn't intend. We collaborate. What Bibi Andersson did made the film more comprehensible for common people and more immediately powerful. I agreed with all her changes.

S: May I ask about a moment in the film that—I think—is very good? It sounds, from what you say, as if Bibi Andersson was behind it. Karin is giving breakfast to her family; everything is close-

B: I know my actors well. We all are closely involved with each other. I know how many parts each carries within him. One day I write one of the parts the actor can play but never has. Sometimes the actors themselves don't know that they can play it. But without actually telling me, they show me the parts they contain.

S: So it is possible for you to write a script because you realize that a particular actress is now ready to play a particular part.

B: Exactly. It's fantastic to be surrounded by so many actors, by so many unwritten parts. All the time the actors are giving you material; through their faces, through their movements, their inflections.

S: Do you sometimes reverse not only the actor but a whole film in the next one you make?

B: I think only a little bit in the relationship between *Through a Glass Darkly* and *Winter Light.*

S: Yes, that's a very interesting case. At the end of *Through a Glass Darkly,* Björnstrand communicates with his son, who had been longing for such an occurrence. The next year we go back to the movie house, and there is Björnstrand playing, in a sense, his own son, only now more

desperately in search of communication with a father (God), who will not or cannot answer him.

B: I think that is fascinating, but I never had it in mind. You are right, but what you say astonishes me.

S: I'm not crazy?

B: No. No. No. You are completely right.

S: If you don't mind then, I'd like to get back to *Winter Light.* I want to ask you—ask you—something to see if I'm right. Isn't it true that whereas you are frequently concerned with the impossibility of attaining corroboration for one's faith, in *Winter Light* you show that the search for corroboration is itself the cause of harm?

B: All the time that I treated the questions of God and ultimate faith, I felt very unhappy. When I left them behind, and also abandoned my enormous desire to make the best film in the world—

S: To be God.

B: Yes . . . to . . . to—

S: Make the perfect creation.

B: Yes. To make the perfect creation. As soon as I said, here are my limits, which I see very clearly and which I will not jump over but only try to open up—technically—then I became un-neurotic—

S: Like a research scientist?

B: Yes.

S: Isn't that how the drama operates in *Persona*? After the credit sequence, the film begins realistically. There is a woman in a hospital, suffering a sort of catatonic withdrawal. She is tended by a nurse. Then, as the film progresses, this realistic drama starts to break from inside (at one moment, the film itself shatters). Is it true that like a research scientist, you were investigating in *Persona* the limits that exist for an artist who wants his imitation of reality to be as true and as complex as reality itself? Don't you say, "Therefore, I will show where the limits are by declaring the artificialities that are my art and by showing them break down or break open at the point where they come closest to touching the truth?"

B: That's very interesting, but it's not what I intended. It's very simple: *Persona* is a creation that saved its creator. Before making it, I was ill, having twice had pneumonia and antibiotic poisoning. I lost my balance for three months. The summer before, I had written a script, but I told everyone it would be canceled because it was a complicated picture and I didn't feel up to it. I was going to Hamburg then to stage *The Magic Flute*, and I had to cancel that, too. I remember sitting in my hospital bed, looking directly in front of me at a black spot—because if I turned my head at all, the whole room began to spin. I thought to myself that I would never create anything anymore; I was completely empty, almost dead. The montage at the beginning of the film is just a poem about that personal situation.

S: With cuts from earlier Bergman films.

B: Because whenever I thought about making a new film, silly pictures from my old ones came into my head. Suddenly, one day I started thinking of two women sitting next to each other and comparing hands. This was a single scene, which, after an enormous effort, I was able to write down. Then, I thought that if I could make a very small picture—perhaps in 16 mm—about two women, one talking, the other not (thus an enormous monologue), it would not be too hard for me. Every day I wrote a little bit. I had as yet

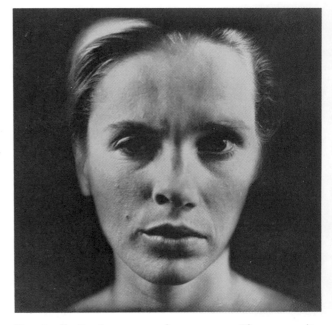

Eventually the two women become one. The composite face of Bibi Andersson and Liv Ullmann.

no idea about making a regular film, because I was so sick, but I trained myself for it. Each morning at ten I moved from the bed to the writing table, sat down, and sometimes wrote and at other times couldn't. After I left the hospital, I went to the seaside, where I finished the script, although I was still sick. Nevertheless, we decided to go ahead. The producer was very, very understanding. He kept telling me to go on, that we could throw it away if it was bad because it wasn't an expensive project. In the middle of July I started shooting, still so sick that when I stood up I became dizzy. Throughout the first week the results were terrible.

S: What did you shoot that week?

B: We started with the first scene in the hospital.

S: But not with the precredit sequence?

B: No, that came afterward. I wanted to give things up, but the producer kept encouraging me, finally telling me to move the company to my island. When we got there, slowly things picked up. The actresses and Sven Nykvist were fantastic; it was a fantastic collaboration. One day we made a scene that we all felt was good. That gave me courage. Then the next day, another scene; then many scenes. It grew, and we began to reshoot what hadn't worked. Exactly what happened and why it happened I don't know.

S: Here's a film you make immediately after thinking you'll never make another film again. You come back to life as an artist, step by step, growing in courage until you can face—utterly without fear—the problems, absurdities, and impossibilities of art itself. And you select as a surrogate an artist who suffers what you suffered, except that Elisabeth *wills* it; she chooses to stop being an artist.

B: Yes, because she is not sick.

S: Let me get at my point another way. When Elisabeth looks at television and sees a Buddhist monk immolating himself in Vietnam, several critics wanted to take this as an uncharacteristic expression of your interest in politics. But I think it must be related to the later scene—in her bedroom—when she studies the Cartier-Bresson photograph of the Jews being led out of the Warsaw ghetto. Both scenes dramatize the awe inspired in the artist when he faces true suffering—which, however, cannot escape some involvement with art, since both the monk and the Jews reach our consciousness through the art of the photographer.

B: Let me explain exactly what I tried to express in the first scene. The monk scares her because his conviction is so enormous he is willing to die for it. The photograph represents real suffering.

S: But it is, paradoxically, also art. And I find it suggestive that during the great scene in *Shame* when you show the people being herded in and out of buildings by the soldiers, you yourself recall the composition of Cartier-Bresson's great photograph. Didn't you feel the recollection?

B: In a way, yes. But I never thought of it. The scene you mention represents humiliation, which is the subject of *Shame*. The film isn't about enormous brutality, but only meanness. It is exactly like what has happened to the Czechs. They defended their rights, and now, slowly, they are being submitted to a tactic of brutalization that wears them down. *Shame* is not about the bombs; it is about the gradual infiltration of fear.

S: So that the low budget and consequent lack

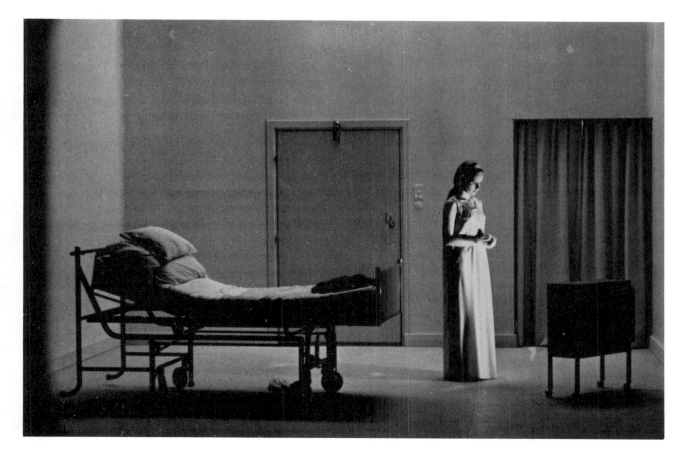

of large war scenes precisely reflect your theme.

B: Yes, but *Shame* is not precise enough. My original idea was to show only a single day before the war had broken out. But then I wrote things, and it all went wrong—I don't know why. I haven't seen *Shame* recently, and I'm a little afraid to do so. When you make such a picture, you have to be very hard on yourself. It's a moral question.

S: Why?

B: Certain things in life are impossible to represent—like a concentration camp.

S: Because the reality is too terrible?

B: Exactly. It is almost the same with war as with murder or death. You must be a hundred percent morally conscious in treating these things.

S: You must not simply shock.

B: Exactly. To see someone dying is false—

S: When we know he will get up after the performance.

B: In the theater it's not so bad because we accept all these conventions, but film is different.

S: Still, you are more successful in *Shame* than you acknowledge. for example, I think that the interview scene creates the horror of war without any false killings. Who are these soldiers? What do they want? How dare they televise their brutalization? How dare they humiliate other human beings in this way: *Life* goes to the end of Western civilization? [Bergman laughs heartily.] Where did you get the idea for this scene?

B: I don't know.

S: It was in the script? You didn't improvise?

B: It was in the script.

S: Do you improvise much at other times?

B: No. I improvise only when I have a plan. Improvising for itself is impossible.

S: Didn't you improvise the interviews with the actors in *The Passion of Anna?*

B: I'm sorry to say that those are very unsuccessful. I just wanted to have a break in the film and to let the actors express themselves. Bibi Andersson and Liv Ullman improvised their interviews, but Max von Sydow and Erland Josephson had no idea what to say, so they said what I told them to. This led to two different films, and I no longer understand why I left the whole batch in, because I always realized that they

wouldn't work. But I like *coups de theatre*, things that make people wake up and rejoin the film. This time, however, it wasn't successful.

S: There are no *coups* in *Winter Light*; the rhythm is even. I want to ask another question about that film. When Von Sydow's drowned body is discovered, why is the shot so distant?

B: Because I always feel that something is more terrifying at a distance. Thus, in *Shame*, when Max shoots Björnstrand, we are far away, and I place the crime behind a wagon.

S: But we are close to Elisabeth when she sucks Alma's blood in *Persona*.

B: Because that isn't real.

S: It's an expression of their relationship rather than an event?

B: Exactly. It's not meant to be terrifying.

S: This brings me to a more general area. Do you exercise total control over camera placement and editing?

B: Yes. When I shoot, I know almost exactly how long a scene will take because I have a sort of rhythm inside that I try to re-create.

S: Do you ever shoot out of sequence, knowing how things will be put together?

B: I only do that when contingencies make it necessary. I always try to start at the beginning, shoot forward, and then reshoot later. I always reshoot the first days' work.

S: There are several possible explanations for Elisabeth's refusal to speak in *Persona*. It is an act of great honesty; since she only imitates the real suffering in the world, she decides not to get onstage night after night and mock reality with her stage grief. It is also an act of aggression against other people; her silence renders them helpless.

B: It is as the doctor in the films says, "Silence too is a role." Elisabeth lacks a sense of humor. Anyone who works in this profession must keep from taking the theater too seriously; it is all a game.

S: Is that why you call *The Magician* a comedy?

B: Yes.

S: Because it is about the game of being an artist?

B: We artists represent the most serious things—life and death—but it is all a game.

S: In *Persona*, why do you repeat the scene when Alma analyzes Elisabeth once with Alma on

Elisabeth stops acting during a performance of Electra.

camera and again with Elisabeth on camera, reacting?

B: Because both actresses are wonderful. First, I cut it in reverse shots, but I felt that something was missing. I felt that a whole dimension was added by repeating the scene with the other woman on camera.

S: Why does Alma break down and speak nonsense syllables before she leaves the island?

B: She has been driven nearly insane by her resentments so that words, which are no longer useful, can no longer be put together by her. But it is not a matter of psychology. Rather, this comes at the point inside the movement of the film itself where words can no longer have any meaning.

S: Do you think that Elisabeth deliberately sent Alma off with the letter [in which she discusses how she is using the nurse] in order that the girl may read it?

B: I never thought about that. Perhaps.

S: Something like that happens often in your films. In *Through a Glass Darkly*, for example, Karin learns how her father has been studying her when she finds his diary. In *The Passion of Anna*, Andreas learns about Anna's lie by finding the letter she left in her purse. Etc. Many of your characters leave evidence about themselves for the very person who must not see it.

B: Letters and diaries are very tempting. I'm extremely, passionately interested in human beings. Anything written or left behind tempts me so much that I'd read it if I could. When my mother died—four years ago—we discovered a diary that we had not known she was keeping daily since 1916! It was a fantastic act to read it because she wrote in a microscopically small script, with many abbreviations. But suddenly we discovered an unknown woman—intelligent, impatient, furious, rebellious—who had lived under this disciplined perfect housewife.

S: I wouldn't dare to discuss your mother, but the characters in your films who leave evidence behind may, in a sense, be lying. After all, you yourself admit that words must arouse suspicion; the self we write about is an artistic construction.

B: Words . . . are . . . always . . . difficult. Now we're back to the beginning. The musician writes notes on a score, which are the most perfect signs that exist between creator and performer. But words are a very very bad channel between writer and performer.

S: And audience.

B: Yes, so I'm always suspicious of words.

S: Interesting fact, though: You use music less and less in your films. Why?

B: Because I think that film itself is music, and I can't put music in music.

S: Why did it take you so long to discover that?

B: Because I've been ambivalent.

S: In *The Touch* isn't the buzz saw that we hear when Karin comes to David's apartment and finds him gone your new way to use music?

B: I think everything on the sound track must complement the image—voices, noises, music; all are equal. Sometimes I feel very unhappy because I have still not found the solution to the problem of sound.

S: Isn't it true, however, that you use commentative sound more frequently now than in your earlier films?

B: Yes, it's true.

S: Another good example of this new use of the sound track is the fog horn in *Persona* that signals a movement out of the real world. One last question about that film: When Alma leaves, you hold for a moment on the wooden statue of a woman which we see again in *Shame*, *The Passion of Anna*, and *The Touch*. Why?

B: It's the figurehead from a ship. On the island where I live, I have her outside my house. She's a friend of mine, and I like her because she is made of hardwood. She represents something to me, for personal reasons.

S: How do you respond to the viewer who has caught such personal references—the reappearing figurehead, all the Voglers and An-

Andreas and the figurehead. The Passion of Anna.

dreases, the discovered diaries and letters, the personal fear of birds that creates the climax of *Hour of the Wolf* but must be invoked even to explain small moments (like the bird dashing itself against the window in *The Passion of Anna*)? What do you say to the person who keeps seeing these things but doesn't understand their significance? Bergman is sending messages, he thinks, but what are they and why?

B: Perhaps these things that mean so much to me also mean something to someone else.

S: You have no specific intention in repeating them?

B: No.

S: But do you see what this does to a spectator who follows you as if you were a writer? This problem has been brought on you by your own genius for creating a unique world that others wish to chart. And it's not a playful world either, like Truffaut's, with all his joking references to favorite directors and his playful casting of friends in minor roles. You don't joke in that way; even in your lightest comedy, the spectator never doubts that serious and typical issues are involved. Your admirers want to understand the layout of your world, to know the names and properties and even the importance of all these lakes, islands, rocks. What advice do you give us?

B: It's irrelevant. All these things are dreams—not necessarily ones that I have dreamed; rather fantasies. When you are dreaming. . . . Perhaps you remember your dreams?

S: Hardly ever.

B: But you know that you dream?

S: Of course. Otherwise I wouldn't sleep.

B: If you didn't dream, you would go mad.

S: Yes.

B: Every night you enter a world of people, colors, furniture, islands, lakes, landscapes, buildings—everything—that belongs to you alone. But if you remember your dreams and start telling them to other people, then maybe the other people will start to know you better.

S: Then it doesn't bother you when critics interpret you through these items?

B: Not at all. Not at all. And let me tell you, I learn more from critics who honestly criticize my pictures than from those who are devout.

S: Why then, very early in our interview, did you insist, "I don't care what you think"?

B: Because I had the feeling that we started with you trying to stress yourself. . . .

S: To make myself the subject of the interview?

B: No. You were so hidden. . . . I saw you had prepared very well, and you remained locked in your preparation. You knew we had little time; you wanted to start in a hurry. So you began to talk to me in a way that was very hard for me to understand. Then I just said anything to break through. Now I think we are in perfect communication. Perhaps our discussion is a little tumultuous, but I like it that way. Now we sit down as two human beings, discussing things in a simple way. When I was impolite and said, "I don't care what you think," I meant it—because all the people who are important to me. . . . Buñuel once said a wonderful thing: "I make pictures only for my friends." And they influence me. They interfere, and I listen to them, and they help me change things. But, you know, I hate the intellectual way of handling things that are very sensual, very personal to me. Do you understand what I mean? So I just said anything that would cut us down to a level where we could communicate. I myself can't say that *Persona* is my best picture. . . . Ten times a month people ask me, "Which is your best picture?" but that is irrelevant to me because some of my pictures are closer to my heart than others. When we meet

and you say, "This is good, and this is bad," I can't stand it, but if you say, "This is closer to my heart; I feel this; I don't feel that," then I can understand you.

S: Then we go on—to the other pictures. *Night Is My Future* is the first film you directed from someone else's script and novel. When you direct in that way, does it feel different from directing your own script?

B: Yes, in a way, but I'm used to it because in the theater I'm always directing other people's scripts. Of course, I like it more in the theater because that is my profession. In films, it's more difficult.

S: When you make such a film, under conditions that come close to stage directing, are you therefore freed for more experimentation with cinematic devices? For example, the opening scene in *Night Is My Future*, in which the hero is blinded during target practice, seems more cinematic than most things in your previous films.

B: The producer cut that whole sequence to pieces. When I made that picture, I would have accepted an offer to film the telephone book. I was a flop from the beginning. Then a very clever producer came to me and said, "Ingmar, you are a flop. Here's a very sentimental story that will appeal to the public. You need a box-office success now." I replied, "I will lick your ass if you like; only let me make a picture." So I made the picture, and I'm extremely grateful to him—he later let me make *Prison*. Every day he came to the studio and told me, "No. Reshoot. This is too difficult, incomprehensible. You are crazy! She must be beautiful! You must have more light on her hair! You must have some cats in the film! Perhaps you can find some little dog." The picture was a great success. He taught me—in a very tough way—much that saved me. I will be grateful to him till my dying day.

S: He saved you from not communicating directly to the audience?

B: Yes. Yes. I was so frightened of the audience that I couldn't communicate.

S: Your next film, *Three Strange Loves*, contains a scene of childbirth. Such a scene recurs often in your films. Why?

B: I have nine children!

S: I have two, both of them sick now—unfortunately.

B: Yes? How?

S: A mysterious ailment. It began with my wife, stayed briefly with my elder daughter, and now my youngest has it most violently. Do you know what hives are? Red weltlike marks that appear on the skin. We now think we may know the cause. We've just built a new house, and the doctor thinks—this is weird!—that a chemical reaction has been set off between the vinyl asbestos tile and the concrete basement floor that somehow causes the emission of a thin gas to which they're all allergic.

B: That is terrible! Your wife is allergic, too?

S: My poor wife is working now for the first time in ten years, and just now she has to cope with the children's illnesses and her own and with getting someone to help out, since I'm not home. Every night the baby wakes up several times, yet my wife must go to work the next morning even though she hasn't slept.

B: It's terrible! Terrible!

S: In *Three Strange Loves*—

B: It started when you moved into the house?

S: No. That would be easy. It started eight months later. Maybe the chemical reaction took that long.

B: Have you tried a temporary move?

S: When she visited her parents in New York, it didn't improve. It's now systemic.

B: It sounds like an allergy that you can be vaccinated against.

S: Allergists can't do that unless they're certain of the cause.

B: Wouldn't sun and sea help?

S: We were in Cape Cod this summer, but it didn't help. We need to see a specialist. Mr. Bergman—

B: What torture! This is torture!

S: It's the uncertainty, more even than the disease itself. Mr. Bergman, in—

B: How did your wife react when the disease began?

S: She itched. But the medicine controls that. Mostly, she's upset for the children.

B: All of them are suffering now?

S: Except for the older child, who only had it two weeks. I didn't get it at all.

B: But your wife has it still?

S: Yes, but the medicine controls it.

B: Does the medicine make her tired?

S: No. But if she stops taking it, the hives return.

B: What is it called?

S: The medicine? Atarax.

B: Calcium or—

S: I don't really know the chemical composition.

B: It's very strange. You know, the relation between a small girl and her mother can be very strange and difficult. If the mother has a pain in the stomach, very often the child will feel the same pain for psychological reasons.

S: I don't believe in doctors, but—

B: Nor I.

S: But they say it's physical and, in this case, I think they're right.

B: The medicine doesn't help your daughter?

S: Only a little.

B: She itches?

S: Yes. And she comes to sleep with us in the middle of the night because she's wakened by it.

B: Terrible!

S: And she's such a good little girl that she feels guilty for spoiling our sleep.

B: Very difficult! It is—

S: Mr. Bergman, why did you make personal appearances in *Three Strange Loves* and in *Secrets of Women*?

B: Lack of extras! [Laughter.]

S: You were saving money?

B: Yes. [Laughter.]

S: Why did you decide at this particular point in your career to make so stylized a comedy as *Smiles of a Summer Night*?

B: I thought it was time for a box-office success, and although everyone disagreed with me, I was convinced that this picture would succeed. Moreover, I have always liked the *pièce bien fait* (Marivaux and Scribe) with its strategical plot construction. In a way, this film is just a play that I desired to write. I hadn't the money to produce it, so I got someone to let me make it into a film.

S: In fact, some people have criticized your films for being too theatrical—particularly the early ones. How do you answer this charge?

B: I am a director.

S: But aren't the two forms different?

B: Completely. In my earlier pictures, it was very difficult for me to go from directing in the theater to directing films. I didn't succeed in making the change. But this is not important.

S: Apropos, is that why you use a narrator in your first film, *Crisis*, and a sort of stage manager who addresses the audience and asks us to use

Two of the first typically Bergmanesque images. Summer Interlude.

our imaginations—unnecessarily, since cinema shows all it wants to—in your second film, *It Rains on Our Love?*

B: Yes. Until *Summer Interlude*. . . . I don't know how many pictures I had made before it—

S: Nine.

B: Nine. Well, I had always felt technically crippled—insecure with the crew, the cameras, the sound equipment—everything. Sometimes a film succeeded, but I never got what I wanted to get. But in *Summer Interlude*, I suddenly felt that I knew my profession.

S: Do you have any idea why?

B: I don't know, but for heaven's sake, a day must always come along when finally one succeeds in understanding his profession! I'm so impressed by young directors now who know how to make a film from the first moment.

S: But they have nothing to say. [Bergman laughs.] Still, I'm very interested in why—and I agree that it is—*Summer Interlude* is a turning point. Might the breakthrough, which you perceive as technical, be related to content? Because this seems to me your first film to achieve true complexity. At the end of *To Joy* the conductor tells the hero, who has just suffered the loss of a beloved wife, that he should find consolation in music, and we close on the strains of Beethoven's "Ode to Joy." *Summer Interlude* has a similar conclusion, but it is far more complicated and ambiguous. The heroine dances off to her new lover, having put the past idyll behind her, but we perceive this as an accommodation rather than a solution. Grief is not facilely transcended.

B: Your question is difficult. I will try to. . . . I don't understand. You are puzzled when the conductor tells the hero to play?

S: No. I'm saying that the conclusions of these two films are similar but—

B: And of *Winter Light.*

S: Yes—but *Summer Interlude* is the first excellent example of this theme, because for the first time you don't seem to feel the need of a simple conclusion. And I think this is crucial to your success. For example, even *Smiles of a Summer Night,* which you call a *pièce bien fait,* is distinguished not by neatness, but by ambiguity. The plot is resolved, but not the problems of the characters. Moreover, though a comedy about love, the film is also a drama about death: Before the lovers flee, you show a medieval clock striking the hour through a parade of wooden figures (recalling the end of *The Seventh Seal*), in which the most prominent is death.

B: That whole film is about destruction. *Smiles of a Summer Night* is much darker than it appears. I made it during one of my most depressing periods, when I myself was near death. Like *Persona,* it saved its creator. Often one makes a tragedy in a good mood and, when in a bad mood, turns to comedy. It is also true, as you say, that in *Summer Interlude* I start to accept life as a compromise. Before you do that, life is difficult and heavy, and things go wrong; at the moment you accept your limits and see them clearly, you have a greater desire to create and more joy in creation.

S: But how could you, in that state, make a film like *A Lesson in Love?*

B: Oh, that's just a *divertissement.* I had just finished *The Naked Night* and was living with Harriet Andersson at a small seaside hotel. She liked to sunbathe on the beach, and I liked to sit down—

S: In the shade?

B: No. It was a fantastic hotel, exactly like the one in *Mr. Hulot's Holiday.* There was a small tower in it where I used to sit and read. I had just divorced my third wife, though I still liked her very much, and, therefore, began writing about her. In fourteen days I finished the script, and fourteen days later we began shooting the picture. The whole thing was just for fun—and money. I was very poor at that time, you know. I

A typical scene from A Lesson in Love.

already had lots of children and a lot of women, and money had to be paid out. A good deal of my filmmaking in earlier years came from lack of money.

S: "Women and children are hostages to fortune."

B: [Laughs uproariously.]

S: Were any of the scenes in *A Lesson in Love* that portray the couple before they're married made in imitation of American "screwball comedy"?

B: No, but I had seen them all, so perhaps unconsciously. . . . You know, I have never been scared of being influenced. I like to use others' styles. I don't want to be unique. I am a cinemagoer. I have no complexes on this subject.

S: Is that because you're sure that you'll always be yourself?

B: Yes.

S: Particularly in the scene where Eva Dahlbeck beats up her former lover, I was reminded of a Rosalind Russell picture.

B: That scene was a one-act play I had written long before and just put in there because it was funny. I wrote it in imitation of the one-act comedies by Chekhov.

S: Back to *Smiles of a Summer Night.* Normally, you show that the woman is wiser than the man in successful heterosexual love, almost like a mother to him. Yet in this film you seem to be arguing that men and women should marry people their own age. Hadn't you previously

suggested, in effect, that all women are older than men? Why the new issue of compatibility in ages?

B: Perhaps you are right.

S: That's one of the reasons I don't feel too optimistic about the lovers' future; hence, I am not too happy at the conclusion. She is far too young and innocent for him. Am I right?

B: Yes, I think so.

S: This film is paradoxical, so much more complicated than it seems.

B: You know, a French critic compared it to *Rules of the Game,* so I wanted to see the film. When an American producer, who wanted to make me a present, asked me to choose one, I requested a print of Renoir's film to put in my private *cinémathèque.* I think it's an extremely bad picture. It is badly acted. Renoir is a very overrated director. He has only made one good picture: *The Human Beast.*

S: You liked that?

B: Wasn't it good?

S: It's awful!

B: It's awful? I saw it when I was twenty, and it made an enormous impression on me. It's not good?

S: No. No. I happen to like *The Rules of the Game* very much, but I think I can guess why you don't. Most of the film was improvised, and there is a tremendous effect of casualness.

B: It is irritating. It lacks style. I can't understand its humor, its complete lack of sensuality. The hunt is good, though.

S: Stupendous. The greatest thing in the film is when the hunters beat the trees to flush the rabbits out. *There* is real brutality! But back to your film: The more often I see *Smiles of a Summer Night,* the angrier I become at Egerman. His wife is dying for him to possess her, yet he is prevented by his own stupid ideas about the possible ways of living with love.

Egerman's folly casts his wife into the arms of his son.

B: He is stupid. He is immature. He misunderstands his affair with the actress. He is a fool.

S: If you could have shot this in color, would you have?

B: No. Because it is more fascinating to shoot in black and white and force people to imagine the colors.

S: Why have you switched to color recently?

B: At the beginning, it was painful, but now I like it. It's more sensual—now that we've learned to use it.

S: *The Passion of Anna* is gorgeous, but—my God!—*All These Women* looks like a bad MGM musical.

B: We started by reading all the books, and we tried to do the right things, but it is—

S: Tutti-frutti.

B: Yes. Yes. [Laughter.] In *The Passion of Anna* we decided to use no blue at all—

S: Yet one feels so cold: gray, but not blue.

B: Exactly.

S: Do you work in color now—to any degree—because you feel that the audience demands it?

B: No. I like it.

S: Why, at the beginning of *The Passion of Anna*, do you show Liv Ullmann using a crutch?

B: All the time I was writing the part I knew Liv Ullmann must play it, and I knew that the crutch would have a powerful effect on Liv Ullmann's feelings.

S: Doesn't it also symbolize the way in which Anna uses her "happy marriage" as a crutch?

B: Of course. But that is a second reason.

S: Why did you make Anna dream a dream from *Shame*?

B: Things sometimes happen for strange reasons. When we made *Shame*, we built that house on the island and landscaped the grounds —all with government permission because, since the island is a sort of animal preserve, you aren't allowed to build houses there without a permit. When the film was finished, the producer told me that we had to tear the house down, and I begged him not to. I told him I would make another picture there even though I had no idea of making one; I just didn't want to lose that house. Inside, I had a strange feeling that I had not succeeded in *Shame*, and I wanted to re-create the film in the place where it had failed. You know, the atmosphere in *The Passion of Anna* is exactly like that of *Shame*: killing, brutality, anonymity, people's sense of their utter helplessness before brutality. Liv Ullmann plays the same role in both films, and the woman in *Shame* might have dreamed the same dreams that Anna dreams. Originally, I indicated the intimate link between the two films through the dialogue, but I eventually cut it out. When Bibi Andersson first comes to Max von Sydow, I had him say, "Two people who disappeared in the war used to live in this house."

S: Why do you make Max von Sydow an archaeologist and then link that not to a former but to a subsequent film? In *The Touch*, Elliott Gould is also an archaeologist.

B: I have always been fascinated by digging and looking for things.

S: You also dig—for the truth about people—

B: Some sort of truth.

S: All right: a truth.

B: No! No! No! No! Excuse me. I dig for secret expressions and relations that we hide—

S: Behind our faces. Thus you put the camera right up close to see if you can get through the face. But you also seem to me to be aware that the hidden truth revealed by means of an actress' face is also a lie because it is art.

B: Please don't talk about the truth; it doesn't exist! Behind each face there is another and another and another. The actress' face gives you, in enormous concentration, that whole series of faces—not at a single moment, but at different moments in the performance or, sometimes, during a long close-up. In each thousandth part of a second an actor gives you a different impression, but the succession is so rapid that you take them all as a single truth.

S: That's the way film itself works: a succession of individual frames perceived by the eye as one moving image.

B: The two things are almost the same; you are right.

S: And in both cases, you pick the ones you want from all the separate expressions and thus make a single truth. So, finally, we get not the truth revealed through the actress' face but your selection of all the instances of it that she has expressed to you.

B: Everything you do in pictures is selection. People who now go out and shoot everything are perverting cinematographic art.

S: You select from the things you've caught with the camera, but you also impose by providing dialogue.

B: That's because I place my people in stylized surroundings and situations where they can express things that are complex and secret—and emotionally stimulating to the audience. Every second in my pictures is made to move the audience.

S: Do you decide exactly how we are to be moved, what we are to feel?

B: No. No. Only that you feel something.

S: Why do you use so much dialogue in your films?

B: Because human communication occurs through words. I tried once, to eliminate language, in *The Silence*, and I feel that that picture is excessive.

S: It's too abstract.

B: Yes.

S: I want to move to *The Silence*, but one last question about *The Passion of Anna*. What is the meaning of the last line: "This time his name was Andreas."

B: [Laughter.] We will be back.

S: I don't understand. It can mean that she's a man-eater, because her first husband was also named Andreas, or it can mean that another human being has been destroyed in the world, "This time his name is Andreas," or that another Bergman character has been destroyed, this time named Andreas.

B: I will tell you; it's much simpler. It means a sort of giving up: "*This* time his name is Andreas." You must feel behind the meaning another that you cannot define. For me, it expresses a feeling of boredom.

S: I don't understand.

B: I mean, "*This* time his name is Andreas"; but I will be back, and *next* time my character will have another name. I don't know what it will be, but this boring character will be back.

S: Also you?

B: Yes. [Hearty laughter.]

S: You know, I think *The Silence* proves my point. Look, I'm not going to try to defend myself anymore, but you should understand that I do disapprove of the totally intellectual response to film—

B: You know, one of my best friends, who lives a completely intellectual life, is emotionally crippled. He's very tight, but I like him extremely because he's so unhappy and nice and, inside, warm. He's his own enemy all the time. Everything I dislike he likes; and everything he likes I dislike. Yet I find it so fascinating to study his reactions, which are always enormously intelligent. His second or third reaction may be emotional, but even that is controlled.

S: I never have only an intellectual reaction.

B: Yes, now that we have spoken awhile, I see that you are extremely emotional.

S: But I must talk to you intellectually because we are discussing your art. . . . Nevertheless, what displeases me about *The Silence* is the exclusiveness of its appeal to our intellects. It gets whiter and whiter as it goes on, bleaching out until I can't see anything. This fits the theme,

but it also starves me. I don't hate *The Silence*, as, for example, I hate a film like *Crisis*, which is of no interest whatever, but I hate it. All it leaves me with are questions: For example, why does the boy look at the picture of the nymph and satyr?

B: This film is very. . . . What shall I say about *The Silence*? I think it is about the complete breakdown of illusions. . . . It's very difficult to tell you. . . . It's about my private life. . . . It's an extremely personal picture.

S: Which is why it doesn't communicate.

B: I think that's true. It is a sort of personal purgation: a rendering of hell on earth—my hell. The picture is so. . . . It is so strange to me that I do not know what it means. I saw it some weeks ago, so it is rather clear in my mind now. Some of

the scenes I liked so much that I was astonished.

S: Such as?

B: One of the best scenes I have ever made is the short meeting between the waiter and Alma in the darkness while the radio is playing Bach. He comes in, pronounces the name Johann Sebastian Bach, and she says, "The music is beautiful." It is a sudden moment of communication—so clean.

S: Also clear.

B: Completely clear. This picture has too many personal references to me and to my life and experiences so that today—ten years later—it seems as if it were made by someone else. But that scene does not.

S: There are two paradoxes about the autobiographical nature of the film. One is the odd excess of impersonal, even routinized

things that were taking place in his life while we were making the film. He had become completely childlike. But his face was so wonderful. So I told him to do whatever he wanted to do, to invent his own business. That was improvised by him to be playful with the boy.

S: All right, but the film is full of perverse sexuality: the dwarfs dressing the boy in girl's clothes, the masturbation, the loveless sex, etc.

B: This is hell—perversion of sex. When sex is completely totally isolated from other parts of life and all the emotions, it produces an enormous loneliness. That is what the film is about: the degradation of sex.

S: And war.

B: Yes, because brutality and cruelty are waiting outside.

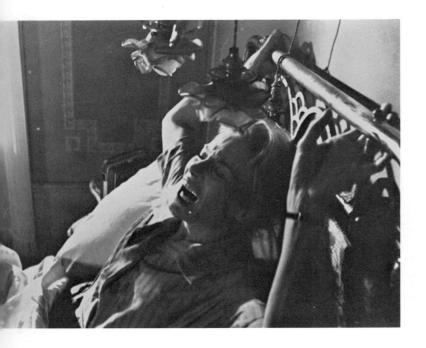

symbolism, largely Freudian. For example, when the waiter bites off the head of the hot dog, certain members of the audience can't resist pointing to the castration symbol.

B: It isn't. The actor I used for the part was a wonderful old man who was sick at the time—owing to a thrombosis, he had lost his memory and couldn't even recall his lines. He even forgot

S: Ready to break through in *Shame*.

B: In 1946, I spent a few weeks in Hamburg, and in Paris and Grenoble, in 1949; all, places where the war had been intense. The hotel in *The Silence* is exactly like ones I lived in. The film has to do with so many things that frighten me—

S: What about the scene where the boy urinates against the hotel corridor wall?

B: He is purging his troubles, his stress. Now he feels a little more courageous.

S: By being naughty, he asserts himself.

B: Yes.

S: Let me move to another kind of difficult film, *The Magician.* Every time I see it I feel differently toward it. Sometimes I love it; other times I hate it.

B: Can't you make up your mind and love the picture? Because it was made with so much vitality and pleasure. You know, I was in a very good mood when I made that film.

S: That's not the way it appears.

B: I'm sorry. We felt the whole time that we were playing a game.

S: Here, I think I *am* speaking for other people. After we've seen *The Magician,* we can't understand why it is called a comedy. At the end of the film, we look at each other and say—

B: "What sort of comedy is this?" A black comedy.

S: That won't do. At least, the moments that are meant to play humorously against the others aren't funny. For example, the whole subplot involving the servants—

B: That was more developed in the original; for reasons I prefer you not to report, I had to cut most of those scenes. You are right that this part of the film is very unsuccessful.

S: *The Magician* seems both to attack and to exploit theatricalism. As a result, I don't know quite how to feel about your apparent surrogate, Vogler. Or is this doubt what I'm supposed to feel?

B: Yes. I don't want you to know how to feel.

S: Even more troublesome is the magician's conception of himself as a priest.

B: He *used* to think of himself as a priest. Once he was idealistic; now he simply does the tricks, without any feeling. The only completely integrated man in the film is Vergerus. He's the one I like, not the magician.

S: Why, then, do you make him a fool?

B: Because he is a fool.

S: Then why do you like him?

B: I like his dream of finding out the truth about magic.

S: You like his innocent scientism?

B: And his passion.

S: But he's an intellectual, a rationalist.

B: Yes, but. . . .

Vergerus contemptuously questioning Vogler.

S: And you don't like intellectuals.

B: No. I do, I do. I do very much . . . and—

S: What differentiates the intellectuals you like from those you don't?

B: A good intellectual, in my opinion, is one who has trouble with his emotions. He must doubt his intellect, have fantasies, and be powerfully emotional.

S: Tell me, are you hostile to people who seem completely sure of themselves?

B: I am very suspicious of them. But, you know, I meet many fishermen and farmers on the island, who are completely free because their lives are so tough and close to them that they are extremely verbal. They are often crazy, but they are sure of themselves because they know their profession. And I always only work with actors who are—in a special way—self-possessed.

S: But your characters are never like that.

B: Not very often.

S: Why?

B: Because . . . it's very difficult to say in English . . . I think one day perhaps . . . I think that in my new film, *Whispers and Cries,* I have created one character who is self-possessed, but she's not intellectual.

S: But why do you generally not create such characters, though you say you like them in real life?

B: To create such a human being, you must be extremely powerful as a writer. I am not yet so powerful because I have so many things that are. . . .

S: Would you like to create someone like Portia in *The Merchant of Venice?*

B: Someone like a Solzhenitsyn character.

S: Let me ask you about *The Touch* now. I am not someone who hated or loved it; I had mixed feelings. I loved the true perceptions about people in the first part of the film, and Karin, by the way, comes very close to being a self-possessed character. In face, one of the film's points is the limitation of her sort of strength, which David lessens. Do you want us to like him?

B: David is . . . it's very difficult to answer that question.

S: Why should I care about him?

B: David and the husband both were created as

much more of the part than there is in it. The guilt for the film's failure is mine. Nevertheless, I think the critical reaction was ridiculous because this film was not made for anything else than to. . . . No. That's not true. I can't understand the critics' aggressiveness.

S: I don't know about the others. For me, the problem is this: Throughout the film, you show that David is doing Karin some good. Church bells often ring when they meet. You include the obtrusive symbol of the madonna, which is being devoured by termites; David tells Karin that the termites are as beautiful as the madonna they destroy—

B: It is very simple. In the beginning of the picture, when it is still romantic, there is a lot of music and beauty. From the middle of the picture, all music, bells, and so forth cease. When he returns to her after his absence, everything has

parts of Karin's life, but then the actress wanted to make the story truer to her heart—wanted more light shed on characters who were made to remain in the shadows. Critics have been very unfair to Elliott Gould. He's excellent; he makes

changed. His beard is off; everything is naked, hard, real.

S: But aren't we meant to feel that even the bad things in their affair have made her a better person?

B: That's because David has brought her suffering and change. She has resources and talents that he brings out.

S: Must one always suffer to develop? Isn't it possible to watch the film and say that she was just as talented before he showed up? One of the loveliest scenes occurs when she is looking at herself in the mirror. Her husband comes to embrace her, and then, without a word from him,

she walks into the bedroom and prepares herself for what is obviously their favorite sexual position. This seems to be poise, richness, understanding.

B: That's true. That's true.

S: I think there's nothing that David does for her that is equally important.

B: Exactly. But you must remember that in the church she tells him that she could live with both men and make a meaningful and proper life. She is much more alive than anyone else. She knows she has enough warmth and human resources to make both men happy and create a new sort of life. She has a richness which he has made her understand.

S: Why, then, in the scene when she goes to his apartment and discovers he's left does she press her hand on the broken glass?

B: There you have an exact example of the difficulty between actress and director. I invented that, but Bibi Andersson could not per-

form it. An actress can do something unsuited to her and make it believable, but Bibi Andersson is so integrated a person that, for her, it is impossible to play something she doesn't believe in.

S: As the author, what did you intend as Karin's motive when she wounds her hand?

B: The pain in her soul is so extreme that she wants to localize it in her body.

S: But it looks different. She enters the room and is dismayed by his absence, yet in the midst of her anguish, she shows signs of exhaustion: She yawns. So, to restore her involvement with the pain, she inflicts a wound on herself.

B: But that is Bibi Andersson.

S: For whatever reason, the scene suggests that David had always appealed to her as a way of quickening her feeling *because* he brought her pain.

B: The whole scene is wrong.

S: It is like a note struck in a piece of music that brings the wrong overtone to the following notes.

B: I quite agree. I'm not very happy about it. It can't be cut out, but it is seductive and wrong. You always have the script, your intention, and the actress. All the time, a fight goes on among these things. It is very fascinating, this struggle. Often it makes things come alive. An example is *Persona*.

S: But *Persona* is not realistic so it can absorb what in *The Touch* becomes a destructive falsity.

B: You are exactly right.

S: This brings me to *The Seventh Seal*, which I also find unbalanced between realism and expressionism. Before I begin, are you willing to offer your opinion about *The Seventh Seal*?

B: *The Seventh Seal* was made in thirty-five days. Most of it was shot in the woods right outside the studio. Everything in it was done in an enormous hurry, and I like it because it expresses a sort of craftsmanship. It's very theatrical and complicated. Some parts of the picture I still like. It is very close to me. When we were making it, each morning brought a new catastrophe because we had to make it cheap and quick. For the beach scenes, we had only three days on location! The actors carried the cameras. We borrowed costumes from the theater. It was all done in a hurry, but with enormous enthusiasm. We were happy even to be able to produce some images each day. For example, the scene with the flagellants was shot from eight A.M. to seven P.M. of a single day.

S: Are you satisfied with that scene?

B: I like it, but of course, I had no time to reshoot anything or even to produce enough shots for the sequence.

S: It does seem to be awfully stagy.

B: Of course it is.

S: You wanted that? These religious people are also putting on a show?

B: That was not my intention. I only wanted it done quickly.

S: Was the script written quickly, too?

B: No. It started as a small one-act play. This picture is enormously theatrical, but I don't care. It was such a fantastic time. We never slept. We only rehearsed and shot. When Raval is dying in the forest, he asks for water, for pity, and he cries, "I'm dying, I'm dying, I'm dying." When we shot that moment, suddenly the sun came out!

S: A miracle.

B: [Laughter.] A miracle.

S: You had fun making it, but it's troubling for the spectator. For example, why does all-powerful death have to resort to such low trickery?

B: The whole film is based on medieval pictures in a Swedish church. If you go there, you will see death playing chess, sawing a tree, making jokes with human souls. It's like a Mexican peasant game that takes death as a joke. Only suddenly does he become terrible.

S: Let me get at the problem another way. It does seem that the sensibility of the medieval artist is totally different from the sensibility behind this film.

B: That's not true. Say anything you want against *The Seventh Seal.* My fear of death—this infantile fixation of mine—was, at that moment, overwhelming. I felt myself in contact with death day and night, and my fear was tremendous. When I finished the picture, my fear went away. I have the feeling simply of having painted a canvas in an enormous hurry—with enormous pretension but without any arrogance. I said, "Here is a painting; take it, please."

S: And internationally, people did.

B: Yes.

S: So you were vindicated.

B: Thirty-five days!

S: Time is running out. Where shall I go? Let me turn to that magnificent early film, *The Naked Night.* Were you consciously imitating Strindberg in that film?

B: Strindberg? I must tell you that I am a specialist on Strindberg, and I don't find anything Strindbergian in that film. People who don't know Strindberg so well. . . . We do. We have a great Strindberg tradition in this theater; I have

produced many of his plays; I have devoted my professional life as a stage director to Strindberg; my version of *The Dream Play* is in its third year, and this is the second time I have staged it. I have staged several of his plays three times each. To me, there is no sign—

S: Let me point to one moment that—

B: No. The picture has something to do with Emil Jannings' *Variety* [a German film directed by E. A. Dupont in 1925].

S: Why?

B: Because it was the first picture I acquired as a collector. It fascinated me so much that I consciously imitated it.

S: *The Naked Night* marks the start of your collaboration with Sven Nykvist.

B: Yes, but he was only one of four cameramen working on that film. It was made in the mess of that circus at a studio which was doing five other films while I was shooting mine. Sometimes other pictures were in my playing area; other times, I was in theirs.

S: How much of an effect has Nykvist had on your films?

B: Little at that time. It started with *Winter Light*, when we began together to examine light. From early morning until late evening, we stayed in that church registering every gradation of the light. Our common passion—and I feel this even on the stage—is to create light: light and faces surrounded by shadows. This is what fascinates me!

S: Yet *The Naked Night* already shows one of your greatest triumphs in lighting: during the scene when the clown is humiliated by his wife's bathing before the soldiers. How was that effect obtained?

B: That was not Nykvist; it was another cameraman.

S: Was it done with overexposure?

B: They thought I was crazy. We made a negative of the print, and then from that negative we made a new print and then a new negative. Eventually we effaced every grain of the image until we got true black and white—and only black and white.

S: There is a related moment in the film that I feel is Strindbergian because—

B: I never thought of it, but perhaps it is Strindbergian unconsciously. If you live in a Strindberg tradition, you are breathing Strind-

Gudron Brost (wife), *Anders Ek* (Frost) *in stills from the humiliation of Frost sequence.*

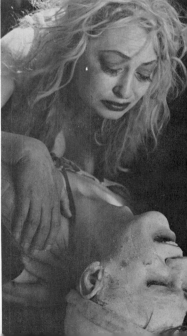

berg air. After all, I have been seeing Strindberg at the theater since I was ten years old, so it is difficult to say what belongs to him and what to me.

S: One of my favorite lines from *The Ghost Sonata*, which is my favorite Strindberg play—

B: Mine, too.

S: —is the young girl's about "the drudgery of keeping oneself above the dirt of life." This I don't see in your films: the dirt, the mere physical act of going on, of tending to things etc.

B: [Very very softly.] That's true.

S: Why? Why, where there is so much life, is

Monika at the low point of her fortunes.

the simple dirt absent? Even in *The Touch*, where it could have been, we don't see it.

B: You're right. . . . I select. . . . First of all, I don't know very much about the dirt of life. I have always rejected it . . . and it's not. . . . I have lived under very bad conditions in my life. I have been very hungry and very sick and sometimes very dirty. With four wives and nine children, you can imagine! But in my pictures I always select, and I find—if you mean real dirt—that it is uninteresting to me. My mind has never been infected by it.

S: One film of yours has dirt, and I love this film: *Monika.*

B: Yes.

S: It's very good.

B: Very good!

S: Very underrated. It has several superb things: the sequence in which they leave Stockholm, the opening shot of Harriet Andersson

that also closes the film. How did you get that? She's listening to a phonograph record, smoking a cigarette, and looking directly into the camera.

B: It just happened.

S: And then you decided to use it at the beginning and end?

B: It isn't in the beginning.

S: In America, it appears under the credits.

B: That is a mistake. At that time, they made a mess of my pictures outside Sweden. I intended that shot only to appear toward the end. When I made it, everyone said I was crazy; suddenly she looks directly at us!

S: Why did you use something like this again in *Hour of the Wolf*?

B: Because television has made it less difficult to accept. Therefore, I have Liv Ullmann tell the story directly to us.

S: Why do you end the film in mid-sentence?

B: Because the whole picture is half-spoken sentences. It is . . . an unsuccessful attempt—

S: Of hers?

B: Of mine, too.

S: Another personal film.

B: Too personal.

S: Indeed, I can't understand what's going on.

B: [Laughter.] Me, too. It's very strange to me.

S: What does the scene with the boy mean? What are the demons doing to the husband? Why does the wife also see them? I have questions and questions.

B: Me, too. To me, however, the picture is extremely real. The demons and the boy. . . . Do you know French? In French, it is called *folie a deux*. The wife is also ill.

S: But we see her as a kind of earth mother, next to a bowl of apples, and—

B: Yes, that's true. But she is also ill.

S: You should tell us that earlier in the film.

B: No. I wouldn't like that. We discussed it, and I decided not to. But she is infected by him. She is really an earth mother, but she becomes infected and will never return to her former self.

S: But she misinterprets her illness. She doesn't realize that she's infected; she thinks the problem was that she was too weak to help her husband.

B: The difficulty with the picture is that I couldn't make up my mind who it was about. Had I made it from her point of view it would have been very interesting. But, no, I made it the wrong way. After it was finished, I tried to turn it over to

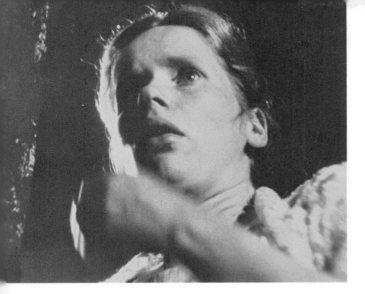

The wife threatened.

Johan and the boy.

The demons.

A demon descends on Johan.

her; we even reshot some scenes, but it was too late. To see a man who is already mad become crazier is boring. What would have been interesting would have been to see an absolutely sane woman go crazy because she loves the madman she married. She enters his world of unreality, and that infects her. Suddenly, she finds out that she is lost. I understood this only when the picture was finished.

S: Do you ever make a film to correct another film?

B: Only with *The Passion of Anna*—

S: Which corrects *Shame*.

B: Yes. And, a little bit, *Winter Light* was made to correct *Through a Glass Darkly*.

S: Yes, and one of the problems—

B: And *The Magician* corrects *The Naked Night*.

S: In—

B: But not consciously. For heaven's sake, it wasn't conscious.

S: You felt it was wrong and—

B: Now I have to go.

S: So we end in midsentence?

[Much laughter.]

Jean Renoir

Beverly Hills, February 5 and 6, 1972

Feature Films: 1924 *La Fille de l'eau* (*The Water Girl*); 1926 *Nana*; 1927 *Charleston, Marquita*; 1928 *La Petite Marchande d'allumettes* (*The Little Match Girl*); 1929 *Tire-au-flanc, Le Tournoi* (*The Tournament*), *Le Bled*; 1931 *On purge bébé* (*Purging Baby*), *La Chienne* (*The Bitch*); 1932 *La Nuit du carrefour* (*Night of the Crossroads*), *Boudu sauvé des eaux* (*Boudu Saved from Drowning*); 1933 *Chotard et cie.* (*Chotard and Company*), *Madame Bovary*; 1934 *Toni*; 1935 *Le Crime de Monsieur Lange* (*The Crime of M. Lange*); 1936 *Une Partie de campagne* (*A Day in the Country*), *Les Bas-fonds* (*The Lower Depths*); 1937 *La Grande Illusion* (*Grand Illusion*), *La Marseillaise*; 1938 *La Bête humaine* (*The Human Beast*); 1939 *La Règle du jeu* (*The Rules of the Game*); 1941 *Swamp Water*; 1943 *This Land Is Mine*; 1945 *The Southerner*; 1946 *Diary of a Chambermaid, Woman on the Beach*; 1950 *The River*; 1953 *Le Carrosse d'or* (*The Golden Coach*); 1955 *French Cancan* (*Only the French Can*); 1956 *Elena et les hommes* (*Paris Does Strange Things*); 1959 *Le Testament du Docteur Cordelier* (*The Will of Dr. Cordelier*), *Le Déjeuner sur l'herbe* (*Picnic on the Grass*); 1962 *Le Caporal épinglé* (*The Elusive Corporal*); 1969 *Le Petit Théâtre de Jean Renoir* (*The Little Theater of Jean Renoir*).

Jean Renoir's house, of pink stucco and brick, is modest by Beverly Hills standards. At seventy-eight, its owner can walk only with the aid of a contraption on wheels, and he cannot speak above a hoarse whisper. But the dwelling is enriched by a splendid collection of his father's works, and Renoir himself, though shrunk from his former girth and liveliness, remains in possession of the lovely qualities reflected in his films.

In each of our meetings, for example, despite his wife's concern and my desire not to tax him, he was self-effacing in his desire that I get enough material, and his endurance was kindness itself. Therefore, I was doubly saddened to hear an ornate clock ticking heavily during the long pauses which it so cruelly explained.

On the second day, after a good night's rest, Renoir seemed more energetic and, because we were discussing particular films, more circumstantial. But at no time did the interview move forward as smoothly as we both might have wished.

Since his reason for faltering was so clearly irrelevant to his talent or sensibility, I have cut and tightened this conversation more than most others. Occasionally running together several of his responses, I have misrepresented the actuality of our encounter, but I have preserved the essentials of its content.

Renoir while shooting The Elusive Corporal.

SAMUELS: For me, one of the most admirable qualities in your films is variety in theme and subject. But most critics today—and I think particularly of the *Cahiers du Cinéma* group—identify directorial excellence with stylistic and thematic unity. I'd like to ask you two questions about this. First, do you agree with the critical emphasis on unity?

RENOIR: I don't know if the emphasis is useful, but I know that unity exists. In spite of yourself, you always express certain ideas; although they develop and seem to change, at bottom they don't.

S: Do you think that unity is necessarily the mark of a gifted director, that too much variety should rouse suspicion?

R: All works of art bear the artist's signature. If there is no signature, there is no work of art. And by "art," I don't mean only paintings, sculpture, films, plays; I mean anything in life that is done well and carefully. In my opinion, our age commits its greatest crime when it kills the author or makes him disappear. Before what we call progress, a man who made dishes was expressing his personality just as much as Picasso does in his paintings. Today this is no longer true.

S: This problem is particularly severe in the conglomerate, mechanical art form of film, where it is difficult to maintain one's personality.

R: Yes, and some people feel that they can only do so by destroying the personality of their collaborators; but that is false. The more you help your partners to express themselves, the more you express yourself.

S: Haven't you ever experienced a conflict between your intentions and those of your collaborators?

R: No.

S: To what do you attribute this?

R: Lack of stubbornness. When I see, for example, that my method is not convenient for the actors, I change it.

S: In Hollywood, the changes are frequently imposed. Do you agree that it is more difficult to produce works of art here than in Europe, where the tradition of the dominant film artist is more firmly entrenched?

R: There are all sorts of artworks. The Hollywood system is not mine, but it has produced some beautiful results. The early period of Chaplin and Keaton, the later films made by Lubitsch or under his influence are marvelous.

Even though Lubitsch was German, his superb films are typically American.

S: But what about the period since then?

R: As you see, I'm ill. For the time being, I can't walk and so cannot see a picture unless someone carries me to the projection room or I can show it here for myself. So I'm a bad judge of recent films.

S: To return then to my first question: What do you regard as the unifying element in your films?

R: Any unity in my films is the result, of course, of my views about the world, for if one feels something deeply it is bound to show. But even more important is what is outside: "Existence precedes essence." The external unity of my films, I think, comes from a certain rhythm and certain ways in which I direct the delivering of dialogue. When discussing the dialogue with my actors, we try to search for reality.

S: You know, I find a characteristic rhythm in your films that I would describe as languid.

R: If so, it is in spite of myself. In fact, I love fast rhythms, but when I write dialogue or change dialogue with the help of the actors during the shooting, I find so many things to add to each shot in which the line is spoken that the result is sometimes longer than I had anticipated. I have too many things to say. Of course, that doesn't always mean that all of them are good, but I'm dying to express them.

S: Since people in real life aren't so ready with their responses as on the stage, is it possible that your slow rhythms are the result of your search for reality?

R: Perhaps, but you know, I am usually the one who wants faster rhythms when we shoot.

S: Then why do the actors slow down?

R: Because I always ask them to consider what they say seriously, and they are always discovering new meanings or business which takes time. I believe that the role of the director is to be a sort of midwife who helps his actors deliver themselves of their performance.

S: Aren't acting and the script more important to you than camera movements and editing?

R: Yes as far as acting is concerned, but I have no commitment to my scripts. I write them very carefully, but the film is always very different from what I started with. I discover things I had not planned, and I would be a fool not to take advantage of them only so that I could stay close to my original script.

S: But the discoveries are about content. What I'm driving at is the dominance of content over form in your films. For example, you seem to me to be nearly the opposite of Hitchcock, who makes films with almost no human content but magnificent structure.

R: Essentially, camera movement doesn't interest me. For example, among the many things that attracted me to the subject of *The Rules of the Game* was its opportunity to minimize camera movement. The classical flavor of the film allowed me to hold the camera still.

S: I'm astonished to hear you say that. One of the things that attracts me to this film is the way in which the camera is a social participant in the scenes, weaving among the characters and allowing us to see and overhear the complexity of their interaction. Isn't that, for example, the way you shot the arrival at the chateau?

R: Of course, the camera is not always still, but if you compare *The Rules of the Game*, for example, to *Grand Illusion* you will see how stable the former is.

S: If I'm not mistaken, the camera movements in *Grand Illusion* are more abrupt (down to the courtyard, up to the battlements), whereas in *The Rules of the Game* the movements slow along with the action.

R: That's because I wanted the movements to be invisible. One must know his technique well enough not to become too involved with the camera. Some directors continually ask their cameraman to move away so that they can look through the viewfinder and push the machine a little to the right, a little to the left; they are perfectionists with camera angles. I never look at the camera. So long as I know what lens is being used, I can predict what the shot will look like.

S: With your relative interest in acting over camera work, might you have been satisfied to become a stage director?

R: No. I went into movies because I loved them and despised the stage. Throughout my early years, I fought the invasion of stage techniques and spirit into films. Probably this was all because of the French theater of my time, which was bad: artificial, full of boulevard comedies, and so on. Yet the best school for movies is vaudeville. I don't know why, but if you look at the great film talents—Chaplin, Keaton, Fairbanks— you will see that they came from vaudeville.

S: So you're not against theater, but only a certain variety. Yet your films owe so much to theatrical tradition, despite your frequent assertions that cinema should be realistic and documentary. How do you explain the paradox?

R: First, I had frequent changes of mind during my career about the proper way to make a film. Second, although we must observe nature, art demands that it be translated. However, the documentary element keeps you from creating fake situations; starting from nature protects you against false overemphasis. Moreover, reality is always more amusing and audacious than our inventions.

S: Yet you don't seem to me to go so far in that direction as, for example, the Italian neorealists. *Toni* is often called a precursor of their style, but when I compare it to, say, *The Bicycle Thief* or *La terra trema*, I am impressed by how much more classically dramatic your film is. It doesn't have that open-ended, slice-of-life quality that you find among the Italians.

R: The word "neorealism" implies a certain style that may not have anything to do with reality. Consider an eighteenth-century play in the style of *commedia dell' arte* and then a modern play or picture about a railroad. In the latter, the actors will wear real grease on their faces, and their hands will be dirty; but if they are hams, they will be hams. If the actor who plays the eighteenth-century shepherd is good and has been helped by a good director, however, he will be convincing and real, even though he is not a shepherd and isn't even authentically dressed like one.

S: In *Toni* and *La Marseillaise*, you worked with nonprofessional actors, as the neorealists often do. Would you have liked to do that more often?

R: No. I believe in professionals. When an amateur is good, it's because he becomes, for that moment, a professional. Of course, there is such a thing as a surprise shot, but I don't like that. For example, you take a dog and call his name. Therefore, he turns his head and for a moment looks like a dog ready to attack. So you keep that shot and pretend in the dialogue that the dog is

attacking. But I don't like that. I don't like lying on the screen.

S: That's why Bresson, for example, does use amateurs. He thinks they are truer, and he even goes so far as to keep them from acting. What do you think of that?

R: Bresson is a genius. His films have nothing to do with the industry or the art. They are Bresson. It is therefore natural that he would oppose actors who might bring something of themselves into his film.

S: You once said that film was dangerous because it was too free. Could you explain what you meant by that?

R: I probably said that after some theatrical experience which made me discover that it is very useful to have a frame. A good way to look at film is as a succession of small frames. For instance, a physical limit is useful. It's easy to write a script like *Grand Illusion* because it is the story of people who are behind walls and cannot get out. Often a film is hurt by loose wandering of the camera. If the script doesn't bind the camera, you must invent ties for it.

S: You've just mentioned physical restraint as an aid to good filmmaking. Are you aware of any other rules that have guided you in your career?

R: I'm not one for rules; I understand them only when the job is finished. However, I can talk about my greatest preoccupation, which is to have the actor create his role without imitation of previous performances. That's why I believe in what we in France call the Italian method. You take some dialogue, sit around a table with your actors, and begin to read, but you do so absolutely without expression, as if you were reading a telephone book. This kills the actor's mania to apply to the present role inflections that he has used in another work. A mother loses her child and has to show her grief. There are two recipes for that situation: tears or hysterical laughter. But maybe the best thing would be to do nothing. You have to discover that, and you cannot discover it if you give a reading of the line or situation before you have absorbed it.

S: Did you discover this method in rehearsals?

R: No. I learned it from Michel Simon and Louis Jouvet.

S: How do your actors move into their performances after shedding their formulas?

R: Sometimes the miracle happens.

S: You don't tell your actors what to do?

R: As little as possible. However, one is always torn between his desire to get the best out of each actor and the need for unity in the entire film.

S: Then your directing is more a matter of correction than of telling your actors what to do?

R: Yes.

S: Isn't this essentially improvisatory method very expensive?

R: Yes. That's why, although I tried to use this method whenever I made a film, I sometimes was forced to renounce it in order to save time.

S: Did producers give you trouble with this?

R: Not often. I usually got along very well with my producers.

S: You've said you are against dubbing, also on grounds of its unreality. But have circumstances forced you to dub against your will?

R: No. If we were living in a period of high civilization, like the twelfth century, and not in our own, dubbers would be burned in the public square for having committed the sin of asserting that one body can have several souls.

S: How then would you react to the contention of Antonioni and Fellini that dubbing is permissible because the essence of film is the visual element. Hence, you can do anything you like to the sound track.

R: I don't agree. The essence of cinema isn't sight; it is sight and sound together.

S: But what about verbal sounds? Do you think that words in films have importance equal to sights? Is there no limit beyond which language mustn't go if a film isn't to become too theatrical?

R: Words can be boring, but they can also be good; it depends on the words. It is true that good theatrical dialogue is sometimes inappropriate in a film, however.

S: What makes dialogue cinematic rather than theatrical?

R: The accompaniment of a close-up. People underestimate the importance of close-ups in film. It brings the actor closer to the audience, and it makes each spectator feel that the performance is directed at him alone. It makes you forget the crowd, as you do not forget it in a theater.

S: Do you also think that cinema dialogue must be less emphatic than what we hear on the stage?

R: That depends on the situation.

S: Because sound is important to you, I'd like to ask how you feel about your silent film period.

R: In those days I was loaded with false ideas. I conceived of the form as a sort of pantomime and tried for stylization in gesture, something close to German expressionism.

S: I don't find that true about The Water Girl. In fact, except for the heroine's dream, that film seems rather more realistic in style than most films of the period.

R: That's because I didn't succeed in doing what I planned.

S: One problem with the film, though, is the number of shots of people mouthing words which, of course, could only be represented through titles.

R: But I loved the titles. When they were wisely chosen, they seemed to me the perfect complement for the image. And I thought that when the spectator had to read the titles, it provided a certain rest, a certain rhythm for the film.

S: Which do you prefer working in, color or black and white?

R: Color.

S: Why?

R: For the same reason that I like dialogue. Color is a dangerous tool because most shots in color turn out to be ugly. But this dangerous game presents a challenge. You mustn't avoid it in the lab, by treating the shots so as to produce a certain impression. The camera should capture exactly the colors of the world in front of it. You mustn't be arty; you mustn't make colors for the sake of making beautiful pictures.

S: You've said that technical developments haven't improved film, but since the art is so essentially mechanical, aren't technical changes necessary for changes in expression? Haven't you benefited as an artist from any new machinery?

R: The only thing which helped and pleased me particularly was the manufacture of lenses with greater depth of field.

S: What about the development of high-sensitivity film stock?

R: Of course. But, you know, technical impediments are useful. Without ultrasensitive film, you have to carry a lot of equipment with you— lamps and so on—and that takes time, and the time allows you to think.

S: In an interview you gave Truffaut and Rivette you said that you particularly liked special effects, but there are few of them in your films. Why?

R: I was very interested in them when I started making movies, but as I grew older, I became more fascinated in discovering reality.

S: When you edit a film, do you tend to cut very much of what you originally shot?

R: No. I always try to be thrifty in my shooting. For example, in the last film I made, *The Little Theater*, I shot many scenes once.

S: Do you normally do few takes?

R: Yes.

S: In recognizing the transience of film, you've said that a film must therefore show its value by its use for a contemporary audience. Isn't this a bit like equating value with popularity?

R: I don't believe that the value of a film is shown by its popularity. Some great films have no success at all. But film is the form of show business closest to hypnotism. It is like the flute played before the cobra.

S: And if the flute stops playing?

R: Sometimes the cobra kills the flutist.

S: This seems a good time to bring up your period in Hollywood. How do you feel about your American films?

R: I had rather pleasant experiences in Hollywood.

S: You didn't feel you were prevented from making Renoir movies?

R: No. What bothered me in Hollywood wasn't interference. I love interference; it produces discussion, and discussion frequently helps you improve your work. You know, I'm not a believer in the *auteur*-king, but I believe that we should feel the presence of the author in a film. What bothered me in Hollywood was the committee method of production that made films too little the result of an individual. The problem in Hollywood is a general approach. It's not that the producer insists that you take a shot in a certain way; it is the general desire for technical perfection that is at fault. People believe that Hollywood producers are very greedy and think only of earning lots of money, but that's not true. Their defect is much more dangerous: they want their films to be technically perfect. Furthermore, they believe that a film made with many stars is more perfect than one made with a few, and that is a false belief. They want the best cameramen, the best

sound engineers; they are afraid of gambling, of play, of taking risks.

S: Isn't this a form of greed? Aren't they trying to secure an investment by taking no chances?

R: I don't blame them; I just don't like to work under such conditions.

S: Were you able to choose the actors you wanted in Hollywood?

R: It was always a matter of discussion. There, as anywhere in the world, a movie usually starts with an actor. He becomes interested in a story, and with his interest you can find a producer willing to back you. Then the producer, the actor, and you discuss the other actors who will join the project.

S: When you began directing in this country, did you encounter any problems dealing with actors who weren't compatriots and didn't speak your language?

R: Not a bit. From the first, my relationships with American actors were very pleasant.

S: René Clair expressed fears about not knowing American mores when he worked in Hollywood. You had no such fear?

R: No.

S: All your American films have happy endings, although not all your French films do. Were you in any way pressured to produce happy endings in Hollywood?

R: No; I like happy endings.

S: How did your experience with American scriptwriters differ from your experience in Europe?

R: In America, the scriptwriter has more influence on the film, largely because it is rare here for the director to participate in the writing. But my collaborations here were not different from my collaborations in Europe. As my English improved, however, I began to write the scripts myself. For example, I wrote the script of *The Southerner*.

S: Why did you make *This Land Is Mine*?

R: To explain to the Americans that it's not easy to be occupied.

S: But this is the only one of your films that could be called propagandistic.

R: No. I made a film to help the Communist candidates in France at the time when Hitler had come to power in Germany. I was back from a trip to Berlin, where I had seen, among other things,

young Nazis forcing an old Jewish woman to lick the sidewalk because that was all a Jew was good for. I decided then to help any anti-Nazis who wanted me, so I worked on *Life Is for Us*, which was made by the Communist Party. The film isn't mine, but I worked on it.

S: What do you think about propaganda in films?

R: When I finished *Grand Illusion*, I was very vain and happy with my work. I thought, "I have made a good antiwar picture." Two years later war broke out.

S: But *Grand Illusion* isn't propagandistic, whereas *This Land Is Mine* is. Even so, did you convey the terror of the situation well enough to make a point in the latter film?

R: Not physically. But it's difficult to answer because I don't remember the film. Probably, it isn't important. If it were, I would remember it.

S: I'd like to get your opinion about a director who seems to me comparable in his interest in culture and the behavior of social classes. What do you think of Antonioni?

R: I've seen *La notte*, and I found it magnificent.

S: It bears some resemblance to *The Rules of the Game* in its concentration on the upper classes and a frivolity or deadness of soul that interferes with love. What would you say was the principal difference between your approach to this subject and Antonioni's?

R: I may be wrong, but I think that I perceived my characters with a more amused eye than Antonioni. My story is as serious as his, but it is also funny. That mixture of tragedy and comedy

is something I tried to achieve in several pictures, but I didn't succeed very often.

S: What do you think of Godard?

R: I like him.

S: What appeals to you in him?

R: His organization.

S: Organization? Isn't he wayward and willful?

R: He managed to popularize his methods with small means. He has a kind of gusto.

S: I'd like now to begin a review of your career. We've already mentioned your first film, *The Water Girl*. Why did you choose to start your career with a film about the besieged maiden?

R: Because I thought it was a good vehicle to show Catherine Hessling, who was my wife at that time.

S: Is that also why you allowed her to wear movie star makeup throughout the film despite the fact that the character was meant to be a waif?

R: We started to make films believing that we would alter everything that had ever been done. We wanted to achieve the effect of a Chinese shadow play or a puppet show. So Catherine tried to appear and gesture like a puppet.

Hessling in Nana.

A Renoir landscape *from* Picnic on the Grass.

S: This stylization is clearer in *Nana* than in *The Water Girl.* But why did you begin *Nana,* which is about sexual passion, with a comic scene in which Nana gets entangled in the stage machinery of her Venus number?

R: Because even that early I was haunted by a desire to mix tragic and comic elements. Whenever I saw the opportunity to produce some laughter, I seized it—always.

S: Why is this so attractive to you?

R: I was brought up to like laughter.

S: That's the influence of your father, isn't it? It always annoys me that whenever critics see an outdoor setting or a tree in your films, they say, "Aha, there you see the radiant light of Renoir *père!*" But landscapes exist in many director's films. It seems to me this shared lightness of attitude is more pertinent.

R: When I started making films, I fought the influence of my father, but I probably didn't succeed in throwing it off entirely. But you are

right to say that the number of natural settings is not the chief sign of his influence. Perhaps it is more a matter of my choice of stories and my preference for ones that mix comedy and tragedy.

S: *Nana* is full of lavish interiors. Why?

R: I wanted contrast between the squalor of Nana's story and the locales in which it took place. Also, I wanted the sets to suggest the social decadence.

S: But why are the sets so immense? I think of the famous scene in which Nana is at her dressing table at the far end of an almost arenalike room.

R: At that stage of my career, I was fascinated with technique. I had developed a system of combining miniatures with real sets. I wanted to show off this invention, so I used these artificially created expanses.

S: Why did you make *Charleston?*

R: Because I had some stock left over from *Nana* and because Catherine and I had just discovered American jazz. So we decided to shoot a little jazz dance with the Negro dancer we had become friendly with at that time.

S: You've called *The Bitch* your first real success, so I'd like to skip over your other silent films and move to this sound picture. This is one of many instances in your work of stories concerning a man ruined by an unscrupulous woman. Few subjects recur among your films. Why is this one of the exceptions?

R: It was a subject very popular in American films; I think I first chose it to express my admiration for them.

S: You handle the subject differently, though. Didn't you feel that the American models were false?

R: Yes, but I loved that falsity.

S: Your film has falsity of another kind. For example, you start the film by showing that the action is like a Punch 'n' Judy show. Why?

R: To announce to the public that this is a show and not real life. The style of the film is real, but I believe in contrast and will never present a subject without it. For example, when I shot another film on this subject, *The Human Beast*,  the producer wanted the big dramatic star of the moment to play the part. She was very talented but melodramatic; I felt that her first appearance on the screen would tell the audience to expect a murder. So instead I chose Simone Simon, with her little innocent Pekingese face.

S: To you, what was the theme of *The Bitch?*

R: The folly of believing in justice. The hero, who kills the girl, should be executed; instead, the young man is punished for Michel Simon's crime simply because no one thinks that a respectable man would have done it and the young man is a pimp.

S: Then you're saying that *The Bitch* resembles not so much *The Human Beast* or *Woman on the Beach* as *The Crime of M. Lange.*

R: Yes. In both *The Bitch* and *M. Lange*, someone who deserves to die is killed, and the killer is not executed for the crime.

S: In your one film strictly in the crime genre, *The Night of the Crossroads*, there is a curious effect of distance, almost of documentary neutrality.

R: I didn't think of it in that way. I simply wanted to create a mysterious atmosphere. In fact, in that film I succeeded too well because no one can understand the plot.

S: What did Georges Simenon contribute to this film?

R: He helped me write the screenplay, he brought me good drinks, and he brought me something more precious than drinks or even a screenplay: He brought me his friendship.

S: For me, it is *Boudu Saved from Drowning* rather than *The Bitch* that is your first major film.

R: Well, in *The Bitch* I discovered Michel Simon, and *Boudu* was a constant improvisation in which he was tremendously helpful. And then the character Boudu exemplifies my belief that reality is more fantastic than the invention of authors. His costume and makeup are stylized, but he is a real person. The plot is theatrical, but the exterior shooting on the banks of the Seine brings reality into the film.

Renoir and Simon (center) working on Boudu.

S: Did you make major changes in the play?

R: Yes. In the play Boudu marries the girl and accepts bourgeois life. As you know, the film shows him rejecting both.

S: You begin this film with the scene of the nymphs and satyrs for the same reason that you begin *The Bitch* with the Punch 'n' Judy show?

R: Yes. I like to remind the public that they are watching a spectacle. If the show contains some lifelike moments, it is good, but I mustn't pretend that life itself is what I am showing. It is pretentious to appear to be presenting life on the screen. Real life is too big. Shakespeare can afford to take real life as his subject, and he succeeds despite the artificiality of his plays; but who can compare to Shakespeare?

S: Do you think the neorealists were wrong to insist by their style that life was what they were showing?

R: No. They were not mistaken. For me, it would be a mistake.

S: Why did you keep introducing the flutist, who is not really a character, into the film?

R: Again, as a little theatrical touch. Also to provide some music.

S: You don't usually have music unless it comes from a real source, do you?

R: Occasionally I've used a score, but I don't like them.

S: Why did you agree to the cuts you made in the final version of *Madame Bovary*?

R: Because it was three and a half hours long and the distributor refused to release it in that form. But I regret my decision; although the film was slow, it was much more substantial than it is now.

S: Did you worry about adapting so great a novel as Flaubert's?

R: Yes. When I can, I always avoid translating masterpieces for the screen. However, I don't think that a plot is very influential for the final quality of a film, but practically speaking, it saves time in the construction of a scenario to begin with a story line taken from a novel or a play. However, when your source is a masterpiece like *Madame Bovary*, you are hindered as much as you are helped. I respected the book too much simply to make use of it.

S: Don't you think that Valentine Tessier was too old for Emma?

R: Perhaps, but a good actress is ageless. Moreover, no actor is ever perfect for a part. Tessier brought the film something precious: a certain nobility and elegance.

S: But Flaubert's Emma isn't noble and elegant.

R: You are right, but Valentine, myself, and all the other participants in that adventure were frozen before Flaubert.

S: Your next film, *Toni*, is certainly a departure from nobility.

R: There again you see the good man ruined by a bad woman.

S: What were you trying to achieve stylistically in this film?

R: I wanted to work closer to nature.

S: Why then did you retain the melodramatically structured plot element?

R: The story happened absolutely as it does in the film. It impressed me very much when it was recounted to me by a friend who had been sheriff in the village where it happened. Yet I thought of the locale even more than of that story. I had wanted to do a quasi-documentary film made in that part of France.

S: Apparently, *The Crime of M. Lange* was one of your most improvisatory films. How did the improvisation proceed?

R: I wrote the story with Castanier, who was a friend and not a professional writer. It wasn't quite as developed as what you now see in the film, but pretty nearly. Then I gave it to Jacques Prévert, who wrote enough dialogue so that we could begin shooting. He would come to the set every day, and we would cooperate in producing additional dialogue. The picture is important to me because in it I discovered Jules Berry, who had never made a film before. I regard his performance of the part of Batala as highly as Michel Simon's Boudu. I tried, with Batala, to create a character who was not real but who represented a certain class of men. I remember the scene when Batala comes back dressed as a priest after he has left to avoid arrest and Lange, who by now wants to destroy him, says, "If I kill you, who will miss you?" Batala replies, "But women, my dear!" This line, which we invented at the last minute, was more revealing for the character than pages of dialogue would have been. And I don't even know which of us— Prévert, Berry, or myself—invented it. My job, when I make a picture, is to put my partners in a certain mood where everything they do and say fits the conception.

S: Ermanno Olmi improvises by telling his amateur actors what the situation will be and then by selecting from the dialogue they invent during their improvisation lines he thinks were best. Have you ever used that method?

R: Yes, but I don't like it. I don't mind the actors changing the dialogue as we discuss the situation, but I don't want to lose the foundation that prepared dialogue offers.

S: When you made that film, you believed in group effort. Do you still believe in it that much?

R: Yes. I believe that to make a film, one must not have partners; he must have accomplices.

S: Why did you decide to actually show in your film made by a group a group making a film?

R: I don't remember, but I did want to make fun of the filmmaking process, I think. Perhaps I was going through a period of doubt then.

S: Do you agree with the message of this film: that it's all right to kill a person if he's bad enough?

R: I ask myself that question every day. I have no answer. It's a dangerous principle, but I made this film during the time of Hitler, you know.

S: Why did you decide to act in *A Day in the Country*?

R: I had always tried to play bit parts in pictures. I was anxious to know how it felt to be on the other side of the camera.

Renoir as Octave in The Rules of the Game.

film. When he asked me to direct it, I agreed because I knew I could use actors in it that I admired, like Jouvet and Gabin. Moreover, because it was a play—even though I had first thought it should be done in Russia by a Russian director—it gave me the chance to do closer shooting of actors than I had done until that time. The script contained many set speeches so that I

S: What did you learn there?

R: Patience. An actor waits and waits under those hot lights, and his work seems to be endless.

S: You also played in your own *Human Beast* and *Rules of the Game*.

R: If I had found an actor who could have been physically appropriate for either role, I would not have taken them. In fact, I wanted Michel Simon for *The Rules of the Game*, but he wasn't free then.

S: In *A Day in the Country* you show the bourgeois characters as essentially sterile and the peasants as virile and romantic. Don't you think that's a rather simple idea?

R: Yes, but the picture doesn't pretend to be profound. I made it simply to take close shots of Sylvia Bataille.

S: In making a film of Gorki's *The Lower Depths* you were going outside your cultural frame of reference. What made this play seem relevant to the France of 1936?

R: I didn't choose the subject. Kamenka, who was a good friend of mine, wanted to produce the

felt that the sacrifice of my belief in realism was repaid by the chance to direct actors in the delivery of these lines. I tried very hard, therefore, not to give any national flavor to the picture. I tried to locate the film in a nonexistent world, thinking that the subject was sufficiently universal not to require exact location.

S: Both this film and *Boudu* imply that the outcast necessarily is attractive to a more affluent person. This reflects your political sentiments, doesn't it?

R: I'm not interested in politics; I'm interested in people. Some of my ideas are reactionary, others are leftist. I don't believe that leftist politics answers all questions.

S: That's why, for example, the aristocrats in *La Marseillaise* come off, in some cases, better than the populace.

R: That's the way they were. Adversity, which they suffered, often brings out the best in people. And in general, money and comfort make life boring. The wealthy are bored with their friends, with their mistresses, with gambling. . . . That's why works of art are so expensive. Rich people need a painting by Cezanne or Picasso to make their lives special, and they pay for it. Poor people want money because they don't know how boring it makes life. And people will never learn. To the end of the world, they will think it's a good thing to have money and, if not money, power. They don't realize that the only happiness in life comes through making something. You are a gardener who wants to grow potatoes, so you have to fight wind, lack of sunshine, rain. Finally, you have potatoes, but they aren't important anymore. The only joy was making them grow.

S: Now we move to one of your acknowledged masterpieces, and I'd like to ask you about one of its best scenes. Did you improvise the moment in the production of the prison camp play in *Grand Illusion* when the soldier comes out dressed as a woman and for a moment the others, who have been sexually deprived, almost forget his sex?

R: I think it was improvised because I recall

that I discovered while shooting the film that one of the actors who played a prisoner was a pansy, so I gave him the pleasure of wearing female clothes in the show scene.

S: Why did you decide to cast Von Stroheim in the film?

R: Admiration.

S: What was he like to work with?

R: In the beginning I thought I would not be able to finish the film with him because he confused the character we had written with the Austrian officer he had been playing all his life. Instead, I wanted my officer to be a defeated man; in spite of his wonderful uniform and power, Rauffenstein is a man defeated.

S: Is that why you gave him a broken neck?

R: Exactly.

S: Did you invent that?

R: I don't know. Probably when I got Von Stroheim to understand that Rauffenstein was a defeated man, he said, "What about giving him a collar?" Von Stroheim was amazed to work with a director who didn't have a full script. The part was originally very small; I wrote it up while we were shooting. Eventually we had a big fight. Von Stroheim wept, I wept, we kissed; after that, our collaboration was perfect. You know, I think it is wrong to despise stars. People think that stars are important only when they are good actors. A real star elevates a film because he is a star. I felt that Von Stroheim would take my picture above

the sordid little prison in which it took place, and I was right.

S: Do you think there is any justice to the charge that you make the prison less terrible than it should be?

R: I think I made it what it was. The only thing I wanted to do in this film was make a picture against war. That's why I didn't make the Germans villains.

S: I think the film isn't antiwar. I think it's about the end of a certain attitude toward war.

R: You are right, but that only happened while we were making the film. I started out to make a film showing that the enemy wasn't wicked so that the audience would wonder why one went to war against him.

S: At the end of the film, when Gabin leaves the woman who has helped him, our relief at his escape is complicated by grief at what he is doing to her.

R: I wanted this. A simple break wouldn't have been deep enough. I believe that you pay for

everything you do. Here liberty is paid for with the murder of a great love.

S: Why did you make *La Marseillaise*?

R: To reconstruct the period. I tried to make the film as if the camera had existed two hundred years ago and I had shot a documentary about the Marseilles regiment going to Paris. I don't like the theatrical distortion of historical characters. That's also part of my motive in making *Grand Illusion*: I wanted to refute the romantic image of the World War I soldier that was common in newspapers and books during the thirties. Soldiers were normally represented with bad slang, a false literary vulgarity. For example, they were always calling the Germans *les Boches*. But when I was in the Army, I never heard this expression; we used to call them *les Fritz*. I always try to fight clichés. For example, movies always pretend that everything leads to drama. Instead, in *Grand Illusion*, when one of the soldiers is told that his wife is sleeping with another man, we would normally expect him to agree when another soldier tells him to forget her. "There's more than one woman in the world," the other soldier says. And the prisoner replies, "Yes, but I have only one." In the same scene, there is a teacher-prisoner who believes in cliché. When he hears they are going to Holland, he says, "Ah, Holland, the tulips, the flowers," and another replies, "Holland, the cheese."

S: Isn't this desire to escape theatrical cliché behind the more mundane, less theatrically efficient rhythm or pace in your films?

R: I'm a bad judge because the rhythm seems efficient to me. I don't ask whether it's slow or fast; I only ask whether it suits the purpose of the scene. You know, *La Marseillaise* is an anticliché picture, too. People think that those who went to establish the republic talked about this as they moved toward their goal. Not at all; they talked about how much the marching made their feet hurt.

S: One of the best scenes in the film is one where the peasant-soldiers are taught to load a musket. Was that in the script, or was it improvised?

R: Improvised. I had an assistant who was an amateur historian of armaments. His sole job in making the film was to reconstitute the military details. I gave him in that scene an opportunity to reconstruct precise details of the arms of the period.

S: Don't you make the events of the Revolution less brutal than they were?

R: Yes.

S: Why?

R: That was not the purpose of the picture.

S: But isn't that falsification? I notice that you always avoid brutality even when there is an opportunity for it in your films.

R: I don't like violence.

S: Don't you think it has its purpose, even apart from truth?

R: I admire violence when it is well portrayed, but you need genius for that; talent is not enough. In any case, I have no gift for it.

S: Do you think *La Marseillaise* is sufficiently coherent?

R: I know that there is something wrong with it—perhaps the lack of a central character, perhaps the lack of stars. The only stars I used had small parts.

S: Like Jouvet. Why did you use him that way?

R: Because he was my friend, he offered to play a part if it was small, because he was very busy at that time. Jouvet's most important characteristic was authority, so he was perfect to play the part of the head of the Assembly.

S: He is also sinister. Why did you want this representative of the new class to be sinister?

R: This bourgeois knows better than the people that the birth of the republic meant the death of the king. He couldn't represent this fact and be cheerful.

S: But he looks like a commissar.

R: Of course. He represents the next ruling class, which will commit excesses of its own.

S: In *The Human Beast* you used some back projection in the train scenes, didn't you?

R: Only once: in the scene when Gabin commits suicide. For the rest, the railroad company had put a few miles of track and a locomotive at my disposal. We had several cars behind the locomotive (a makeup wagon, one for the electricians, etc.); it was a rolling studio.

S: Do you think there is too much documentary footage on the railroad in the film?

R: No. While I was working on the script, slowly the Zola subject of heredity began to yield to my more characteristic subject of the relationships among people. I am interested always in relationships among a group of people, like those imprisoned together in *Grand Illusion*, or working together, as in *Toni*. In *The Human Beast*, the railroad becomes a little world. Actors sleep with actresses; bosses sleep with their secretaries; the train operator in *The Human Beast* sleeps with the wife of the dispatcher.

S: There is a curiously untypical moment in the film. When Gabin and Simone make love in the little cabin near the tracks, as they sink to the floor, you pan to a sluice of water entering a barrel. That seems unusually blatant symbolism.

R: Good or bad, it was the only idea I had that could keep me from having to show them making love. I felt I needed something to fill the screen as the camera withdrew from them. You say you find my rhythm too slow; but it is the right rhythm for me, and I work hard on it. At the moment you mention, I felt that it would be too fast if we cut away from them when they go down to the floor, but also that there would be a certain emptiness if I didn't move to the detail you indicate.

S: Most people think *The Rules of the Game* is your finest film. Do you agree?

R: I can't say. As with everything one does in life, sometimes I love it, sometimes I hate it. Perhaps you will find this strange, but for me it belongs, among my works, in the same category as *French Cancan*.

S: I do find that strange.

R: Both films show the same type of society.

S: But *The Rules of the Game* is so much more serious a film.

R: What is a serious film?

S: Well, I think that *The Rules of the Game* says much more about life than *French Cancan* does.

R: Yes, *French Cancan* is more limited to the evocation of a certain period. In *The Rules of the Game* I was portraying a class that exists in many periods. These people are lovable, charming, pleasant to spend a weekend with, but they have a frantic desire to commit suicide. Like Rauffenstein and Boeldieu in *Grand Illusion*, they

fear that the world doesn't need them anymore. Even today, we see what has always been true: that revolutionaries often rely on financing by the rich; the rich subsidize those who will destroy them. I wish I could make that film again about America at the present moment.

S: Radical chic.

R: Yes.

S: I'd like to ask some specific questions about this film. Why, for example, in the scene when Robert goes to his mistress' apartment to tell her that their affair is over, do you show them in the reverse cuts standing next to Chinese statues?

R: You know, when you have a good subject for a picture, you are hoping to find symbols which help to clarify things. By situating them near those Chinese statues, I associated them with an endless unchanging and formal society.

S: In general, don't you make greater use of objects in *The Rules of the Game* than in your previous films?

R: Yes. It wasn't deliberate; it happened while I was shooting. In a film my nephew made of Picasso at work, Picasso says, "Don't leave holes, don't leave empty spaces." That's a rule I try to follow, even if I do so unconsciously.

S: What is Christine after in the film?

R: She doesn't know herself. Probably when she was a young girl she read some love stories, which she still reads, and she is disappointed because life is no romance.

S: Could she have been happy with Octave?

R: No. He is a bum, and Christine is very proper.

S: Was the *danse macabre* a symbol of the fate of her class?

R: Yes. That was an easy symbol; perhaps too easy, but it was very tempting.

S: It works, however, because they don't regard it as a symbol. They don't know how portentous it is to play what they only regard as a game. So far as you're concerned, what is the rule that Jurieu breaks, causing him to be killed?

R: He is like this Japanese soldier I've just read about who spent thirty years in the jungle by himself. Jurieu has entered a world in which he doesn't belong.

S: I have a somewhat different interpretation. I wonder if you think I'm wrong.

R: You can't be wrong. If a film is good, it leaves room for collaboration by the spectator.

S: But I could be collaborating stupidly.

R: I know, but still the film must allow you to create some of it. For example, after *Grand Illusion* came out, I received letters from people asking me if the escapees would return to the front, if Gabin would marry the girl, etc. Others actually created their own conclusions about these questions.

S: I'm talking about something a bit different: not what happens to the characters after we leave them, but about what they mean during the film. To me, Jurieu is ironically far too much like the world he enters. After all, he doesn't run away with Christine; he stays long enough to ask permission from her husband.

R: No, if he were really part of that world, he would simply go to bed with Christine, without asking her to marry him.

S: All right then, why doesn't he run away with her without marriage?

R: Jurieu is like a foreign substance entering the organism. In a chateau very much like the one shown in the film, one hundred years ago a man brought a catfish from America that he introduced into the lake around the chateau. After a while, that catfish devoured the local fishes, multiplied, and then began to devour his own kind. Jurieu has great respect for the rules and is very charming, but the others instinctively know that he is dangerous because he is not one of their species. So they eliminate him.

S: As you say, if he were a member of that class, he simply would have slept with her. But he doesn't have two choices; he has three: adultery, marriage, and flight. Why doesn't he follow Christine's own wishes and accept the third?

R: The rules of the game.

S: So, as I say, he is not a total outsider. Do you think the class you portray in this film has any capacity for love?

R: In a way. La Chesnaye loves his wife and his mistress. He would even accept their infidelity, although it would pain him at first.

S: Then what brings havoc to this society in the sphere of love?

R: The stupid jealousy of the women.

S: Then you approve of the multiple liaisons?

R: No. I don't approve of this morally; I simply find it practical. Being immoral, however, it carries the potential for danger. Fidelity is to be preferred.

S: What made you turn to India after the Hollywood period of which we've already spoken?

R: I had read a review in *The New Yorker* of Rumer Godden's *The River*, which regretted the fact that this well-written novel was not likely to find a large audience. I purchased a copy and, after reading it, was certain it would make a good film. I tried to interest people in Hollywood, but no one wanted a film about India that didn't show its more colorful side—elephants, tigers, Bengal Lancers, etc. Godden's novel about young girls in a proper house on the banks of the Ganges didn't seem box office to them.

S: But India doesn't really influence the action much.

R: It influences it by making the English family more English than they would be if they were at home. You know, I tried in this film to show that colonialists could be good people. I don't believe in heroes or villains, and one's social role doesn't say all there is to say about you. We are all like trees, rooted in a certain earth, but you cannot call that earth moral or immoral.

S: Why did you include the narrative about Krishna in the film?

R: Because I wanted to show something purely indigenous. The English family so dominates the story that I needed something to balance them.

S: Why did you move to Italy for your next film, or rather why did you stay so long away from France?

R: I don't know.

S: It was an accident?

R: Everything in life is an accident.

S: Do you agree with those critics who call your Italian film *The Golden Coach*, Pirandellian?

R: No. Pirandello establishes a confusion between theater and real life. I start with this confusion, but I quickly resolve it. I want to show that life is life and the stage is the stage.

S: How was Anna Magnani to work with?

R: She was marvelous, unique; I know of no one like her. Her outstanding quality is perhaps sincerity; she can throw herself into a part so completely that she forgets the real Anna

Magnani. More important, she has a natural tempo. She knows how to walk, to run. I think I showed her talent off in that scene when she walks down the staircase after winning over the council and getting the right to keep the coach.

S: She shows there her amazing ability to appear beautiful without really being so.

R: She used to arrive on the set in the morning exhausted from a night spent in a café. In this condition, she was impossible to show on the screen. I remember that my nephew, who was the cameraman, used to quarrel with her for looking so bad. I would tell her just to make up and we would see what happened. She did, we had two or three rehearsals, and acting transformed her into someone twenty years younger.

S: In *Picnic on the Grass* you make the representative of science and intellect such a fool that you seem to be stacking the deck.

R: But I do believe that many scientists are fools.

S: But since Meurisse is such a fool, there isn't much development in the film.

R: Perhaps I'm a bad judge, because I love Meurisse's performance so.

S: I agree that Meurisse is marvelous, but the role is a problem.

R: I'm a bad judge of that, too, because I wrote the role.

S: Why in your last film did you decide to go back to the subject of *Grand Illusion*?

R: Having made a film about a war of gentlemen, I found it interesting to consider a war fought under more sordid conditions.

S: Yet oddly enough, *The Elusive Corporal* is more of an entertainment than *Grand Illusion*.

R: Probably because that was the only way I found to make interesting a situation that wasn't inherently so. I didn't choose the film, though I very much enjoyed making it.

S: I was puzzled by the end of the film, when the two men meet on the bridge and pledge a return to fighting. It almost seemed like a call to maintain a military posture for the audience, though, of course, there was no war going on when the film was made.

R: Very frankly, I didn't know how to end the film and wrote several versions. That happened to me very often. I didn't know how to end *Grand Illusion* either. I wrote that last scene just before shooting it. In *The Elusive Corporal* I just wanted an excuse to end with this bridge and the panorama of Paris, because I wanted to show very clearly that we had left Germany and come back to France.

S: When you made *The Little Theater of Jean Renoir* for television, you originally intended one segment about revolution against war. Why didn't you make that?

R: Budget limitations and my failure to find the right actor for the part. I needed a young Michel Simon, as he was during the time of *Boudu*, but I couldn't find him.

S: I want to end with a few general questions. Have you been much influenced by critics?

R: Certainly; I'm a human being and am influenced by everything in my surroundings, just as you are.

S: Was any critic particularly important to you? Bazin?

R: Undoubtedly. He made me feel that I was doing something significant.

S: Have you felt generally well treated by critics?

R: Yes. And also by the public.

S: When I told René Clair how odd it was that directors who hated each other all liked Godard, he said that he found it odd that directors hated each other. He said that when you, Delannoy, and he began your careers, there was no rivalry between you.

R: Clair is too kind about the earlier period. When I started making films, I was convinced that all French pictures were bad and that I was, perhaps, the only man who could make good ones.

S: Clair also had few copies of his films, which disturbed me. What about you?

R: I have some that I produced myself or that the producer made me a gift of.

S: How is it that directors of stature are not given prints as a matter of course?

R: First, color films can't easily be reproduced. Black-and-white films can be duplicated, but the dupe threatens the business of the original owner. What happens, for example, when the director or writer dies? Will his heirs sell off all his effects, including the prints, and to whom?

S: My last question: You've spoken eloquently about the dangers of money and a mechanical attitude toward filmmaking. Would you have preferred to work under less commercial circumstances, and have you felt hampered by the conditions under which you did work?

R: Noncommercial films are rarely good. When you make a film just for yourself, the chances are high that it won't be a good one. Moreover, even though I was often prevented from doing what I wanted to, my ambition was to belong even more than I did to the world of commercial films. I believe in professionalism. I may sometimes have been stopped from making a film, but once shooting started, I was always free.

Alfred Hitchcock

Universal City, February 28, 1972

Feature Films: 1925 *The Pleasure Garden*; 1926 *The Mountain Eagle, The Lodger*; 1927 *Downhill, Easy Virtue, The Ring*; 1928 *The Farmer's Wife, Champagne*; 1929 *The Manxman, Blackmail*; 1930 *Juno and the Paycock, Murder*; 1931 *The Skin Game*; 1932 *Rich and Strange, Number Seventeen*; 1933 *Waltzes from Vienna*; 1934 *The Man Who Knew Too Much*; 1935 *The Thirty-nine Steps*; 1936 *The Secret Agent, Sabotage*; 1937 *Young and Innocent*; 1938 *The Lady Vanishes*; 1939 *Jamaica Inn*; 1940 *Rebecca, Foreign Correspondent*; 1941 *Mr. and Mrs. Smith, Suspicion*; 1942 *Saboteur*; 1943 *Shadow of a Doubt, Lifeboat*; 1945 *Spellbound*; 1946 *Notorious*; 1947 *The Paradine Case*; 1948 *Rope*; 1949 *Under Capricorn*, 1950 *Stage Fright*; 1951 *Strangers on a Train*; 1952 *I Confess*; 1954 *Dial M for Murder, Rear Window*; 1955 *To Catch a Thief*; 1956 *The Trouble with Harry, The Man Who Knew Too Much*; 1957 *The Wrong Man*; 1958 *Vertigo*; 1959 *North by Northwest*; 1960 *Psycho*; 1963 *The Birds*; 1964 *Marnie*; 1966 *Torn Curtain*; 1970 *Topaz*; 1972 *Frenzy*.

Since no other filmmaker has been interviewed so usefully or at such great length as Alfred Hitchcock (in François Truffaut's *Hitchcock*), I was at a special disadvantage in this case. Although I prepared my questions to ensure novelty, duplication turned out to be unavoidable. Directors who are artists—individual sensibilities rather than faceless craftsmen—exhibit characteristic themes and techniques; logically, their comments about themselves must show a similar confinement. I should not have been surprised to find Hitchcock answering my questions by so frequently referring to anecdotes he had offered Truffaut.

As a consequence, however, I omitted from the transcript much of a talk that ranged over a five-hour period in the well-appointed quarters of Alfred Hitchcock Productions at the Universal studio. Because his general remarks reflect confrontation with a view of Hitchcock's talent distinctly different from that of Truffaut's, I retained most of those. Since comments on individual films proved less original, I render the summary of his career rather sketchily.

Additional description is also unnecessary for the corpulent figure that is Hitchcock's well-known trademark. But I can report that the dour voice and manner of his television appearances are clearly fabricated. "Agreeable" and "almost avuncular" come closer to describing his behavior—at least, as interviewee. Perhaps "imperturbable" might complete my impression. In responding to questions or objections, Hitchcock has the air of a man wholly confident of his credo. This he expressed in our talk, emphasized in minor revisions he asked to make in the transcript and summarized in a personal letter with which he accompanied its return.

SAMUELS: Your long distinguisged career has taken you through every technical revolution in cinema. Were there any you would have preferred to miss: sound, Technicolor, Vista Vision, etc.?

HITCHCOCK: So far as screen size goes, I never liked what is commonly referred to as the letterbox screen. It leaves you with a good deal of empty space that causes the audience to wonder what it's there for. A painter is able to choose the canvas size that fits his subject. (I happen to own a Dufy that was painted on a long, narrow canvas; but the subject is a harbor and therefore suitable.) Filmmakers, on the other hand, are bound by the screens available throughout the world. You can't compose for a New York screen only; you've got to think, say, of the screen in Thailand. I've always believed in film as the newest art of the twentieth century because of its ability to communicate with the mass audiences of the world. In any case, I suppose that oversized screens were devised when the industry was searching for novelty, which, of course, led to Cinerama. But I can even remember films, in which, out of pure showmanship, the screen size was altered to produce a climax.

S: As in DeMille's *Samson and Delilah*?

H: Yes, or *Portrait of Jennie*, where there was a lighthouse and lots of water that lent themselves to the process. But I don't think it enhanced the story.

S: Isn't it generally true that technical impediments are useful? For example, you seem to me to change vistas without an expansible screen in a film like *The Thirty-nine Steps*, and therefore, to excite us by your skill. Through your editing, you alternate open and closed spaces.

H: You can do anything you want with montage. Cinema is simply pieces of film put together in a manner that creates ideas and emotions. The tragedy is that people don't make films that way now. Because I'm bound by consensus to make thrillers—

S: May I interrupt for a moment? Would you have liked to release yourself from this binding?

H: I'm not sure. The cobbler should stick to his last, you know.

S: However, you began your career with a variety of films. Why did you narrow your focus later?

H: Unfortunately, one's employers expect certain things from you, so I've been more or less forced to stick to my genre. But, you know, people confuse what I do with mystery. I don't believe in mystifying an audience. I believe in giving them all the information and then in making them sweat. It's no good devising a film to satisfy only yourself. The subject doesn't count either. You get your satisfaction through your style of treatment. I'm not interested in content. It disturbs me very much when people criticize my films because of their content. It's like looking at a still life and saying, "I wonder whether those apples are sweet or sour." Cinema is form. I see many good films that contain very fine dialogue. I

don't deprecate these films, but to me, they're not pure cinema. Trying to make them cinema, some new directors find odd angles to shoot from, but they still only produce what I call "photographs of people talking."

S: I agree with your objection to weird angles. That's why I was puzzled in *Spellbound* when you shoot Gregory Peck drinking a glass of milk by aiming the camera at the glass that's being drained.

H: I was playing with white there, in preparation for the denouement, which had to do with snow. Throughout the film, I wanted to make a sort of leitmotiv of that color.

S: In view of your characterization of yourself as a formalist who just happens to work in the thriller genre, why have you, on occasion, made something like *Under Capricorn*?

H: *Under Capricorn*, I made to please Ingrid Bergman, who was a friend of mine. I was looking for a subject that suited her, rather than myself.

S: You've said you like to achieve your effects through editing. What do you think of directors who don't rely on it so much, like Antonioni and Bergman?

H: Antonioni is almost a surrealist.

S: But he's as visual as you are.

H: No question!

S: Bergman is rather more complicated because he relies so much on words.

H: And yet he has indicated on one occasion that he learned a lot from Hitchcock. He uses the visuals as much as he can, whether in the form of gigantic close-ups or natural objects; you know, the sapling trees against the sky and so on. What Truffaut appreciated from my technique was the use of the subjective treatment. A typical example is the film *Rear Window*, where the central figure is a man in one position whose viewpoint we study. His viewpoint becomes his mental processes, by the use of the camera and the montage—and this is what I actually mean by subjective treatment. The objective treatment, however, is also used when necessary; but for me, the objective is merely an extension of the theater because you are a viewer of the events that take place in front of you, but you are not necessarily in the mind of the person. Subjective shooting puts the audience in the mind of the character.

S: You obtain your best results, I think, by creating sharp intrusions of the subjective in an otherwise objective narrative. For example, I'd instance the change to subjective camera angle in *Notorious* when Ingrid Bergman has to meet all of her husband's Nazi friends and convince them she's a Nazi, too. By making the camera her eyes, you convey the intensity of the threat.

H: Yes. I wanted to say visually, "Here is Ingrid in the lions' den; now look at each lion!"

S: These alternations we've been discussing—between open and closed vistas, subjective and objective camera work, etc.—indicate what I believe to be the essential musicality of your films.

H: I, myself, use musical terms when I direct. I say, "Don't put a great big close-up there because it's loud brass and you mustn't use a loud note unless it's absolutely vital." Cinema is the orchestration of shots.

S: In *The Thirty-nine Steps* you orchestrate not only shots, but music itself. You begin and end with natural music in the music hall, have a bit more of it in the Salvation Army Band scene, and use background music very sparingly: a bit in the moor chase and a few romantic bars when Madeleine Carroll returns to the inn room after learning that Donat has been telling her the truth. Yet in your American films you tend to use background music more generally. Why the shift?

H: A matter of conventions. Moreover, when I first came here, I didn't have the complete freedom I'd had in England. One had to conform. Don't forget, I came in a period when the producer was king. I suppose the most flattering thing ever said to me—not immediately after *Rebecca*, but two or three years later—was Selznick's: "You're the only director I'd ever trust a picture with." In those days—although I'm now speaking heresy—I never understood how, for example, Selznick could say, "Thalberg's great with a finished picture." A producer like that used to take a finished film, rewrite it, reedit it, and so on. I first experienced this when I started *Rebecca*. I'd rehearse a scene, but before I could get ready to shoot it, the script girl would come up and whisper, "I have to phone Mr. Selznick now." He had to okay the final rehearsal before I could shoot! That's how heavy the hand of the producer was in those days. Another example is retakes. When I used to complain of a technical defect and ask to reshoot a scene, he'd say, "No retakes!" "Why not?" I'd ask. He replied, "It may not be in the picture." The producer used to assemble the film, arrange the credits, even outfit it with a temporary score taken from the music library. Within three weeks of the last day of shooting, you'd have the sneak preview.

S: How did you manage to become invulnerable to this kind of interference?

H: Very simply: I was loaned out. As soon as I was working for someone I wasn't under contract to, the supervision was lessened.

S: I had understood that you evaded interference by shooting things out of order.

H: No, I just normally work that way. To me, a picture must be planned on paper. People are always asking me why I don't improvise on the set, and I always reply, "What for? I'd rather improvise in a room with the writer." My method is very simple. I work out a treatment with my screenwriter. In order to do this, you've got to have a visual sense. I never look through the camera; I think only of that white screen that has to be filled up the way you fill up a canvas. That's why I draw rough setups for the cameraman.

S: You're making live-action animated films.

H: You could say that. If I wanted to, I could draw every frame of the finished picture. But when I have a good cameraman, I don't need to go that far. I simply tell him what elements I want to include or exclude in any shot. What I do with the writer is involve him in the direction of the picture and have him collaborate in the creation of the story line, including dialogue. After having completed this process, I leave it to the screenwriter to write his dialogue within the framework of the finished, agreed cinematic story line. I know every shot we'll end up with because the planning stage has been so complete. What mystifies me is why so many other filmmakers need to see things on the screen before they edit, whereas a musician can hear his music simply by looking at the notes and lines of his score. Why shouldn't we do the same?

S: Can't you plan so carefully and definitely because of your genre? After all, your films work precisely because they manipulate the spectator. Yet there are other sorts of films. Andre Bazin argued, for example, that deep focus and long takes left the spectator free to choose the elements he wished to pay most attention to and thus were to be preferred.

H: Is a listener allowed to choose the notes he'll hear? If you free the spectator to choose, you're making theater, not cinema.

S: I'd like to talk about a different kind of freeing the spectator. What do you think of the disinterested quasi-documentary style of neorealism—a film like *The Bicycle Thief*, for example?

H: It's very good, but it's no different from any chase story.

S: But the emphasis is not on effect. Rather it is on the social realities reflected in the situation.

H: Yes, but De Sica takes the audience into whorehouses, soup kitchens, homes. . . .

S: But not so as to produce a sharply defined emotion in each case. A panorama is created. That's not your intention.

H: I go further than a film like *The Bicycle Thief*, which shows a man and a boy walking in front of a panorama. I believe that your backgrounds must be involved in the story. For example, in *North by Northwest*, when Cary Grant gets trapped in an auction room, I use this setting by making Grant start crazy bidding.

S: What I'm driving at, however, is my suspicion that you're not interested in documenting a social reality without regard to evocation or the solving of an esthetic problem.

H: Where else is the dramatic impact for the ordinary spectator? You've got to remember that *Bicycle Thief* wasn't a success with the Italian audience. It's funny you should instance this picture. We have a home in Northern California, and in the period of *The Bicycle Thief*, we happened to have an Italian couple working for us who spoke not one word of English. One day my wife and I took the mother and her daughter into San Francisco, where my wife and the girl had to do some shopping. Since I didn't know what to do with Mrs. Chiesa, I decided to take her to see *The Bicycle Thief*. It was an Italian movie; I thought it might interest her. There was a knot of about twenty people in the theater—it was a road show, I remember, at the Geary—and we watched the film. Do you know, she only gave one exclamation the whole time: when the father cuffed the little boy. So when we got outside, I asked her how she'd liked it. She said, "Okay. But why didn't he borrow a bicycle?" Of course, she demolished the whole thing. So I said, "Mrs. Chiesa, what films do you like?" "Ah," she said, "I like a Betty Grable musical."

S: You may direct your films at the Mrs. Chiesas, but your style seems to me to require some sophistication in anyone who wishes to appreciate your work.

H: Yes. I don't expect the average spectator to go beyond his emotional reaction; then, if the others like to examine the way. . . . You know, this may explain why occasionally one of my films is indifferently received and then, a year later, it becomes a classic. I never understood the delay.

S: Can you give me an example?

H: *Psycho.*

S: But wasn't the first response to *Psycho* due to a brutality unexpected in a Hitchcock film? Your films aren't usually brutal. Why, in *Psycho* and *The Birds*, did you suddenly change that?

H: But *Psycho* was designed to throw a violent moment on the screen and then reduce the violence as the film progressed, while keeping its effects alive in the minds of the audience. Furthermore, brutality was inherent in both subjects. It's like *Frenzy*, which is the story of a man who is impotent and therefore expresses himself through murder. I only show one of the women being murdered; the rest I leave to the audience. I show a second murder this way: I bring the man and his victim along a corridor through an extended shot that takes us up the stairs, around the turn of the stairs, along the passage; then, I show them entering the room as the door closes, and he says something to the effect that she's his type. Then I cut and take the camera back the very way we've come—I had to have a special rig built for this—until we reach the street. As we're coming down, the traffic noise has been getting louder. Then I take us all the way out into the busy Covent Garden Market until we can see the full façade of the building. I then deliberately bring the street noises up to such a volume that the audience must say to itself, "No one will ever hear the poor girl's

screams." I'm not interested in showing brutality. I made *Psycho* in black and white purposely to avoid the blood. Red would have been unpleasant, unnecessary; I wouldn't have been able to treat the blood cinematically, as in the editing of its flow down the drain and so on, had the sequence been in color.

S: Since you've raised the subject, what do you think of working in color?

H: Color should start with the nearest equivalent to black and white. This sounds like a most peculiar statement, but color should be no different from the voice which starts muted and finally arrives at a scream. In other words, the muted color is black and white, and the screams are every psychedelic color you can think of, starting, of course, with red. Years ago I answered this question by describing a murder in a park, where you'd pan down to feet struggling in a flower bed full of white asters. Since it's night, you still haven't gone much beyond black and white. Then you dolly in to one petal of the white aster till it fills the whole screen; then suddenly there's a slash of red.

S: I understand Chabrol does something like this in *The Butcher*, where a sandwich suddenly has blood dripping on it.

H: Has he?

S: Is it true that you regard your actors only as elements of composition?

H: Well, the actor must be an element because film is montage. But I do explain the cutting to him so he knows why I've asked him to cooperate.

S: Do you let your actors see rushes?

H: Certainly.

S: You don't try to make your actors become other than what they are, do you? I mean, you seem to me to select your performers for qualities they inherently possess.

H: Well, if you take what I call a fantasy chase picture like *North by Northwest*, it's good to cast a known personality in the role of the endangered hero. That way the audience worries more about the character. We always are more deeply concerned by what happens to someone near to us than by something we might, say, read in the paper.

S: Am I not right, however, in thinking that the acting in your films is generally low on the list of your priorities?

Bernard Cribbens and Anna Massey.

Vivien Merchant.

H: No. The tiniest role is just as important as the bigger roles.

S: Your minor characters always seem better to me.

H: In *Frenzy*, for example, I have more character parts than I've had in years because the London stage actor is willing to play a moderate size part. So, I've got Vivien Merchant, Alec McCowen, Bernard Cribbins, Anna Massey, and so on. They're all leading players, you see. Vivien Merchant actually brought the character to me.

S: In view of the technical brilliance of most of your films, I wonder why you so often settle for bad backdrops. I think, for example, of the mother's street in *Marnie*, where you show an obviously painted ship and an obviously painted sky in the background.

H: That was a technical mixup, and something of which I did not approve. We were very pressed for time, or I would have scrapped the whole thing and started over. I wanted to show something that had always fascinated me—I think I'd seen it in Copenhagen and London, as well as in Baltimore, where *Marnie* takes place—

a row of houses and suddenly a ship looming above them.

S: You would shoot on location whenever you could, then?

H: Of course. On the other hand, some location shooting has become terribly cliche. I mean, if I see any more people walking along sidewalks and made to appear as if they were dancing because of the use of a long focus lens! We've got an awful lot of people nowadays who'll say, "Ah, I must symbolize the traffic." So they use a ten-inch lens that makes the cars all shimmer. If I see any more out-of-focus flowers in the foreground!

S: Your films constantly show respectable people secretly attracted to crime. Why?

H: Can you give me an example?

S: Remember that little woman in *Strangers on a Train* who is so excited to learn that her cab is being commandeered by policemen chasing someone. She's a very minor character, but your films are full of touches indicating the same generalized attitude.

H: I think this is a little quirk; there's no deep significance in it.

S: But you often show that people find crime

sexy. I think, for example, of the Peggy Ashcroft character in *The Thirty-nine Steps*. She is attracted to Donat, of course, because he's from the big city, which she longs for; but she is even more attracted when she learns he's a fugitive.

H: I think this must have something to do with my being English. Crime is much more literate in England than in America. In England, unlike America, crime novels are first-class literature. Not only are the English more attracted by crime, but the crimes themselves are more bizarre.

S: English eccentricity?

H: They are eccentric, especially the intellectuals. I remember what happened, for example, to the poet Lascelles Abercrombie when he was challenged to a duel. Offered his choice of weapons, he chose steamrollers. I'll tell you how deeply interested the British are in crime. There's a group in London called Our Society. It meets regularly on Sunday evenings at a fashionable restaurant in a private room. The members include lawyers, writers, journalists. When they meet, they rehash a recent *cause célèbre*, effectively trying the case among themselves. They borrow exhibits from the trial and so forth.

S: What do you think differentiates the British interest in crime from the American?

H: The British interest is esthetic.

S: Did you then change your style of treating crime when you moved from England to America?

H: I'd say that until *Frenzy*, and setting aside *North by Northwest*, I haven't had as much opportunity to introduce the British type of humor in my American pictures.

S: So *Frenzy* takes you back to something like *The Lady Vanishes*?

H: Except that that was a fantasy and *Frenzy* isn't. The closest I think I came in my American films to the humorous portrayal of character along with the crime was in *Shadow of a Doubt*.

S: I think that film also comes rather closer than usual to having content.

H: That's true.

S: I'd like to hear what you think of my version of this content. Aren't you showing that the girl in the film isn't quite so superior to her murderer-uncle? When he first comes to town, she's happy to have the relief he brings her from small-town boredom, but when she realizes that he threatens the status of her family, she pretty ruthlessly tries to get rid of him.

H: She switches from adulation so suddenly that she becomes paranoid. The horror of learning what he is makes her switch loyalty almost viciously.

S: Aren't we meant to find her ruthless?

H: She is ruthless. She comes down those stairs wearing that ring and thus tells him he must leave or be executed.

S: Our sympathy is split between them. He's a murderer. . . .

H: But a very attractive man. That's something I always insist on. Movies usually portray murderers as tough and unsympathetic. That always makes me wonder how they ever got near their victims.

S: You wouldn't be interested in a murderer who didn't get close to his victims, would you?

H: No. I've never been interested in professional criminals. The audience can't identify with their lack of feeling. I'm also not interested in the conventional detective. That's why, for example, in *Frenzy* I invented the chief inspector's wife so as to permit myself to place most of the discussion of the crime outside a professional context. And I get comedy to sugarcoat the discussions by making the wife a gourmet cook. So, this inspector comes home

every night to discussion of the murders and overrich meals.

S: In the early scene of *Shadow of a Doubt,* when Joseph Cotten is being chased, why do you select such a high-angle shot?

H: For clarity of effect. It was like saying, "Here we are above a maze, where you can see both the exit and all the people who are trying to keep him from getting there."

S: Why did you have the niece fall in love with the detective at the end of the film?

H: I think that was a commercial concession, really.

S: You do, occasionally, introduce a love element that isn't strictly necessary. Why don't you resist this convention?

H: I'm not self-indulgent where content is concerned; I'm only self-indulgent about treatment. I'd compare myself to an abstract painter. My favorite painter is Klee.

S: But can't a commercial concession in content hurt the form? After all, the end of *Shadow of a Doubt* is corny.

H: It is corny. In *Frenzy,* I have dared— because times change—to kill off my love interest.

S: Speaking of daring, why do you so often show lovers, who are forced by circumstance to bed down for the night, behaving like virgins, even though it's quite clear that they've had

plenty of experience? This happens, among others, in *Rear Window* and *Foreign Correspondent.*

H: Well, the Laraine Day character was a Quaker. And, in *Rear Window,* I think the audience is thinking about another problem; I mean, how did they do it with his leg in a cast? Anyway, we weren't as permissive in the period when those films were made as we are now.

S: Yet *The Thirty-nine Steps,* which is earlier, is also more risqué.

H: In Hollywood, we had the Breen Office. We couldn't even show a husband and wife in bed together.

S: Well, let's go back then to *The Lodger,* which you've claimed was your first characteristic film. In connection with the subject I've been interested in, your detective in this film is inferior to the criminal: he's stupid, lascivious, uncharming, etc.

H: He's a local; he hadn't the lodger's finesse. He's a constable off the beat, that's all. Since those days, however, as you'll see in *Frenzy,* the level among inspectors has gone up. They've a police college now.

S: How did you get the idea for that marvelous shot of the lodger's hand moving down the banister?

H: All such touches were substitutes for sound. I wanted to show, by means of that shot, that the woman downstairs was probably hearing a creaking noise.

S: You repeat this sort of shot several times, as in *Foreign Correspondent* and, most famously, *Vertigo.*

H: Staircases are very photogenic.

S: Why do you make the young girl in the film so sexually aggressive toward the lodger?

H: She's goaded by the idea that he might be Jack the Ripper.

S: Another instance of the attractiveness of crime. Aren't you attributing to your characters your own delight in excitement?

H: I must refer again to the English attitude. Did you ever read *We the Accused* by Ernest Raymond? It's based on the Crippen case, although he alters the locations and circumstances. Raymond shows the whole process of English law. He shows the police to be kindly, but also the murderer, who did nothing worse than rid himself of a bitch of a wife. He takes us right up to the hanging, when the governor walks into the condemned man's cell and says, "Good morning." Then the hangman steps forward and says, "Put your hands down at your sides, old chap." And then his hands are strapped, and the procession starts. The white cap goes on, the noose goes on, and the assistant executioner straps the ankles. Then the hangman gives the condemned a friendly tap on the arm and pulls the lever. On the way to prison, when they were originally arrested, the murderer was asked what type of tobacco he wanted, and the girl for whom he killed was offered a choice of magazines.

S: In *Blackmail*, you've said that you wanted the first sequence to illustrate duty, but doesn't this throw us off a bit? The film begins almost as if it will be a documentary about a day in the life of a policeman; then it becomes a thriller.

H: I wanted the whole film to have that effect, but I was prevented. I wanted the film to open with an ordinary criminal being apprehended by detectives who behaved like men working in an office, just doing a job. In the last sequence, the detective's girlfriend was to give herself up, and then I would have repeated the same routine as I started with. The whole idea was to show his conflict between love and duty, with duty winning out.

S: But that isn't thriller technique; that's content.

H: Yes. The only thriller technique in the film would have been the girl's suspense about whether or not her murdering a rapist will be discovered.

S: Doesn't this alteration suggest that you might not have become so totally a director of thrillers had things worked out differently?

H: I think you'll find that the real start of my career was *The Man Who Knew Too Much*.

S: But might you have gone on to make films which, though effective and cinematic, had a more thorough grounding in the complications of real life?

H: Well, I did make a film out of Galsworthy's *Skin Game*.

S: But you're not fond of it.

H: Because it's too theatrical.

S: Do you think you would have branched out beyond thrillers more often had you written your own scripts?

H: No, I'd probably have narrowed down.

S: Why don't you write your own scripts?

H: I do.

S: But not the dialogue.

H: I do now and again, but you can't be jack-of-all-trades. Dialogue writing, out of which comes character, is a job of its own. I'm busy enough with the cinematics. I work with the writer, as I've told you, very closely. You know, our first treatment can run as long as one hundred pages.

S: In the murder scene in *Blackmail*, did you allow Cyril Ritchard to sing because he was a singer or because you wanted him to?

H: Because it was my first talkie and the producers wanted it. It's like that old talkie *In Old Arizona*, which thrilled everyone so because it allowed them to hear bacon frying.

S: The opening of *Murder* is notable as a forecast of your later combinations of suspense and comedy. You pan across a sinister street but then show the inhabitants doing funny things: In one apartment, a man is taking his teeth out of a glass; in another, a girl tries unsuccessfully to get into her bloomers, always putting both her legs through the same opening.

H: That last detail was taken from a night when I went into my mother's room during an air raid in World War I. The whole house was in an uproar, but there was my poor Elsa Maxwell plump little mother, struggling, saying her prayers, while outside the window, shrapnel was bursting around a search-lit zeppelin—extraordinary image.

S: Do you make references to your own experience often in your films?

H: Odd bits here and there, but very rarely. *Murder* was an interesting film, though, because I intended it as a satire on the theater. In those days, the actor-manager was king: Sir Henry Irving, Sir Herbert Beerbohm-Tree, Sir Gerald du Maurier. Du Maurier used to have an office over His Majesty's Theater, called the Dome, where he conducted his business. That's why I dressed Herbert Marshall, who plays the hero, in black coat and striped pants, like a cabinet minister. They never went into the provinces. So, when my actor-manager does, he finds himself experiencing conditions which, up to then, he had disdained. When he starts investigating the murder there, he feels he's suffering the indignity of a lower order of actor.

S: In the finished film, doesn't the comedy get restrained by the thriller element?

H: Yes. But I still keep the theater business alive with the play within a play, when Marshall makes the murderer read from a play dealing with the crime, like Hamlet making Claudius witness his own crime to see if the man will expose himself. You know, I modeled the murderer on a circus performer of the period. He used to enter the ring, dressed like a woman, accompanied by a trim maid, and then go into his trapeze act. Oddly enough, the girl who plays the thief in *To Catch a Thief* did a high wire act in the circus, too.

S: Since the murderer is a homosexual in this film, why do you make his motive shame at being a half-caste? It hardly seems the more serious problem.

H: He was a half-caste homosexual. In those days, being a half-caste was very serious. Being a Eurasian in India, for example, meant you belonged to neither side, so that you weren't accepted. But the element is surely dated now.

S: In *Rich and Strange*—

H: One of my less successful pictures.

S: But it has many good things in it.

H: Yes, I like it.

S: Is the opening sequence with the umbrellas what gave you the idea for the umbrella scene in *Foreign Correspondent*?

H: Two different purposes; in *Rich and Strange*, I simply used the umbrellas to express the life of ordinary clerks in the city of London.

S: Do you ever reuse a device deliberately, though?

H: Can you give me an example?

S: In *Rebecca*, Joan Fontaine's employer puts out her cigarette in a jar of cold cream; in *To Catch a Thief*, Jessie Royce Landis puts hers out into an egg.

H: I was aware of *that* repetition; the second example was used to show my utter dislike for eggs.

S: Why did you use place-name titles in *Rich and Strange*? Wasn't that a rather anachronistic device?

H: Oh, you had to. You've got to remember that some people in the audience won't be able to identify a remote place just by seeing it. In *Frenzy*, I've got a shot of London taken from five thousand feet up, yet I put a crest over it as though it were a map. I want to make certain that everyone realizes we're in London.

S: *The Man Who Knew Too Much* has a great deal to do with place.

H: You know how I wanted to start the original version of that film? I wanted to show the hotel window in St. Moritz, which reflects the beautiful Alpine scenery, suddenly shattered by a bullet, so that the whole window cracks and smashes to the ground. But I was told that a bullet would go right through and simply make a hole.

S: Why do you precede the killing with the comic bit of the unraveling sweater?

H: To show that death comes when you least expect it.

S: Isn't the final episode, in which the kidnapped child is rescued, rather anticlimactic, coming as it does, after the Albert Hall sequence?

H: No, because the film is about the kidnapping; the assassination is just my McGuffin. The characters in the film are worried about the McGuffin, but the audience isn't.

S: What made you decide to use Doris Day in the remake?

H: I'd seen her in a film called *Storm Warning*, where she gave a good nonsinging performance.

S: Didn't this produce the same problem that you have in *Blackmail*, where an inappropriate musical number is forced into the film because your star is a singer?

H: No, here the singing becomes part of the story.

S: One of the most charming scenes in the remake is the dinner in the Moroccan restaurant. Was that improvised?

H: Yes. That place is brick for brick, fabric and all, exactly like a restaurant in Marrakesh. I let the actors improvise their behavior with the unusual food, though, as you say.

S: Why did you change the dentist's office in the original into a taxidermist's in the remake, particularly since the latter turns out to be a false lead?

H: Dead right. I don't know. That was a mistake.

S: Although *The Man Who Knew Too Much* was your first success in the thriller form, wouldn't you agree that *The Thirty-nine Steps* is a better film?

H: Yes. The speed was perfect. You know, people say that you can cut a film and make it go fast. I don't believe that. Speed is preoccupation. In *The Thirty-nine Steps*, there was no dead footage, so the audience's absorption creates the impression of speed.

S: One small thing that bothers me in this film is the superimposition of the dead spy's face—talking to Donat in the scene right after she's murdered.

H: I don't remember why I did it, but I wouldn't repeat it today. What was the last scene in the version you saw?

S: Donat and Carroll, who were handcuffed together, now clasp hands in love, with the now useless handcuffs dangling between them.

H: You know, originally, I'd shot another scene. They drive away from the theater in a cab. Donat says, "Now that's all over, and I can start paying attention to my wife." "Your wife?" she says. "Are you married?" "Yes, I'm married to you." "How?"—and he tells her that the rule in Scotland is that if you declare yourself man and wife in front of a witness, you are man and wife, so they'd been married while hiding at the inn.

S: It's a good thing you cut that. The present ending is much better. Why did you make a film of Conrad's *The Secret Agent*? I thought you disapproved of turning literary masterpieces into films.

H: It was a project I was assigned by Gaumont British. I only read the book once. We go to all sources for material, don't we?

S: Were there any complaints at the time that you were making a thriller out of what was originally a political satire?

H: The question never came up.

S: Why did you change Verloc into a theaterowner? Did censorship keep you from showing his seedy little shop with its pornography?

H: No, I just thought there would be more dramatic opportunities this way—as there were—for example, in the scene when his wife comes home after her brother's death and sits in that flea pit of a movie house, where they're playing the cartoon *Who Killed Cock Robin*?

S: Would you agree that *The Lady Vanishes* is your best British picture?

H: Well, it did have that guaranteed movement provided by a train. Gilliat and Launder had written the script, but I wanted to make several

changes. Their script ended when the lady is removed on a stretcher. I added the whole last sequence where the train is held in the woods and also the bit in the middle about the illusionist. I don't think that Launder and Gilliat were too pleased when, after the film came out, it was referred to as a "Hitchcock picture." I believe that's what made them decide to produce and direct their own scripts, which they've done with great success ever since. They had written the two English comics as silly-ass types. I decided to cast the roles against type. I found Naunton Wayne and Basil Radford, who were used to playing absolutely different parts. Later they made a career out of their combination.

S: You also provide a strong patriotic motif. The British eventually come through with characteristic grit.

H: That's the way they would have behaved.

S: In general, your British heroes seem to me to result from more acute social observation, whereas the characters in your American films seem almost allegorical. Is that true, and is it a consequence of your expatriation?

H: I think you'll find the answer to that in *Frenzy*, which has all the social detail you're talking about. That film is full of characters who belong to their background.

S: Is the relative abstractness of milieu in your American films a response to your sense of being foreign?

H: I guess so. I'll give you an extreme example—though it comes from my British period. When I made *Murder*, I made a German as well as an English version. In the German version, Alfred Abel played the Herbert Marshall part. When it came to directing that, the producers wanted to change so many things it would have made for two separate pictures. I had a scene in the original where Herbert Marshall is brought a cup of tea by the landlady. Her kids come into the room, climb all over his bed, even let their kitten get under the bedclothes. Meanwhile, Marshall sits there trying to preserve his dignity. The German actor wouldn't do it. He insisted that you couldn't make fun of so important a man. He wouldn't allow himself to be dressed as Herbert Marshall was—in tweeds and a raincoat—when visiting the suspected murderess in jail, either. I'd already satirized the black coat and striped pants and wanted to show him now in the role of amateur detective. Abel demanded that he be allowed to wear the more formal costume to visit a young lady. What we British would have found funny, the German found improper.

S: In your American films, the humor does seem to lie not in the character, but in the lines.

H: I think my British films use humorous understatement. You'll find the same kind of understatement in *Frenzy.*

S: It seems to me that your American characters are quirky without respect to their national origin. Your humor in these films is more psychological than sociological. I think, for example, of Bruno in *Strangers on a Train.* You even use the setting, which is clearly American (Washington), rather allegorically. So we have Bruno standing in black before a white pillar of the Jefferson Memorial.

H: Bruno becomes sinister, standing in front of all that white.

S: Then, to get back to *The Lady Vanishes:* What was Michael Redgrave like to work with?

H: It was his first screen part. When we started, we rehearsed a scene, and then I told him we were ready to shoot it. He said he wasn't ready. "In the theater, we'd have three weeks to

Michael Redgrave and Margaret Lockwood.

rehearse this." "I'm sorry," I said, "in this medium, we have three minutes." But he learned the new way quickly.

S: Why did you include that single shot of the train hurtling over the viaduct?

H: That was a miniature. The whole film was made in the studio. I don't recall the reason for that shot, though.

S: I think it sustains the sense of danger because of the height and so forth of the viaduct.

H: Yes.

S: You were very clear to Truffaut on the flaws in your next film, *Jamaica Inn,* but I'm still puzzled by the slowness of its pace. It's almost as if you wanted to accentuate the problem.

H: Don't forget, I was associated with two extremely difficult men: Erich Pommer, the producer, and Charles Laughton.

S: *Foreign Correspondent* is very patriotic; it even ends with "The Star-Spangled Banner." Was that your idea?

H: That was Walter Wanger and Ben Hecht.

S: Don't you think it was the wrong package for all your fine thriller ideas?

H: Got me a telegram from Harry Hopkins!

S: I'd like to move now to what seems to me an outstanding example of your American period, *Strangers on a Train.*

H: I liked it very much, but, you know, I had terrible trouble getting my treatment dialogued. Eight writers turned me down. They couldn't visualize the story. This shows that some writers don't look at the screen. They think only of the written page.

S: The film is full of brilliant images, like the anonymous feet at the beginning. I wonder whether others were so clearly planned as that one. I think, for example, of the scene in the dining car, where Farley Granger is in clear light, but Robert Walker, the sinister character, is always barred by shadows cast by the venetian blinds.

H: That's a trick of staging. I remember in *The Lodger* when Novello goes to the window, I made one shadow of the lattice cross his face and the other come down between his eyes.

S: In the novel, Guy pays for his crime, whereas he doesn't in the film. Do you think the notion that Bruno is the embodiment of Guy's murderous impulse is compromised by this?

H: You could say that, but after all, what made him guilty?

S: He willed his wife's death. That doesn't warrant death for him, but in the film, you let him off completely.

H: If he were punished, I think the audience might leave the theater feeling dissatisfied, and you might lose all that went before.

S: Don't you think today's audiences would accept a downbeat ending?

H: No question. In *Frenzy*, the heroine gets killed.

S: Do you at all regret yielding to commercial considerations of contemporary audience response?

H: I come back to my previous remark about cinema as a world medium. No other medium can reach so wide an audience. A film can go to South America, as well as Japan. I mean, there is some satisfaction in knowing that one's cardboard head stands in the middle of a Tokyo marquee with the two stars on either side, even though I'm given Oriental eyes. I'm reaching people a long way off.

S: You used a double for Farley Granger in the tennis match.

H: Two. I even had a machine made for that scene that could project balls under the camera. Granger is always hitting right into the lens. We had to have a very strong spring arrangement so that the ball would go way over just before the cut.

S: Since you've agreed that, in general, you stay away from stories with deep content, why did you choose to make *I Confess* and *The Wrong Man*?

H: I guess I was persuaded by the gentleman I formed a partnership with during that period. He knew quite a bit about cinema. He founded the London Film Society, which almost amounted to the introduction of foreign films into English-speaking countries. *The Wrong Man* I needn't have done. I was under contract to Warner Brothers then, for whom I'd made three pictures in a period when I might have made four. The contract was up, but since I'd been paid the equivalent of four pictures, I decided to let them have one for nothing. This script was the available project.

S: In *I Confess*, why do you allow Anne Baxter and Montgomery Clift not to age very much during the film, though it covers a considerable time span?

H: It's difficult to do. If you show your characters lined in one scene, you've got to line them through the whole film. If you make them younger in the earlier scenes, you've got to give them such heavy makeup that all their character would be gone in close-ups.

S: Many people thought *Rear Window* in some sense self-referring. Were you conscious of the photographer-spy as in any sense, a self-portrait?

H: Not at all.

S: Why did you use a set rather than a real apartment house?

H: We had thirty-one apartments across that courtyard, twelve completely furnished. We never could have gotten them properly lit in a real location.

S: What do you think about the prominence that *Vertigo* has assumed for your European critics?

H: I think they understood the complexities of the situation.

S: But do you agree with those among them who say the film refers to you: You change Kim Novak into Grace Kelly, just as Jimmy Stewart changes her from one girl to another?

H: No, there's nothing in that. Here's a good

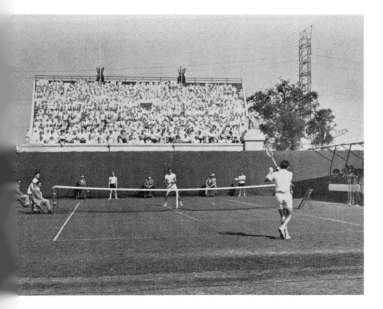

The apartment house set from Rear Window.

example, though, of the importance of the subjective treatment we spoke about a while back. You remember the scene when Kim Novak comes out of the bathroom, dressed like the original girl and wearing her hair blond? She comes closer to him, as I lift away the green haze in which the scene is shot, and then he takes her in his arms. Then I pan around from them over a special set I had built—showing the stables where he had last embraced what he thought was a dead woman. I put Stewart and Novak on a little platform and turned them around so that with back projection, I could seem to be moving from the hotel room, into the stables, then back into the hotel room. In this way, I could illustrate Stewart's feeling that the kiss is taking him back into the past. A lot of people would have shot this objectively, dissolving from the hotel room into the stable, but that would have lost the subjective effect.

S: Why did you shoot the climactic Mission Dolores scene on a set?

H: Because there was no tower on the spot. I matted the tower in. I remember telling the monsignor that he'd have a lot of visitors to his nonexistent tower after the film came out. You know, he did!

S: Why do you superimpose the painting of Carlotta when Kim Novak comes out wearing the same jewelry? Don't you think this unnecessarily obvious for the same viewers that are able to understand Stewart's rather complex psychology?

H: No, because this was a very important detail that would later give the girl away. Audiences' eyes wander. You need to underscore something that important.

S: *North by Northwest* seems to me your most consistently inventive film.

H: Took a whole year to write. Ernie Lehman and I decided, as in *The Thirty-nine Steps*, to fill out every inch of the film. We decided to make a picaresque thriller with lots of locales for the chase.

S: It also seems to be audaciously gratuitous.

H: That's right. I even reduced the McGuffin. When Cary Grant asks Leo Carroll what James Mason is after, Carroll says, "Let's say he's an importer-exporter." "What of?" "Government secrets." I realized by this time that the audience doesn't really care about the McGuffin; it's the excitement of the chase that counts.

S: *Psycho* contains some of your most brilliant effects, notably in the editing of the shower murder, but I'm bothered by bits of cheating here and there. For example, when Norman's "mother" enters the bathroom, she is in total darkness though it is dazzlingly lighted. There's also the business of having "her" lines spoken by an actress in the beginning of the film, and the cut to a high-angle shot when Norman takes her body into the fruit cellar so we won't realize that she's dead.

H: For the bathroom, you must remember that the bathroom light is shining right into the camera. In fact, we had to use a projector lens to get the right effect. We committed the cardinal photographic sin—shining a light into the lens—but that causes the audience to subconsciously realize why they can't see the face of the assailant. As for the mother's voice, it was a bit of a cheat, but it was necessary to the story and I doubt that Tony Perkins could have produced the right falsetto.

S: Why did you end the film with the psychiatrist's explanation?

H: Because the audience needed it. Otherwise, they'd have a lot of unanswered questions. You'd run afoul of the icebox trade.

S: The "icebox trade"?

H: The people who get home after seeing a movie, go to the icebox, and take out the cold chicken. While they're chewing on it, they discuss the picture. In the morning, the wife meets the neighbor next door. She says to her, "How was the picture?" and the wife says, "It was all right, but we discovered a number of flaws in it." Bang goes your word of mouth!

S: In *The Birds*, I'm puzzled by the relationship between the family's situation and the attack of the birds.

H: I only wanted to show that life goes on with its petty interests even when they are dwarfed by

some cataclysm. Substitute an air raid and you'd have the same meaning.

S: But there's an awful temptation to see the horror as some sort of symbolic emanation from the personal drama. Why did you give us so much of the latter if you didn't want us to feel that the personal situation is primary?

H: Because I didn't want to bring the birds on too early. You know, I think it was Fellini who said he wouldn't have had the nerve to make an audience wait so long for the birds to make their appearance. But I wanted to show how much was going on of minor importance, before this terribly important event takes place. Great catastrophes tend to wipe out lesser human foibles and troubles. And there was a certain amount of truth in that film. A farmer in Bodega Bay told me that he'd lost a number of lambs to birds. They used to peck the animals to death. In Oceanside, once, a house was invaded by starlings coming down the chimney.

S: Why did you have so much trouble with the ending of *Topaz*?

H: I had a lot of trouble with that. It originally ended with a duel in a huge football stadium at early morning. A little knot of men enters, and the duel starts. Then one of the characters becomes frantic and tries to stop the duel. But the referee refuses. Then, at the moment the two men take aim, at the top of the stands a sharpshooter, with a telescopic rifle, shoots the spy in the back. Someone asks the hero what happened, and he says, "Obviously, the Russians have no further use for him." A lot of the film had problems: You had Frenchmen speaking English to Frenchmen; Cubans speaking to Frenchmen in English. How can you believe that?

S: Is your dissatisfaction with *Topaz* what sent you back to London?

H: No. I'd been trying to work out the *Frenzy* story for some time. Last year I had three writers on it, but things didn't go. Then a publisher sent me a book with a totally different story, so I started a new *Frenzy* all over again, with Anthony Shaffer writing the screenplay.

S: A moment ago you spoke of the need for a subject that led you to *Topaz*. Have there not been times when, in retrospect, you found it would have been better to wait and not make a film?

H: I've dropped many projects. I brought a couple of writers over from Italy for one project, but unfortunately, there was a language barrier. I wanted to work up a treatment of an idea I've had since 1935. It takes place in a big hotel, managed by a family of thieves, brought over by one of their members from Italy. Now, however, the manager is such a big shot that he doesn't need to be a thief anymore. Suddenly, an important woman arrives with a collection of valuable coins. So the manager is stuck with the problem of putting her up in the hotel and keeping his family away from the valuables. From then on, you have adventures. And while they take place, I'd show the whole workings of the hotel: the kitchen, the laundry, etc. It would have been a comedy-thriller with the whole mechanism of the hotel featured. But the script never worked out for the reason I indicated.

S: Have you ever been prevented from making a film by your studio?

H: Sometimes.

S: Why didn't you do it anyway?

H: I'd have loved to make a film of *We the Accused.*

S: Since you've had such subjects, why didn't you make an Alfred Hitchcock film, with all the Hitchcock mastery, outside the commercial considerations to which, as you've said, you sometimes made concessions you later regretted?

H: What do you mean by "outside commercial considerations"? Films about "the human condition"?

S: No, just something made without any worry about the box office.

H: Well, the subject would have to offer opportunities to tell it my way.

S: Have you never had such a subject?

H: I own one now: J. M. Barrie's *Mary Rose* but at present, it doesn't seem to have any commercial potential.

S: Why can't Alfred Hitchcock make anything he wants to?

H: That's a privilege I have, but one mustn't take advantage of it. My contract gives me complete artistic control. I can make any film I like, up to three million dollars. But such privileges are a responsibility to the studios, which I obviously cannot, and would not, take advantage of. I don't have the right kind of conceit. I want to please everyone if I can. We live in an industry. A lot of people have jobs here: five thousand of them. If every film we made lost money, where would we all be? Many films never get beyond New York's East Side. I didn't walk into this business without proper knowledge of it. I've been a technician; I've been an editor; I've been an art director; I've been a writer. I have a feeling for all these people. I fill my responsibility to myself by the manner in which I make films. The subjects I choose, however, are chosen so that I'll not indulge myself at the expense of others. You've spoken of commercialism; I don't look at it that way. We should use the power of film to reach a world audience.

Index